From Data to Profit

How Businesses Leverage Data to Grow Their Top & Bottom Lines

Vin Vashishta

WILEY

Thanks to my mother for providing me with a library to grow up in, my father for the Atari 2600 that I took way too far, and Kiran and Erin for a life worth living.

About the Author

Vin Vashishta's fascination with technology began at an early age, reading science fiction books by Isaac Azimov and Arthur C. Clark. His study of strategy began when he watched the company he worked for go from industry leader to insolvency in 2 years.

Vashishta wrote his first computer program at 12, and what hooked him was the creative freedom to build anything he wanted. He began his career in technology in 1996, working on databases, building websites, and installing PCs. A career as a software engineer wasn't a sure bet back then, but he enjoyed the work.

He did everything from writing specifications to software engineering. Next, he built and led cross-functional teams. Vashishta spent a decade in the corporate world and was laid off twice during that time.

Both layoffs made him acutely aware that he wouldn't last long at any company if he didn't produce value instead of just technology. After the second layoff in 2012, Vashishta founded V Squared to build data science products for clients.

He recalls that no one else would give him a chance to do that work as an employee, so he made opportunities for himself, building a client list and a track record of success, one pitch and solution at a time. In 2015 he gained recognition on social media as a thought leader. He's a two-time LinkedIn Top Voice, is a Gartner Ambassador, and has been recognized by dozens of industry groups.

Today, Vashishta is a C-level technical strategy advisor, and he teaches gap skills to data professionals.

Contents

Introduction

Businesses are thinking about technology backward. Many business leaders think that 2020–2023 brought about the fastest digital transformation in history, but in fact those three years were the slowest technology will ever change again. Technology and therefore business will never move this slowly again in our lifetimes.

Businesses today are in adapt-or-die territory. Apple CEO Tim Cook said, "We don't believe you can save your way to prosperity. We think you invest your way to it." As such, Apple is looking for new markets to expand into, using innovation to drive growth. Amazon is slimming down and reallocating its war chest with the same goal. Both used smart investments during the Great Recession to become the companies they are today.

The last time Amazon snapped its fingers, half of retail disappeared. Amazon combined digital and web technologies to disrupt the retail industry and become a titan. Even retail giant Walmart seemed invincible until Amazon leveraged technology to reveal the weakness in Walmart's operating model.

Amazon is looking for ways to be a disruptor again. But Amazon won't be alone this time, and the disruption will touch every competitive industry, not just retail. Microsoft and OpenAI's partnership was the major technical story of 2022 and revealed the potential scope of AI applications. Nothing in recent memory has captivated people's attention in the same way.

ChatGPT reached 1 million registered users in just 5 days and soon after became the fastest application to reach 100 million registered users. GPT-4 has propelled OpenAI and Microsoft further into the public spotlight. Microsoft is looking to duplicate ChatGPT's growth trajectory by building Copilot into its suite of enterprise applications and regain its dominance in the space.

The fast-follower applications from tech giants such as Google, SAP, and Salesforce have created even more interest. With multimodal models, video, images, audio, and text are generated together seamlessly. The rate of technology change isn't slowing down; it's accelerating.

The more people use and share their results, the more front of mind the technology becomes for CEOs. AI was once viewed as speculative and often attracted indifference. Now data and AI are leading a wave of new solutions. New business models have emerged in the first half of 2023, and investment continues to flow into AI startups. Even in an economic downturn, AI is experiencing growth, with some speculating that it will drive a turnaround.

A Novel Asset Class with a Greenfield of Opportunities

In late 2022, I talked with a reporter and said cautiously, "This feels like the real thing." Past false starts with data and AI have jaded the entire data science field. I was hit by the first hype cycle, the one most have forgotten, in the early 1990s. The data science career that I imagined took almost 20 years to materialize.

I am a skeptic, but even I must acknowledge how capable AI models have become. The first half of 2023 has proven cautious optimism to be warranted. However, the grandiose predictions will fail to materialize because this wave is focused on practical applications. But the time between a new tool being released, practical applications being delivered, and revenue materializing is getting shorter every year.

Data and AI are driving this wave of tools and products. The World Economic Forum classifies data as a completely new asset class, unlike any we've seen before. It's not the new oil. It's more potent than that. The rapidly improving product landscape is filled with examples of the new monetization paradigm.

Use a gallon of oil or an ounce of gold once and they're gone. A gigabyte of data can be reused to generate value across the firm. The models it trains are never depleted. They can return value for years with minimal overhead. Partnering with large model platforms opens even more opportunities.

A 2021 Accenture study discovered that companies with a holistic data and AI strategy generated 50 percent more returns than their peers. Over the last 2 years, dozens of surveys have been published with similar findings. However, it took real-world applications to turn skeptics into promoters.

C-level leaders spent 5+ years investing in data teams and infrastructure. There's a mountain of evidence that the ROI hasn't materialized for everyone. Inconsistent results have revealed that the problem doesn't have a technical or tactical solution. Hiring talent and buying tools support technology delivery, but something is missing.

Talk to data scientists, and the same story plays out repeatedly. The business doesn't get it, and leadership doesn't buy in. Data teams are developing reports and simplistic models. Their capabilities and value are trapped just like the value in the company's data. How do we unlock it?

It begins with technical strategy. This book focuses on data and AI strategy, but I will reveal the bigger picture that businesses need to survive in the modern competitive marketplace.

The Road from Laggard to Industry Leadership

When Satya Nadella took over Microsoft, the company was at a crossroads. The business thought of itself as the industry leader. Customers had the opposite opinion. This is where Google finds itself at now. Microsoft executed a brilliant turnaround, and Google needs to take a page from its book to navigate the challenges to its search dominance.

Microsoft adopted a challenger's mindset and abandoned hopes of regaining dominance in its traditional core business lines. It took a completely different approach to its development tools. Microsoft restructured the business around the next technology wave and went all in on the Azure cloud platform and building a services ecosystem on it.

Its partnership with OpenAI marks a new transformation to AI. Azure is the core infrastructure supporting the collaboration, and Microsoft has launched its GPT 3.5 and GPT 4–enabled services there. OpenAI leverages Azure to train some of the most complex models in the world.

Microsoft's cloud services began a long journey back to technical dominance, but it has always looked ahead with AI firmly in its sights. At the same time, transformation doesn't come in giant leaps. Digital yielded to the cloud, then data, and now AI.

Microsoft has realized that opportunities for revenue growth come in waves. However, a business built to monetize software and services would fail to monetize the cloud. A company built without best-in-class cloud capabilities would fail to deliver best-in-class AI products. Microsoft needed to transform again to monetize the models in development with OpenAI.

It has proven to be a successful technical strategy, and Microsoft will leverage what it has learned to transform in the future as new technological waves roll in. Microsoft has become AI-first this time, but the next wave is already on the horizon.

Azure is at the center of its OpenAI partnership. All its attention is funneled to products and services customers can buy today. In fact, Microsoft is teaching a master class on monetizing advanced models. I'm not talking about multiyear time horizons. Products hit the marketplace months after new models are developed.

Technical Strategy as a New Top-Level Construct

What is the key to Microsoft's growing track record of success? Satya Nadella is a technical strategist. VCs are now looking for the next generation of technical strategists. Investors have realized the connection between the hybrid capability set and business success. In 2022, at the World Economic Forum in Davos, Jim Breyer, CEO of Breyer Capital, said, "We invest in technical strategists." We are at the front of a sea change in strategy and technology. Businesses need a new partnership between C-level leaders, strategists, and technical experts to unlock the value trapped in their data and organizations.

Supporting that partnership is a new top-level strategic construct, the *technology model*. Everything in the business that creates and delivers value to customers needs a strategy. Firms are transferring an increasing amount of their business and operating models from people to technology.

The transfer began with digital transformation and cloud adoption. Data and AI are the next stages. The Internet of Things, virtual reality, augmented reality, and 5G are potential amplifiers. This is the nature of the technology-enabled marketplace. Disruption isn't coming. It's here, and the impacts are playing out in rapid cycles.

Transformation now comes in waves. In the mid-to-late 1900s, the spaces between technological advances were more than 10-year spans. Since 2000 we have seen new software, the Web, mobile, cloud, data, IoT, analytics, AI, platforms, and more on the horizon. Each wave supports greater technical capabilities, so more parts of the business and operating models can be transferred into the technology model.

Businesses' reliance on technology will never be this low again. In this book, I will explain the climb from where enterprises are now to where they must be to survive the next 5 years. It is a techno-strategic process that blurs the lines between data scientists and strategists.

I will explain how strategy planning and implementation follow the data science life cycle. The two domains have more in common than most realize.

Strategy is prescriptive and forward-looking. It informs decision-making across the enterprise. Strategy reveals multiple paths for achieving business objectives, allowing the business to adapt to changing conditions. Optimization and efficiency are core objectives.

Reread the previous paragraph but replace "strategy" with "machine learning" or "AI." The sentences still work.

Reliable machine learning models manage complexity and reduce uncertainty. They have predictive, prescriptive, and diagnostic capabilities, which increase a business's learning rate and accelerate continuous improvement cycles. Revenue and efficiency gains compound and make the company more productive and profitable with each cycle.

I will explain the new user-technology relationship paradigm. People view software as a tool like a hammer or a screwdriver; this is human-machine tooling. They look at models and AI as team members; this is human-machine teaming. Stable Diffusion and GPT-4 are the leading edge of the third transformation, which is human-machine collaboration. I'll explain the opportunities and how to seize them in this book.

The software paradigm handles logical processes with easily defined, stable steps. Models manage intelligent processes that require the synthesis of knowledge to novel scenarios. Today, people are handing over autonomy to models for some intelligent workflows. The number of intelligent processes that data and AI can manage and that people trust the technology to handle will multiply in the next 2 years.

This book explains how to go from a legacy business with early data maturity to competitive maintenance, advantage, and industry leadership. I will detail what needs to happen for early investments in data and AI initiatives to break even, generate revenue, and become the primary source of new growth.

The book will cover three pillars that are critical for success: frameworks, road maps, and technical implementations. This book's frameworks are lightweight and designed to generalize across businesses. They are flexible and adaptable. Road maps connect strategy to execution and value creation. Technical implementations and real-world examples will drive concepts home, making this all actionable instead of aspirational.

This book is written for data scientists, leaders, product managers, and project managers. Businesses must operate from a common playbook or transformation moves in competing directions. Business units must understand their role as part of a connected enterprise. Technology is just a tool. Companies must be rebuilt to monetize technology in partnership with people.

Playbook for the Enterprise

The book begins with the path to alignment. Continuous transformation requires a new business culture that must be rapidly implemented. Goals and incentives must align with it. As I'll explain, talent must be developed internally because external sourcing is unsustainably expensive and time-consuming.

Technical progress cannot happen without strategy informing and aligning decision-making across the enterprise. Internal adoption does not occur without operating model transformation and internal training. Value cannot be delivered to customers without business model transformation.

All three top-level strategic constructs must move together, or data and AI will fail to thrive. C-level leaders face pressure to quickly pivot from compelling transformation stories to capable execution. Investors are looking for tangible progress, a track record of successful deployments, and measurable returns.

Pressure is growing for data teams too. Budgets receive greater scrutiny, and data professionals are no longer untouchable. The risks are reinforced daily by the latest round of layoff announcements. Any group that isn't profitable now finds itself on the chopping block. Last year, Amazon, Microsoft, Alphabet, and Meta wound down unprofitable business units. The rest of the business world has followed.

The decade of bottomless budgets for innovation without expectations is over. Activist investors pose challenges to CEOs who haven't executed. They prefer companies that invest responsibly and show returns quickly. Investors expect businesses to navigate the current uncertainty by leveraging data effectively. It's not enough to keep repeating a data-driven story.

When companies like Nike are forced to confess that they don't have visibility into their inventory, stock prices plummet. Intel could not execute supply chain derisking and continues to struggle with execution. Its share price has been punished.

Companies such as Apple have used data to minimize supply chain disruptions and avoid excess inventory traps. This is the standard that other businesses are being held to. Leaders know the value that mature data capabilities deliver. Now business leaders are looking for people in the data organization to step up.

New roles are emerging. The emphasis on data and AI products has pushed a new type of product manager into the hiring plan. Data strategists are increasingly common, and C-level data leaders are seen as critical. Demand for people who can monetize the technology is growing faster than for technical practitioners.

This book is a training manual for these emerging roles. I explain how they work together and ensure the execution that CEOs need. Now more than ever, businesses must align and work together.

Systems, Models, and Frameworks

This book teaches systems, frameworks, and models. What is a system? Systems are anything that we interact with. A marketplace is a vast, complex system with multiple players and objectives. The business itself can be viewed as a system. Supply chains are systems.

This book's frameworks are designed to help readers navigate these systems. With systems, models, and frameworks, I will provide you with domain knowledge and expertise I've developed over the last 11 years of working in data science and more than 25 years in technology.

I had to figure out how to give readers a full view of what's going on across the business and make it work for several different types of companies. It took me a long time to develop a different way of explaining these constructs that goes beyond memorizing facts and definitions.

There's no step-by-step sequence of events that holds across businesses. Intuitively we all know that rigid frameworks and monolithic approaches are flawed. The most talented people can synthesize their frameworks and experience to novel scenarios. How?

Every business has domain knowledge. In this book, I'm passing on the domain knowledge that my company (V Squared) and I have accumulated. Strategy is, in a way, a representation of the business's domain knowledge.

When I tried to boil *domain knowledge* down to its most basic form, I came up with this: the set of biases, assumptions, and heuristics that the business uses to explain its marketplace view, processes to create value, and decision-making process.

Developing and continuously improving the business's domain knowledge is exceptionally important. There's so much value in that institutional knowledge. In the modern competitive landscape, it's more critical than ever.

The business is continuously transforming. We can introduce data into the business and influence domain knowledge. By leveraging data, we're trying to determine what's right and what can be improved. The purpose of data is to introduce new knowledge into the business.

I had to figure out a way to deliver this information knowing that you will be working with different types of domain knowledge and expertise. That's why I developed systems, models, and frameworks.

I'll explain systems and give you models and frameworks to adapt to those systems. Everything is designed to adapt and improve.

Introducing Data to the Enterprise

Unfortunately, strategy planners experimented in production in the past, which is obviously a worst practice. Without data and models, what else were they supposed to do? Business strategy resulted from best guesses, because it's all we had.

Now we have data, so I must explain what happens when we introduce data into the strategy planning process. Continuous transformation is the constant theme, and the technology model sits underneath it to help the business manage technology's value creation.

These technical strategies inform decision-making, and each framework will focus on decisions. The purpose of the strategies is to help people without all the information they need to understand the enormously complex systems they are making decisions about. We are giving them models and frameworks so that they can adapt to make decisions and be more successful.

The frameworks in this book are the same ones you'll teach to everyone else. The technology model supports decisions about what should transition from the operating model into the technology model. Technology-supported process or workflow automation initiatives can be planned to implement that transition.

Next comes the core-rim model, which I'll explain in depth. Technology lives at the core, and people handle the irreducible complexity at the rim. One layer deeper sits the value stream, which connects value creation to workflows and explains how individual tasks create value. Using that, the business can decide what should be transferred into the technology model. These changes enable continuous transformation to take advantage of each technology wave.

How do we measure it? I explain AI strategy key performance indicators (KPIs) at the end of this book. One of the KPIs you can use at the lowest level of granularity is the percentage of workflows generating data, leveraging data, and leveraging models.

These frameworks are like layers of an onion. As we get deeper into each framework, we get closer and closer to implementation—the KPIs track execution from the value perspective. We can't drag senior leaders into managing the technology or workflows. Frameworks allow them to continue to manage value creation.

Frameworks go from very high-level abstract constructs all the way down to managing the value creation of each one of these initiatives. Everything is a system, and we need a model to understand the system and a framework to interact with that system. Those help the rest of the business do their parts too.

That's where alignment comes from. Transformation becomes more efficient when the business works together from a single playbook. When the goal is to adapt and improve from day 1, business culture changes to support the data and AI-driven firm. The business takes back control, so value creation drives transformation.

Without these frameworks, businesses risk losing their autonomy to technology. When technology drives strategy, the results are catastrophic. These frameworks allow people to maintain autonomy while reaping the benefits of data and AI. Everything this big needs a justification. In Chapter 2, "There Is No Finish Line," I'll explain what's changed to force this level of transformation.

1

Overview of the Frameworks

Profiting from data, analytics, and more advanced models is complex without using frameworks. Costs rise too quickly for more than the simplest of initiatives to be feasible. Most businesses are just coming to terms with the big picture of what it takes to monetize data and AI, but I've worked with it for more than 11 years.

I developed the frameworks covered in this chapter to optimize the process of technical strategy and monetizing data and AI. There are layers to the challenges, and there are layers to the frameworks. Introducing them up front in Chapter 1 will help you to keep track of them and answer some of your questions before you ask them.

This chapter serves as a quick reference for each framework. As you get further along in the book, revisiting earlier frameworks will be useful. For example, *continuous transformation* will take on an expansive meaning the further you read. The *technology model* and *opportunity discovery* will grow increasingly critical over the course of the book. The need for *business culture changes* gains urgency once I explain the big picture and maturity models.

As you work to monetize data, analytics, and more advanced models, you'll encounter a range of challenges. That's when you should come back to the frameworks in this chapter. Where in the process is the challenge emerging? The answer to that question will point you to the appropriate framework. How can you implement a framework to overcome the challenge? That will point you to the next steps to overcome the challenge.

Continuous Transformation

The *continuous transformation* framework explains what has changed and what businesses are adapting to. Technology is advancing faster than ever, and each technology implemented could deliver a competitive advantage. The business can't build data and AI products with software engineers. It must develop new internal capabilities to build with new technology. New products will be possible, and existing products will be refreshed with new functionality.

Each technology wave could transform the business in small or large ways. How SHOULD the business transform? That must be a strategic decision because technology threatens to take over if senior leaders don't have frameworks that help them retain autonomy.

Each wave will impose a cost on the business, so each wave must also deliver significant returns. When transformation happened slowly, companies could recoup their costs over several years. Waves are currently 3 to 5 years apart, but that span is reducing rapidly. Think of how quickly generative AI has moved forward, and you'll get a sense of the new speed limit.

Continuous transformation is part of each framework because it drives the modern competitive business. This is the root cause of emerging opportunities and threats.

Three Sources of Business Debt

Transformation should be easy, but it isn't. Adopting new technologies should be straightforward, but it's the opposite. Three sources of business debt are to blame, and businesses need frameworks to manage each.

Technical debt is accrued by making technical decisions without the continuous transformation framework. Each technological wave is inevitable. It's coming, and while we can't see all the impacts with 20/20 vision, there are obvious implications that every business should be preparing for. Building today with a high-level plan for how subsequent technology waves will impact what we're building lowers the cost and time to transform with the next wave.

Technical decisions today must amplify the value of future waves, and those subsequent waves must amplify the value of current products. Technical debt creates interference waves, while continuous transformation creates amplification waves and cycles.

Strategic debt is accrued by building a monolithic strategy that ignores technology's increasing role in the business and products. Leadership can turn to technology and the technical teams for help overcoming challenges and achieving strategic goals. Most companies don't integrate technology into strategy planning or opportunity discovery. As a result, a critical source of growth and competitive advantages sits on the sidelines instead of being elevated to partner status.

Strategy must continuously transform with each technological wave, and C-level leaders need frameworks to make technology decisions strategically. Enterprise-wide alignment on transformation and technical maturity is possible. These frameworks create the connection between technology and value creation.

Cultural debt is accrued by the business's evaluation, accountability, and incentivization structures failing to transform to support new technology waves. Technology must be integrated into the business's workflows, but most cultural artifacts are not designed to support integration. Some artifacts punish people throughout the company for leveraging new technologies. Others make people accountable for workflow outcomes that result from workflows that technology now controls.

Cultural artifacts must continuously transform to reinforce technology adoption and monetization. New frameworks support data-driven and increasingly technology-dependent business and operating models. Decisions must be made with transparency into the cultural artifacts they disrupt.

Evolutionary Decision Culture

Data and the business's technical capabilities continuously transform, which improves the quality of data available to support critical decisions. The business gathers new data and develops higher-quality models. Both introduce new information to the business. As a result, strategy planning must transform.

Strategy must be built with the best available data to avoid analysis paralysis. It must also be reevaluated when data and models improve. No decision should be considered final because there may be good reasons to change in the future.

People must be incentivized throughout the business to make decisions with their best available data and improve them as data improves. In some cases, that will lead to the business walking away from significant investments and firmly held beliefs. Transformation often requires quitting to improve.

The Disruptor's Mindset

Disruptors are critical for transformation. They challenge firmly held beliefs and what the business is working toward today. This mindset supports a culture of experimentation and rapid improvement. The big innovations come from the disruptor's ability to see flawed assumptions and the implications of replacing those assumptions with new knowledge.

Cultural artifacts must be built to support disruptors. People must be incentivized to find and replace flawed assumptions. Experimental frameworks must be implemented to enable disruptors to prove or refute their ideas rapidly. Value-centric frameworks must be implemented to prevent disruptors from derailing the business with experiments that cannot be monetized.

The Innovation Mix

Businesses cannot be innovating all the time, and a lack of innovation puts the business's future at risk. C-level leaders need a framework to decide how much innovation the company should be working on. Too much innovation and the business will fail to exploit its current opportunities. Too little innovation and margins will drop until the business's current opportunities run dry.

An innovation mix helps the business to continuously transform the resources it dedicates to innovation initiatives. The mix swings like a pendulum to meet the business needs of today and the next few years.

Meet the Business Where It Is

Technical strategy is often aspirational. Initiatives are built for an ideal business environment. Every business is at a different maturity level. Each has strengths and challenges. Not every company will choose to become AI-first or build massive internal capabilities.

We must meet the business where it is and plan technical strategy with a connection to the business's strategy and goals. We must assess the business's current maturity levels and make an opportunity-centric decision about how far it will mature to seize those opportunities.

The Technology Model

C-level leaders need a framework to make strategic decisions about how the business uses technology to create and deliver value to customers. Technology makes many things possible, but that's not how decisions should be made. Technical feasibility doesn't always lead to monetization.

The *technology model framework* introduces a top-level strategic construct that sits with the business and operating models. It makes technology a core pillar of business strategy. C-level leaders can make decisions based on business value without getting dragged into technical or implementation details.

They choose which parts of the business and operating models to transfer into the technology model based on the opportunities they see. These align technical initiatives with business value and strategic goals.

Individual technical strategies inform decision-making about the value-generating advantages each technology wave delivers better than alternatives. Digital, cloud, data, AI, IoT, and other technologies have unique strengths supporting different monetization strategies. Technical strategy is a thesis of value creation that explains why the business uses an individual technology to create and deliver value to customers.

The Core-Rim Model

Data and AI are novel asset classes, and a monetization strategy must be a core driver for technical initiative selection. There is a second aspect to the strategic decision process. Data and models can take over an increasing number of internal and customer workflows. But can they handle the complexity?

The logical steps performed in each workflow are only a fraction of the process. Dig deeper into workflows, and sometimes we find hidden complexity. Intelligent processes don't follow easily defined steps, and decisions are made based on expert knowledge. Are data and models reliable enough to manage the complexity?

C-level leaders need a framework to assess what workflows should be transferred to the technology model and which ones the business doesn't trust technology to manage. *Core-rim* provides support for those decisions.

Transparency and Opacity

Businesses have a hidden giant of data-generating processes. Where do the processes of data gathering and model development begin? The mistake most companies make is to try to gather everything. There's simply too much, and most data does not deliver much value to the business.

Transparency and opacity is a framework that aligns data gathering with high-value workflows. These workflows can be internal user or customer workflows. Data gathering must have a framework for prioritization; otherwise, costs spiral out of control, and value creation is not guaranteed.

This framework supports opportunity discovery and estimation, which lay the foundation for prioritization.

The Maturity Models

Continuous transformation must reach down into strategy implementation and execution. Without that connection, strategy is aspirational. The maturity models support implementing continuous transformation and technical strategy across four key pillars. This is the most challenging connection to make because it spans products, business units, customer segments, and technology waves. The big picture of continuous transformation is massive, and the maturity models create alignment with a lightweight framework set.

- The business's data and AI capabilities continuously transform to deliver higher-value products. The *capabilities maturity model* keeps that development aligned with products and initiatives. Capabilities should be built in line with business needs so talent and infrastructure maximize their returns to the business. This framework supports value versus technology-focused decisions about capabilities development.

- Products continuously transform to seize opportunities with each technological wave. The *data product maturity model* explains how digital products evolve into data, analytics, and advanced model-supported products. This framework supports decision-making about initiative planning. Products can be built today with space for the inevitable transformations coming next. They can be monetized at each phase, so incremental delivery creates incremental returns for the business. Transformation is sustainable, and costs are minimized.

- Data gathering capabilities transform to seize opportunities as product lines grow into platforms. The *data maturity model* supports moving the business from opaque to transparent while delivering value at each phase. It's the connection between data engineering and monetization. Initiatives support bringing new information and domain knowledge into the business for high-value workflows.

- Data and model development capabilities transform to deliver increasingly reliable models. Use cases have levels of reliability requirements depending upon how much of the workflow is turned over to technology. The way people work with technology, especially data and advanced models, must be taken into account. Breaking initiatives down to support internal users' and customers' reliability needs is supported by the *human-machine maturity model*.

The Four Platforms

The business must create a vision and product strategy to prevent product lines from delivering inconsistent experiences. Disconnected products transform in different directions and create expensive redundancies. Internal users and customers adopt these products at lower rates because they lack a coherent alignment.

The maturity models enable initiatives to be designed in alignment with business value, capabilities, and how people engage with technology. The platforms connect products as they progress through the maturity models.

- The *product platform* handles customer workflows.
- The *operations platform* handles the tasks performed as part of internal user workflows.
- The *decision support platform* provides data to improve the decision chains associated with internal user workflows.
- The *operating system model and AI app store platform* support partnering with large third-party models to deliver value to customers and internal users.

Each platform needs a vision to articulate where it is today, what's being built this year, and what the platform will be in three to five years. The vision explains how each transformation supports technical strategy and top-level business strategic goals.

Top-Down and Bottom-Up Opportunity Discovery

The business needs frameworks to support nontechnical leaders and domain experts in discovering high-value opportunities. Most companies depend upon the data team to put forward opportunities, but they aren't the closest to strategic goals, internal business needs, and customer needs. Opportunity discovery is more successful when technology teams partner with the business.

Top-down opportunity discovery provides a framework for C-level leaders to surface large opportunities that align with strategic goals. It's an evaluation process that helps leaders separate hype from reality. Opportunity discovery is managed based on technical viability, proven value estimates, and technical feasibility.

Bottom-up opportunity discovery provides a framework for mid-level leaders and frontline workers to surface opportunities based on the needs they are closest to. It creates a prioritization framework that prevents data teams from being overwhelmed with low ROI work and ad hoc requests. That justifies delivering data literacy training and self-service tools to manage those requests. The highest-value opportunities are estimated and added to the product road map for rapid delivery.

Large Model Monetization

OpenAI's GPT presents new monetization opportunities, and businesses need a framework to support decision-making. The operating system AI and AI app store frameworks explain the new paradigm in nontechnical terms so C-level leaders can surface opportunities for near-term value creation. Familiar paradigms provide context for decision-making and opportunity discovery.

Maturity model leapfrogging explains the new competitive paradigm. Businesses can leverage operating system AI to deliver high-maturity products without developing those capabilities internally. They work for only some use cases, and leapfrogging helps C-level leaders decide which use cases to move forward with.

Data curation and operating system AI retraining explain mid- and long-term opportunities created by this paradigm. C-level leaders leverage this framework to direct data capabilities maturity and data engineering initiatives that align with high-value opportunities.

The Business Assessment Framework

Meeting the business where it is requires an initial assessment. Nothing works until the business moves forward with a common understanding. The *business assessment framework* defines the current data and AI maturity level on seven assessment points.

The information gathered as part of the assessment feeds into the data and AI strategy document. The information helps develop the product, infrastructure, internal training, and hiring road maps. The first rounds of opportunity discovery are completed as part of the initial assessment process.

The assessment marks the boundary between planning and implementation. It's where the work begins. One of the critical artifacts is the data monetization catalog. It defines data as a novel asset class by connecting the business's data to the use cases it supports. Companies can put a value next to each data set and see where it derives the greatest value from.

The data monetization catalog enforces the need for value and use cases to drive data curation instead of gathering everything and finding value later. This avoids data swamps and high-cost, low-value data engineering initiatives.

The Data and AI Strategy Document

This framework outlines the key components of the data and AI strategy document. The purpose of the *data and AI strategy* is to inform decision-making across the enterprise about the technology. It should create alignment and continuity.

The data and AI strategy document must explain why the business uses data and AI to create and deliver value to customers. It must provide actionable information about how external teams will be impacted and their motivation to transform. It introduces the data team and describes its place in the business.

The document creates certainty about what comes next and why C-level leaders have chosen this direction.

Data Organizational Development Framework

The *data organization* must build in alignment with the maturity models. Meeting the business where it is often means there are existing resources in place today. Those serve as the starting point, but scattered resources and disparate teams don't support rapid maturity.

The data organization goes through a three-phase transformation. The initial assessment identifies where resources are today and what they are accountable for. The transformation strategy and capabilities maturity model defines where the team must go to deliver. In this first phase, the data team does not own everything it needs to deliver data, analytics, and model-supported products.

The second phase centralizes talent and infrastructure. Functional and project deliver improvement cycles optimize product quality and delivery speed.

The third phase distributes resources to the business units and product teams they support. The closer they are to the workflows and needs, the higher-value products become.

The data organizational development framework provides support for the three phases and rapid capabilities maturity.

More to Come

Throughout this book, I will define smaller supporting pieces and frameworks. I support each framework with implementation cases and examples pulled from the real world. The goal is to deliver a common playbook for the enterprise to follow.

Each framework supports and amplifies the others. They are lightweight and adaptable. Everything is meant to transform because, as I'll explain in the next chapter, there is no finish line for transformation.

2

There Is No Finish Line

This chapter and framework is step 1 of a much longer journey. I don't expect you to follow my lead blindly. Instead, I will explain the drivers and help you understand why taking these steps is crucial. The modern competitive landscape is fundamentally different than ever before and at its core is technology.

The business world understands technology has had an impact on the modern competitive landscape, but few understand the extent. Technology is a critical part of the business. The modern firm relies on it to create and deliver value to customers. Technology is not a static entity, and companies cannot be static, either.

Google provides an excellent example of what happens when even the most innovative company stands still. Google developed advanced data science and machine learning capabilities. However, it isn't enough to innovate and be technically competent. Monetization remains elusive if the business doesn't transform along with technical capabilities. That's how Google got caught flat-footed.

As technology evolves, the business must adapt to that new technology. In this chapter, I start by explaining what that means. Continuous transformation is a framework to manage the evolutionary nature of technology. It enables businesses to control technology's value creation. There's a massive difference between having data, analytics, and advanced models and actually monetizing those technologies.

By the end of this chapter, you'll understand what has changed and have the first tool in the technical strategy toolkit: continuous transformation. Each chapter adds a new capability and framework to help you navigate the modern competitive landscape.

Data and AI strategy paints a grand vision for data science in the enterprise, but the journey there is incremental. Transformation has no finish line because conditions continuously change as technology advances. The business's capabilities must grow to integrate new technologies and adapt. However, monetization requires the rest of the company to transform as well.

Where Do We Begin? With Reality

Today the business could be deep into digital transformation or cloud adoption, but that's not the end. Data, analytics, and AI come next. Behind them are other technology waves. However, the pervasive mentality is that transformation will come to an end. Technology will stabilize, and progress will return to where it was in the 1980s.

That's not going to happen, and businesses must adapt or be swept aside by rivals that have. Not everyone in the business understands the magnitude of the risks and opportunities. Transformation would happen faster if they did.

It's not just the technology that must change, so we can't ignore where the business and its people are today. They won't magically catch up after the data team puts the technology in place. The process is more efficient when the business transforms on an aligned road map. When technology leads the way, monetization is elusive, and adoption rarely materializes.

So much of what data scientists do fails because we refuse to meet the business where it is and let it dictate the pace of transformation. The current maturity level is rarely perfect, but this is the reality we face. The first guiding principle I will introduce about data and AI strategy is this one: "We must meet the business where it is, not where we want it to be or think it should be. We must transform at the business's speed, not the technology's."

Transformation is more successful when it meets people where they are now and accepts how they think. This book would work in a company like Meta or Google, but most companies aren't technology-first and have no aspirations of becoming a Meta rival. Most companies' challenges start at an earlier maturity phase, which is fine.

Few initiatives require advanced machine learning and deep learning methods. The majority of businesses will not develop high-end models in-house. They will partner and purchase. The value most businesses will generate and benefit from comes from straightforward approaches, simple descriptive models, and advanced analytics.

The work required to transform the business to that maturity level is often underestimated. The focus and investment are skewed toward the technology and data team. We're in a time of "adapt or die" for companies across industries. The urgency is high, but to succeed in continuous transformation, we must meet businesses where they are. We must acknowledge that transformation is two-sided.

We must also support the business through imperfect stages of transformation. I would love to live in a world where people read this book and suddenly became data-driven mental powerhouses. I have been working with businesses in various phases of their data journeys for more than a decade, and believe me, we don't live in that world.

These frameworks apply to real people at actual companies. I wrote this book for humans, whereas most books in the data field seem designed for the ideal business with perfect people. Transformation begins humbly and imperfectly. It never stops because if it does, the company will fail.

It's the same with people. People never stop learning, growing, and improving their capabilities in technical fields. There's always a new programming language and model architecture to learn. Continuous transformation is a framework for helping the business come to terms with a reality that's been with people in the technology field since the beginning.

Defining a Transformation Vision and Strategy

The purpose of these frameworks is to create a company that's better tomorrow than today. Technical strategists must provide a future state and big picture, the main components of the vision. At the same time, there's no finish line to this journey. The vision will help the business see where they're going, but getting to that point isn't the end.

We need to be forward-looking and prescriptive to support senior leaders. Just like everything else that has been disrupted by continuous transformation, the vision will evolve and improve. Anytime I get better data or a more accurate model, my vision for the future may change or become more certain. The central theme of this book is continuous transformation.

Continuous transformation supports the most granular initiative level and enterprise level so each phase can deliver incremental returns. The business can structure transformation to align with its business goals. C-level leadership should decide how fast and far it wants to go with each technology. To achieve that objective, they need a framework to manage value creation versus technology.

Continuous transformation helps the business make timing decisions about adopting data, analytics, and AI. Longer term, there are more technology waves on the horizon. When will a company be ready to move to platforms and, potentially, even evaluate quantum computing?

These technological waves are inevitable. No matter what the business's transformation rate, each phase is still unavoidable. Companies will leverage each technology wave, so decisions should support technologies that are further out on the transformation timeline.

In the early 2000s, we made a huge mistake, and I was part of it. We built applications for the old paradigm, scaling by incrementally adding on-premises hardware and infrastructure. We should have built incrementally, knowing we were going to the cloud eventually.

When the inevitable cloud migration happened, it was harder to get buy-in because it was so expensive and time-consuming. We were forced to rebuild core components. It would have been faster and more cost-efficient to have taken a long-term view. Even in a technology organization, we fought the inevitable transformation.

Taking a continuous transformation view would have been the better choice. The entire business would have been on board with cloud adoption because the changes could have been deployed incrementally. Most of the pushback we received was rooted in the disruptions that rapid adoption and years of poor decision-making had led to.

The cost per quarter would have been more manageable, and the impacts on the product release schedule could have been minimized. There wouldn't have been a scramble to hire, select infrastructure, and retrain technical staff.

We know the business will adopt data and AI. As we're building digital apps and adopting the cloud, we should gather data differently, with AI in mind, as part of creating digital solutions. Businesses have not taken that approach, and the lack of intentional, incremental transformation makes each future wave more expensive.

Paying Off the Business's Digital Debt

Data teams inherit a massive amount of technical debt that comes from early digital transformation initiatives. The business has been working to become a digital enterprise for the last 10 years or more. This transformation focused on moving from a manual to a digital business.

Digital transformation began for some companies in the late 1990s. The goal was to transform paper records into digital equivalents. The paper record's layout became the front end and the user interface. The information people put on those paper records was captured by an application for storage in a database. The application's back end was the logic that took data where it needed to go and delivered it when users needed it again.

Then people realized that the logical back end was capable of so much more. It could enforce some business logic and handle some tasks faster than people do. PCs were transformed into the hammers and then the nail guns of a new type of business. Applications took on increasing amounts of work and equal levels of complexity.

As applications became more capable, our paradigms did not evolve to see the implications. Digital thinking still holds on to the original tenet: taking paper forms and turning them into applications. Data is saved to be redisplayed to users in the same format as the old paper form.

Senior leaders were told that everything was going digital, which is how they rebuilt the business. Influencers to Big 5 consultants told the business it must become digital and move to the cloud. The shift and associated transformation were labeled as once-in-a-generation changes.

Businesses built everything on digital foundations, which create data silos. Each organization has apps or platforms that they use. Those apps follow a basic tenet: keep data close to where it was gathered and where it will most likely be used.

The best practice of keeping data close to where it is gathered is a worst practice in the data world. Applications gather data to use later. The application's scope and functionality dictate what data is gathered and how. Keeping data in these application domain-specific silos makes sense if digital is the endgame.

The marketing team has apps that collect data that lives in those apps. It made sense because those apps needed to access the data to serve it back to the marketing team (users). A silo was inadvertently built around that data.

The sales organization has another set of apps and another silo. We have software engineering, which should touch all parts of the business because it needs to get requirements from and service different business units. Even their apps are siloed. When it comes to data, almost nothing is open and easily accessible outside of these silos.

With the data paradigm, any team could potentially need data from marketing or sales. People across the business or even customers might need a report on how an R&D initiative is progressing. In this paradigm, data silos that don't talk to each other become barriers to progress.

In the past, apps haven't needed to connect. In the rare cases where they did, it was handled by some really kludgy APIs. It's painful to get data from one app or platform to another.

Most data is gathered accidentally and haphazardly. Contrary to popular belief, there are such things as too much and worthless data. Metadata wasn't part of the gathering process, so it isn't available to support data science initiatives that now need it for reliability or compliance reasons. The data team needs access to data from multiple silos.

Digital wasn't the endgame. Data and AI are the next waves, so we should make decisions during digital transformation to support them. Digital architecture and data gathering that fits the next wave makes it less expensive to transform. The business sacrifices a little during digital transformation to get a lot more back during the data and AI waves.

Short-horizon decisions have made it harder to implement data tools, infrastructure, data engineering best practices, and data curation. Those decisions lead to low-quality data sets that are often useless for analytics and model training. As a result, the cost of cleaning and transforming data to get some value from it is higher than it should be. Most initiatives aren't feasible from a cost or technical perspective because the business believed transformation was a one-time activity and that digital was the end state.

Each transformation is more expensive than it needs to be because businesses doesn't make forward-looking technical decisions. Transformation vision and strategy provide the first components required to change that. Continuous transformation implements a framework and new way of thinking.

Some digital products in development now will transition into data products or support data products in the future. If we act on that knowledge, we can make decisions today that amplify the value of future waves. The continuous nature of technical change comes to the front of the planning process, where it should be.

Continuous transformation requires incremental transformation to deliver incremental returns. The digital product should have a near-term break-even point. Moving to the cloud should have its own near-term break-even point. If each phase doesn't, what's the point? Today, many technical decisions are made with ambiguous promises of future returns. Technical strategy keeps decisions grounded in value creation.

Continuous transformation strategy emphasizes prioritizing and designing initiatives to return value to the business as soon as possible. Each phase should demonstrate the potential for that technology to deliver value. Most companies have a great transformation story but struggle to demonstrate execution incrementally.

Delivering value at each phase is one way the technical strategy and data teams can support the C-suite. Incremental product delivery, improvement, and returns show that transformation isn't just a story. A CEO that invests in Q1 can talk about returns in Q2 or Q3. There's a path to break even and profitability built into each initiative.

Managing the Value Creation vs. the Technology

Continuous transformation enables each initiative and technology to be managed from a value-creation standpoint. The company has a tool to answer the question, "How far should the business go in data, analytics, and AI maturity?" The technology supports a range of maturity levels, but the business shouldn't mature just because it's possible. Maturity level must be justified by returns.

Maturity levels must be defined by C-level leaders' objectives for each technology. How much new revenue will be booked on data, analytics, and AI products? This is measured in the percentage of the business's growth that will depend upon each technology. The more revenue and growth C-level leaders attach to a technology, the more capabilities and maturity must be developed to support the goal.

Continuous transformation creates a link to justify initiatives, allowing the business to decide its target maturity level using simple questions. We've established that the business will transform to adopt data and AI, but how mature should it become? This defines what must be built today by providing a vision for the company's future state.

Will data and AI be leveraged for competitive maintenance? The business will keep pace with competitors and match their moves. C-level leaders don't see opportunities for significant cost savings or new revenue generation but realize there will be competitive pressures.

Will data and AI be leveraged for competitive advantage? The business will go further than most competitors because C-level leaders have discovered significant opportunities to reduce costs, improve productivity, and generate new revenue.

Will data and AI drive most of the business's growth in the next 3 to 5 years? Companies will leverage leading-edge approaches, commit to becoming an innovator in the industry, and release best-in-class products based on the technology. C-level leaders see opportunities to become an industry leader by leveraging the technologies.

Those three decisions correspond to revenue, so the technical maturity level is connected to value. The future state isn't defined in technical terms. The transformation vision and strategy are defined by setting expectations for value creation. Opportunity discovery becomes a critical process, and I explain those frameworks later in this book.

How mature does the business need to be with a given technology? That depends on how much revenue growth, cost savings, and productivity improvement each technology must deliver to the company.

If data, analytics, or AI will be the business's primary growth engines, it must become an innovator. This level requires building capabilities out the furthest. It represents the largest transformation for these technology waves.

If the business keeps up with the marketplace, that will be the smallest buildup. The company will not create a competitive advantage or peg any growth to the technology. The goal is to maintain its position in the marketplace, and this transformation takes the least investment. The fewest initiatives will be attached to those technologies.

Framed that way, the decision evaluates opportunities relative to the competitive marketplace. Are there opportunities for significant growth and competitive advantage, or are the only opportunities the business has limited to competitive maintenance? How far will other companies in the space decide to go? Suppose the incumbents don't move fast enough. Will new competitors see the opportunities left on the table, enter the marketplace, and use a technology wave to take market share?

The continuous transformation strategy connects value creation to a high-level idea of how far the business must go from an investment and capability standpoint. Infrastructure, which is notoriously difficult to justify and express in terms of ROI, also fits here.

Early data initiatives and proofs of concept are small wins with short-term revenue gains at most companies. Continuous transformation allows the technical strategist to support a long-term vision by showing that short-term initiatives can be set up for longer-term wins. These early projects changed the perception of technology.

When CEOs think of innovation, they imagine distant, uncertain returns and long durations before breaking even. Continuous transformation reframes that perception. Each phase of an initiative (digital, cloud, data, analytics, AI, platform, quantum, IoT, 5G, and whatever else is available), and each adoption wave amplifies the value of the next. Initiatives deliver short-term returns while setting up for the next technology phase, which also provides short-term returns.

A Master Class in Continuous Transformation Strategy

Microsoft is demonstrating how this will play out. There's space in its digital tools, like Word and Excel, for cloud and AI-supported features. Putting the cloud pieces in place was a painful transformation because Microsoft didn't begin with that goal in mind. Part of Satya Nadella's turnaround of Microsoft involved transforming the business with a cloud-first strategy, but he saw the long game extending to data and AI.

Office 365 took application functionality into the cloud to deliver value for customers that's platform and device agnostic. The transformation made sense because the cloud provides those better than alternative technologies. This introduces another critical tenet of continuous transformation. With all these technical options, which ones should the business leverage? The technology must deliver value better than any alternative technology.

Microsoft transitioned Office 365 to the cloud because that technology delivered customer value in a new way that Microsoft could monetize. The cloud helped them maintain their competitive positioning in the enterprise productivity apps marketplace. It was a choppy road because the transformation was unplanned. Microsoft should have seen that Office 365 would eventually migrate to the cloud because of the technology's value proposition.

For Microsoft, moving to the cloud met changing customer needs. Users wanted access to Office apps from anywhere and on any device. Relying on an app and using a per-seat license plan doesn't work in a multidevice reality. The cloud disrupted the digital paradigm, and competitors showed Microsoft's customers the benefits of apps built in the cloud.

For Microsoft, it was an adapt-or-die moment. Nadella helped the business survive by going all in on the cloud, but he knew that wasn't the endgame. AI was on the horizon, and if Microsoft wanted to avoid repeating past mistakes, it needed to make decisions to support the next phase of transformation.

GPT is transforming traditional digital features into more capable model-supported features. The rollout speed across its software platforms and apps shows that Microsoft was ready from the start. Microsoft envisioned the opportunities that would eventually be made possible by large foundational models. Over the span of years, Microsoft made space in products and platforms for the inevitable transformation.

By evaluating initiatives on longer time scales with the continuous transformation framework, CEOs can manage the value creation of technology adoption versus having technology adoption drive their strategy.

Most transformation strategy is tactical. Whatever the technology enables is what the business believes it must do to survive. Strategic factors should drive the decision; the only guarantee is that the business will end up with a lot of expensive technology. The decision process involves the marketplace, business model, operating model, current customers, product portfolio, and competitors.

The continuous transformation strategy should be driven by opportunities the business has access to that align with those strategic factors. Technology cannot dictate strategy to the

C-suite. What's technically possible shouldn't drive how far the business should transform and how much they should invest.

The C-suite needs this framework to regain control over the technical direction and make decisions based on strategic objectives and opportunities. Here are some key considerations:

- What other opportunities does the business have access to, and is there a better technical strategy?

- Is there a more responsible way to invest those dollars that will return more to the company than in data, analytics, AI, or platforms?

- Would a more conservative technical strategy result in higher margins?

- Is the business model set up to adopt the technology for internal efficiency?

- If not, how much will it cost to make that transformation, and how does that compare to the cost reduction opportunities?

We should encourage the business to question the value of adopting data and AI. In most companies, that's not allowed. The business is a large part of this transformation journey, so people outside the data team must be bought in. Meeting the business where it is forces us to answer uncomfortable questions.

The reality is the business doesn't have to spend a dime on data or AI. Buy-in gets a lot easier when C-level leaders invest based on the opportunities they see instead of feeling forced into the decision. Strategy is an evaluation of trade-offs, so data and AI must sing for their suppers.

Evaluating Trade-Offs

At a strategy level, technology competes against things like stock buybacks. Google ($155 billion), Meta ($108 billion), Microsoft

($116 billion), and Apple ($409 billion) have done significant stock buybacks in the last 5 years. The first three companies are fairly tightly clustered in the amounts of money they've put into stock buybacks. Apple sits at three to four times the others.

Apple believes the best way to use its free cash flow is to return it to investors directly through stock buybacks instead of investing in high-growth initiatives. Meta is at the lowest end of this group because it holds the opposite thesis. Meta believed investing in growth opportunities was the best way to generate long-term shareholder returns. Meta saw significant opportunities and threats on the horizon.

Meta believed that putting the extra billions into things like the Metaverse would return more to shareholders, in the long run, than investing in a stock buyback or dividends. Meta has pivoted back to AI and has a much more modest platform strategy today. Conditions changed, and it was strong enough to adapt its strategy. Even strategy continuously transforms and improves, but only if the business has the right culture and mindset.

Microsoft invests in partnerships with companies like OpenAI. It sees AI as a growth engine and has a mature strategy for monetization. In the middle of 2021, its buybacks dropped sharply, hinting at their $10 billion OpenAI investment.

Microsoft is also investing in developing Azure, making it more capable, because the company sees it as the growth engine for the future. Microsoft's vision includes GPT-4 supporting Azure Cloud to drive adoption. It believes investing in Azure, and advanced AI capabilities will return more to shareholders than stock buybacks. This is an excellent illustration of continuous transformation.

Decisions made during Azure's development amplify the value they get from the OpenAI partnership. Their cloud-based apps present further opportunities to monetize the GPT-4 line. Copilot is everywhere, and Microsoft continues to find new ways to monetize GPT-4. It has transformed across digital, cloud, data, analytics, AI, and platforms. Progress in one wave amplifies the others because the company has aligned continuous transformation and technical strategies.

Google's buyback level is low relative to Apple but significantly higher than Meta and Microsoft. It gives shareholders more returns through stock buybacks. It's a sign that Google doesn't see as much potential for returns in putting that money back into the company.

Relative stock buybacks could have clued us in early that Google was slowing down its investment in the future. It made them vulnerable to a company like OpenAI delivering an LLM platform first and rivals leveraging their platform to leapfrog their search dominance. OpenAI and Microsoft invested more to develop faster. Google didn't recognize the magnitude of the opportunities and threats.

Google had similarly capable models to GPT-4 but wasn't developing them quickly until its code red response to Chat-GPT's release in 2022. Google's strategy didn't see the same growth opportunities, not because they weren't there but because Google wasn't built to seize them.

What Happens When the Business Loses Faith in Data and AI?

Technology competes for budget with alternatives. A company's technology budget has felt like a money spigot for almost a decade. That changed in 2022. Now C-level leaders are closely monitoring increases in spending, which has significant implications for data and AI strategy.

What else could the business put an extra dollar into that will produce more revenue than investing that dollar in data and AI? Strategy is an evaluation of trade-offs in an attempt to optimize the business. Sometimes the trade-off is not reinvesting that dollar into the company and new development but buying back stock or providing a dividend.

For any advanced technology like data and AI, that's a trend to monitor closely. It means the business doesn't want to accelerate investment in the data team as much as they want to put money back in investors' pockets. They may not believe in the long-term prospects of data and AI. This is an assumption, but is there data to support it?

Returning cash to investors versus reinvesting in the business for growth means the company has given up on developing faster or delivering more initiatives. C-level leaders and the board have lost their optimistic view that the business can grow by increasing its investment in these technologies. Technical strategists must answer the question, are they right?

Mark Zuckerberg, CEO of Meta, in the Q4 2022 earnings call, said the word "efficiency" 41 times. He said the word "Metaverse" seven times. Meta's focus shifted away from investing as much as possible into the Metaverse and pushing the technology development as fast as possible. Meta wanted to be there first and full speed ahead.

Mark Zuckerberg is a new convert to the cult of efficiency. He said he tried it for nine months and thought it created a better business. He likes Meta more now that it is a smaller, more efficient business that spends money more thoughtfully. He likes this leaner organizational structure and believes it better executes his core vision. The reduction in spending is an optimization, and Meta has slowed the pace of Metaverse platform development.

Meta is doing more with less, converting Mark Zuckerberg to efficiency. It announced a $40 billion stock buyback and then a second round of layoffs. Meta believes it doesn't need to invest as much into the Metaverse and should generate returns by passing profits directly to shareholders. It is the signal of a change in investment, but it's one that started a year earlier.

Meta struggled with stagnating revenue growth. The early signs of a slowdown deeply impacted ad revenue. Its ad business also had significant impacts from Apple's decision to restrict the user data it had access to on iPhones and devices.

Meta's first response was to invest in technologies where there were growth opportunities. Conditions have changed significantly since the Metaverse strategy was announced in 2021. Reevaluation was the right call.

Meta signaled the turn to efficiency recently, but investors, in their reaction to Meta's 2022 earnings calls, signaled their demand for efficient growth well in advance. Zuckerberg is one of the strongest-willed leaders and controlled the final decision-making at Meta. If anyone would stay the course and resist calls to streamline, it was him. Zuckerberg's capitulation is a sign of things to come.

Meta's shift in focus is critical to understanding what happens at other companies for data and AI investment. If the ROI isn't there, hype and optimism always give way to pragmatism. Data and AI are inevitable, but so is the Metaverse. Eventually, that technology wave will have its day, but Meta now believes those opportunities are further out in the future. Zuckerberg has decided to double down on the AI wave because the potential is more tangible, and returns are closer at hand.

As I said earlier, most businesses aren't Meta, so for them, data and AI are their cutting-edge technology investments. A slowdown in spending on data and AI initiatives indicates a lack of confidence that moving faster or spending more will result in higher rates of return.

Reducing the investment in what the business previously thought of as a growth area indicates either that leaders believe they can grow more efficiently investing elsewhere or that they don't see the same potential returns materializing as they once did.

The business sees an alternative that will return more efficiently. Strategy is an evaluation of trade-offs or an optimization process. As a result, data and AI must demonstrate higher returns for the business than an alternative investment to maintain its budget.

What happens if we find ourselves in a company reevaluating its investment in data and AI? The reality is that most businesses are reevaluating every dollar spent. Technology must deliver short-term returns. One of the major themes behind continuous transformation is we should be generating significant returns at each phase of adoption and transformation.

Several frameworks I present in this book optimize the time to break even and profitability for data and AI initiatives. We're in a new reality, and technical strategy must come forward to answer tough questions and deliver immediate returns. The value must be proven with improved productivity, cost savings, and new revenue generation. Most of all, it must be efficient, so we must choose the best technology for the job.

Each initiative must have a shorter time to achieve those milestones than in the past. Businesses are unwilling to wait for two or three years to break even. Initiatives should deliver in three to six months and have a purpose beyond setting up for the future with unclear returns. We need a long-term vision of continuous transformation, but it can't come at the expense of today's returns. This represents a new balancing act and is yet another reason why technical strategy is so critical.

What's Next?

In early-maturity businesses, technical strategists are the only ones with a long-term vision. Once the technology establishes a track record of success with early initiatives, they can bring more opportunities to the business and define the bigger picture.

Implementing continuous transformation into initiative design gives the CEO more than a cool-sounding story to explain their increases in spending. They have projects to point to with proven returns. If investors question their decision to spend money on data, analytics, and AI versus a stock buyback, dividend, or preserving free cash flow, the CEO can push back. They can support the expenditure with execution and results.

Strategy planning evaluates trade-offs, and continuous transformation allows C-level leaders to decide how far the business transforms. All they manage is the value creation piece of transformation. They aren't dragged into managing the technology.

When senior leaders are forced to manage technology, they're taken out of their comfort zone. They go from the strategic, managing value creation, to the tactical, managing technical implementations and execution. We want to give C-level leaders frameworks that allow them to stay in their comfort zone and perform their highest value-creating activities.

The mistake technical teams make when working on getting buy-in is dragging C-level leaders into the technology. The purpose of continuous transformation is to separate value creation from technical implementations. At the top level, we should focus on opportunity discovery, not how we get there. Feasibility is part of opportunity discovery, but C-level leaders shouldn't be dragged down to that level as part of the process.

Immediately behind continuous transformation strategy is the technology model. Continuous transformation sets the stage to decide how much of the business and operating models should be transferred into the technology model. That also connects to opportunity discovery.

Each technology wave has a strategy because each technology manages a different type of value creation better than the other alternatives. One purpose of the technology model is to simplify this process. Leadership doesn't need to determine which opportunity or initiatives will leverage a given technology.

It's a simpler determination. The business is transferring pieces into the technology model. Those pieces can be part of a product or internal operations, and it doesn't change their calculation. The business plans to move a piece into the technology model because they see an opportunity to create and deliver customer value with a more efficient, effective, or new process.

Senior leaders and external business units see the top level of the technology model. They are given technical strategies, so they have a framework for decision-making from a value-creation standpoint. They have a framework to evaluate alternatives and understand the opportunities created or enabled by each technology.

Before we go there, though, we need to provide the business with frameworks to support adopting continuous transformation. That means culture change. Nothing else works without the next two chapters because people in the business are punished for adopting data and AI. We need to fix that so the business can move forward in alignment.

3

Why Is Transformation So Hard?

Continuous transformation and data break traditional business culture. That's why change doesn't come easily. Continuous transformation, data, and AI have institutional barriers to overcome.

Continuous transformation and enterprise-wide alignment sound awesome until you see them play out in the real world. Both constructs face significant challenges because legacy strategy, which most businesses are built on, is foundationally broken. Technical strategists must overcome not only digital debt but also strategic and cultural debt. We don't succeed in anything else if we don't make changes at this level.

In this chapter, I will introduce you to the sources of strategic and cultural debt. There's a reason so many well-run businesses have failed to implement a data-driven business. The challenges are structural, and understanding the root causes will help you to move forward.

By the end, you'll have a better grasp of how we got here and why buy-in is so challenging to get. You'll see the barrier to adoption more clearly and be ready for the solutions in the next two chapters.

Cautionary Tales

CNN+ was the streaming version of the first 24-hour news channel. The business allocated a total budget of $1 billion to developing, launching, and growing the new streaming offering over 4 years. It was touted as the future growth engine for CNN in a changing content marketplace.

Cord cutting is an existential threat to CNN's business model, and the streaming version was seen as the future. The business case was built on comparisons to the *New York Times*, a completely different business model. There were some similarities but not enough to make a data-supported case for CNN+. The counterfactual case and changing business realities were largely ignored.

Discovery was acquiring CNN while all this was going on. CNN+'s leadership decided to push the product out before the merger went through so the service would have time to grow before the new leadership came in. If anything, it would have made more sense to slow down and reevaluate once the merger was completed.

Discovery attempted to launch several niche subscription streaming products, but the ROI never materialized. GolfTV and the Food Network were notable cautionary tales that should have been evaluated before setting the strategy. In their focus on

New York Times and all the positive data that case provided, leadership ignored the data, which went against their already decided upon strategy.

CNN+ was launching just as subscriber growth at Netflix showed signs of slowing. Disney+ was publicly demonstrating how much it costs to fill a content pipeline that sustains significant subscriber growth. Despite the growing number of reasons to pull back on the launch, CNN+ went full speed ahead.

The platform development timelines had to be pushed out to deliver a high-quality product. HBO already had a platform it could have leveraged but didn't. Costs and complexity increased.

The pricing strategy failed to align with the changes in product strategy that were inevitable after the merger went through. To attract early customers, CNN+ offered a lifetime $2.99 monthly subscription. The pricing disincentivized customers from switching to a bundle of Discovery streaming products that included CNN+.

The goal was to reach 2 million subscribers by the end of the year, but after a brief initial subscriber pop, those numbers became infeasible. The service had between 4,000 and 10,000 daily viewers, indicating a steep decline in subscribers. Still, CNN+'s leadership advocated for the service to keep running.

Despite the best available data showing the decisions made around CNN+ were flawed, leaders held firmly to the slim data that supported their views. CNN+ was shut down just a few weeks after launch and a loss of somewhere around $300 million. The project should have ended much sooner when losses were nowhere near that level, but strategy planning and business culture don't support that approach.

A variation on that theme played out at Disney. Disney+ has been losing money since its inception, and Bob Chapek needed to turn that around. Investors were growing tired of the drag on profitability in the name of subscriber growth.

Chapek did something unthinkable to prop up subscriber growth. He ordered new releases to bypass the theaters and go straight to the streaming platform. That decision made some sense during the pandemic, but once theaters reopened and attendance rose, holding to that strategy was a major contributor to Chapek's eventual firing. Disney+ reaped small rewards while the core business suffered significant damages.

He alienated talent and movie makers with the decision. It cost Disney massively at the box office and reputationally. All of this was done to cover up the underlying business model issues with Disney+. The data proved it was time to look for new ideas. Chapek attempted to cover up the problem with a strategy that conflicted with the best available data.

The culture of data cover-up was on full display when Chapek increased park admissions pricing to offset the amounts being lost by Disney+. Disney's CFO reportedly went to the board to reveal the attempts to make financial data for Disney+ look better than it actually was by offsetting losses with gains in other parts of the business.

Leaders must stop creatively using data to support a narrative, or the data's value never materializes. We have cultural barriers to overcome that start at the top.

Data-Driven Transparency

The primary purpose of data curation for decision support is to help the business understand its critical internal and customer workflows. Data brings transparency with new information and insights. Everyone in the company should love that idea and get behind it. A more transparent business is a more efficient business.

Some will resist because their survival depends on opacity. CNN+ would never have launched if the company had been data-driven and used the best available data to make better decisions. Bob Chapek would still be running Disney if he had reacted and responded to data sooner instead of covering things up. Instead, he used data to support a narrative. In his mindset, the choice was a matter of survival.

Not every business unit produces value efficiently. Disney+ does not produce a value efficiently yet. It must continuously improve and transform. It must look for opportunities to leverage all available technologies to become more efficient.

Disney has world-class technical teams from digital, through data, and even emerging technologies. It should leverage these capabilities to determine how to make Disney+ produce value more efficiently.

At legacy businesses like Disney, C-level leaders don't bring their most significant challenges to the technology team. In a technology-first business, that would be the first place the CEO goes for help making business units run more efficiently.

People will resist transformation because it's a matter of survival for them. Instead of adapting to the change, they are still held back by legacy strategy constructs. Bob Chapek could not transform because admitting that Disney+ costs too much was equivalent to admitting failure. What would have happened to him? He thought he would get fired by deciding to change or pivot.

There is often a cover-up when business units cannot produce value efficiently. Many business units depend on opacity to function. I hate to say it, but entire parts of the business are intentionally siloed.

People are told not to talk outside of the organization. They think that if the rest of the business knew what they were doing, something terrible would happen. Their leadership wants to present a very controlled image to the rest of the company. If a business unit produces value inefficiently, its leadership is threatened by the introduction of data. Data scares their teams and is a significant threat to their existence.

As a result, some people in the business will resist to maintain the status quo. This is the culture technical strategists must fight. I hate to say it that way, but introducing data into the strategy planning process introduces transparency. That sounds great to us, but not everyone reacts so positively. Legacy thinkers will reject the data.

The Nature of Technology and FUD

Businesses should be using technology to support strategy. With each transformation, the company should look for ways to leverage these technologies to support the business's core strategy and goals. Each wave should reinforce the next one. The business should use technology only when it can be monetized. Technology should be leveraged only when it will support the business or operating model.

The key word is *should*. It implies an evaluation of trade-offs instead of letting what could happen dictate what should happen.

The fear of missing out is thick in our current business climate. As other companies succeed with AI, we see the fear play out in front of us. Snapchat released an internally built competitor to ChatGPT. That move has many of us scratching our heads trying to figure out why Snapchat wouldn't just partner with OpenAI or Anthropic. It doesn't make sense from an ROI perspective.

At the same time, Elon Musk announced that Twitter would develop an unbiased version of ChatGPT. OK, unbiased according to who and, again, what's the monetization? There's no definition of where this model will fit and why Twitter would take this on with all its other issues.

At this moment, it doesn't make strategic sense for most businesses to develop a large model. It just sounds cool, and that's the problem with fear, uncertainty, and doubt (FUD). It can drive strategy, and by extension, whatever is driving the FUD takes over strategy. In this case, technology is taking the wheel.

When technology drives strategy, the business gets a lot of technology, but it doesn't necessarily get much value from it. We should normalize asking, "Why should the business use data? Why should the business leverage analytics, AI, platforms, cloud, or digital? Why are we using any of these things?"

The purpose of data and AI strategies is to answer that question. Technical strategists must give the rest of the business the frameworks they need to manage this new kind of firm.

There's another harsh reality about technology: it doesn't care about the business. Technology doesn't care about society. Technology doesn't care about the marketplace or customers. It doesn't act in response to them.

Technology is an entity that's continuously improving and evolving independently of business and economic systems. Humans have an interesting relationship with technology and innovation. It's in our DNA. We are inventors by nature. No matter what's happened in the rest of the world, people will continue to invent stuff because that's just what we do.

Technology will perpetuate itself. That's its nature. It doesn't care if every business stops innovating. Technology would still advance, and companies would be built from nothing to exploit new technologies.

We must internalize this technical governing dynamic. It will continue progressing, just as AI did, without a business in the driver's seat. When OpenAI released the original GPT, its go-to market was, "Tell me what you would do with this."

In the past, that was a terrible business model. You shouldn't build something and then ask the rest of the world, "Well, what would you do with this? Can you make any money off this? Does this look good to you? What would you like to do with this?"

That's not the way successful products have emerged in the past. With venture capital, innovative startup business models are subsidized. Innovation can just happen on its own. Often, a business steps forward like Microsoft did and sees the potential. Microsoft evaluated GPT and saw multiple opportunities to monetize the model across its platforms.

Technology doesn't need a business or academia; it just needs humans. As long as there are people, there will be innovation and invention. The nature of technology is to perpetuate itself. Businesses must adapt technology to support strategy. It's one of the big reasons these frameworks are so vital to business.

Change is continuous, so businesses must look at each one of these technology waves and decide.

- Should we use this technology to create and deliver value for customers?

- Is this a promising technology for us to gain a competitive advantage or become innovators?

- Do our business and operating models fit? Could it make sense to pivot the business or operating models to adapt to this new paradigm?

The answers will differ from business to business, so it must be a strategic decision. The decision cannot be made by seeing that the technology exists; therefore, the business should build something with it. That's legacy strategy thinking and FUD. Everybody else is doing it, so our business must be a fast follower. We must get in there.

In that mindset, the decision is all about technology. Companies believe that if they build the technology, they'll just figure it out as they go. None of that works. The culture must adapt and transform to adopt technology and monetize it.

The Business Has Been Lied to Before

This is something that Rita McGrath articulated very well in *The End of Sustainable Competitive Advantage*. Businesses must continuously adapt and transform because competitive advantage cannot be based on a single technology. Technology evolves too quickly, so competitive advantage based on technology is transient.

Companies are expanding horizontally into other marketplaces to disrupt incumbents. They leverage technology to take market share. Competitive advantage is no longer sustainable because technology has foundationally changed how businesses and the marketplace function. Everything is continuously transforming.

The strategy planning process must continuously transform and evolve. The business's culture must continually transform and evolve to adapt to these new paradigms. Companies aren't designed or built to support any of this. In fact, some processes in place now block parts of the business from using data and becoming data driven.

I can't blame leadership for making the technical decisions that they did. A small army of people told them, "All you have to do is become digital, and that's it. You're good. Everything will follow and be easy from there."

Continuous transformation is the new reality. Even platform providers are returning to C-level leaders with a new message, "That digital paradigm that we told you about . . . so you actually do need to centralize your data." Vendors are introducing data mesh and other architectures to cover up the fact that they created a massive problem by siloing data next to the applications that used it. Today they must walk their way back, and I can't blame C-level leaders for being frustrated by it.

Businesses invested heavily to rebuild themselves for digital, and now they are being told to transform again. Transformation is hard because we have users who have been lied to. We may not have lied to them, but they don't care.

We are part of this amorphous technologist group that keeps coming to them and telling them that they must change. We tell C-level leaders they must invest more money into infrastructure and architecture. They must figure out data mesh and all these other technologies they don't understand meaningfully.

Most businesses are in a digital paradigm, and the culture was built to match. Data and AI are a different paradigm, and data can be used anywhere. We look at workflows as connected entities that flow from one side of the business to the other. *Recruit to retire* is one of these life cycles. HR needs data from every system across the company to support it.

Pricing models are another excellent example of data living all over the enterprise. I have built pricing models for very large companies, and it's horrifically painful to get data from these different silos. That was a significant contributor to the initiative's cost and the business's resistance to it.

If you're working at a technology-first company, you've probably never encountered any of this. Some of your customers or competitors can't adapt as quickly because they have massive technical, cultural, and strategic debt. Most businesses have legacy systems and legacy thinking. They can't simply implement a pricing model like Amazon, Meta, and Microsoft can. It takes longer because there are digital silos between the business and its data. As a result, transformation is painful.

Is It Sci-Fi or Reality?

We're advocating for dramatic change, so there must be something equally dramatic that the business is responding to. The paradigm shift is bigger than data and AI versus digital thinking. I tell a dramatic story to help explain just how significant this transformation is and how it will ripple through businesses for the next decade.

Strategy implementation ties into monetization. It's complex because data and models are novel assets. OpenAI, Google, Baidu, and NVIDIA have driven home the potential of human-machine teaming, but that's not the end. It's just a view through a keyhole.

What's on the other side will challenge your thoughts about monetization potential. The AI class of 2023 demonstrated the value proposition of one model category. This category is primarily aimed at automation and augmentation. They improve productivity and, in some cases, increase our capabilities.

What's being overlooked is a different class of models that are capable of time travel. Just like GPT-4 and other large language models (LLMs) made a big splash this year, this class of models will have equally significant impacts.

We don't think in long time scales, and things like strategy implementation occur on long timescales. The purpose of strategy is to help us deal with complex concepts across long timescales. It feels like it's getting more complicated, but it's always been this way. We haven't investigated the systems we interact with deeply enough to see the complexity.

Instead, we created deities to handle what we didn't understand. In Hawaii, the goddess Pele holds the volcanoes because those were once random actors. Today, we have some level of prediction capability to explain volcanos. We understand some of the systems behind volcanos and can predict them better than in the past.

Through logical explanations and increasingly accurate predictive abilities, we lost the need for Pele. Interestingly, we still have her with us in Hawaii, and her legend touches our behaviors. Locals will not take rocks from a volcano. You would have an easier time pushing a Hawaiian off a cliff than getting them to take a lava rock from one of the island's active volcanos.

We're horrifically superstitious, and there's no logic to it. The belief is built on a collection of stories about people who took a rock from a volcano and had horribly bad luck. Then everything turned around when they returned the rock to the volcano.

It's irrational, but when someone has a series of unfortunate events befall them, we look for a pattern and causes. We resort to these deities and beliefs if we can't find them. We've relied on the supernatural throughout history to manage complexity.

I am as data-driven as it gets. I would decline if you offered me $5,000 to take a rock from Volcanos National Park. The risk that I believe offsets the monetary gain is based on mythology and childhood stories. Yet, I cannot shake its grip. How can data succeed against our nature?

Introducing the nature of decision-making into data and AI strategy is essential. It is one of many aspects that we are working to transform. The changes that must take hold to support data and models go beyond the technical solutions. The head of data at Ally Financial said, "What I thought was a last-mile problem was really a first-mile problem."

He meant that Ally Financial began adopting data and AI by solving technical problems. Early initiatives and transformation begin by developing technical capabilities and buying infrastructure components. The objective is to deliver technical solutions, and that mission is accomplished. The tough questions begin when value fails to materialize.

It's only after several post-mortems and business soul-searching that the gap is revealed. No one defined what all those technical resources should be building or why. Focus on technology and the business will get it. Focus on value creation and the equation changes to include the business.

Strategy must lead technology for the returns to materialize. Evaluating technology for monetization first forces us to confront transformation's cost, complexity, and uncertainty. Can a business continue to make decisions the same way it always has and simply drop data into the process? Will that succeed, or is a transformation necessary before data can improve decisions?

The Coming Storms

We are constantly making decisions faced with uncertainty and complexity. Data and models allow us to handle both better than we could in the past. Today, we can forecast hurricane paths with remarkable accuracy. Growing up in Hawaii in the 1980s, the cone of uncertainty around the hurricane's path might as well have been the entire ocean.

Hurricanes moved across the Pacific, and we had no idea what would happen from day to day. If they approached the islands, we had to prepare as if each one would hit us. I was 5 when Hurricane Ewa came straight at us. It looked at Hawaii and said, "You know what? I'm taking a vacation right there."

We got hit by a category 1 hurricane, and going through it shaped many of us. That one-time event was so extraordinary. We had a power outage for over a week and had to boil water. Trees were shredded, and debris littered the streets. Street signs became projectiles and embedded themselves sideways into houses. I remember very little from that time in my life, but I can describe the sound of the wind hitting the windows in vivid detail. Those and dozens of other memories stuck with all of us.

Each time a hurricane approached, we bought batteries, prepared our radios, and ensured we had food and water for 10 days. Most homes had a hurricane survival kit, and we knew where we would go to evacuate. We had a primary room to ride out the storm and a fallback location in case that one was compromised.

We were overprepared for a hurricane strike. For years, the warnings came, but nothing happened. Time passes, memory subsides, and we forget the hurricane's severity. We were no longer conditioned to believe the inference being served to us by weather forecasters. Many hurricanes over 10 years just coasted straight past us. We became numb to the weather predictions and warnings to be prepared.

Hurricane Iniki was tracking far to the south and was predicted to miss the islands. It would cause some surf on the South Shore. I was ready that morning to go out and catch some fantastic waves. I woke up at 4 a.m. and put on my headphones to tune into the surf report. Instead of hearing a surf report, surprise, Iniki made a hard right, and it was coming straight for either Oahu or Kauai.

I could see the beach about a mile from my house. The same beach that this category 4 hurricane could be passing directly over. It was one of the most significant hurricanes ever to hit Hawaii, and no one was ready.

Few people were awake early enough to hear the warning. Civil Defense didn't put the sirens on until 7 a.m. because they feared waking people up. That's how numb we were. You might die, but we're going to let you sleep in.

It's a decision that shows our irrational natures as completely irrational actors. I had already lived through one hurricane, but the memory had faded, so I stopped preparing for the next one. A rational actor would have remained vigilant, but people don't fit that description.

The only reason that I got what I needed from the grocery store was because I was awake early to go surfing. The entire island appeared at the grocery store when the sirens rang. Camera crews documented the chaos.

Cars clogged the roads, trying to evacuate, but it was too late. People on Oahu, especially tourists, were mainly concentrated on the South Shore, right in front of the ocean and wouldn't have gotten to safety. They got really lucky that Iniki went over Kauai instead of Oahu.

We are terrible at using our experiences to develop effective heuristics, even in catastrophic circumstances. Data doesn't have a chance if we don't address an initial transformation in our work. What does that look like?

Time Travel

Our hurricane models have gotten a lot better. In the southern part of the United States, the Gulf Coast has strong experience reinforcement loops. People have been hit by hurricanes and remember the impacts. Anytime a hurricane warning is issued, most people take it seriously. Our models have a track record of success, and people are willing to act on the predictions they serve.

The impacts of high-value data and advanced models play out every hurricane season. Most of us can't remember when we didn't have weather forecasts integrated into our lives. Without forecasting, we wouldn't know a hurricane was coming, and our decision frameworks would be very different.

It would begin to get stormy, and we wouldn't know that we needed to get into a shelter until the hurricane really picked up. Residents might have an hour to prepare, so we had to act differently. We needed to be consistently prepared for days without access to clean water and the ability to get food.

Hurricanes delivered massive disruptions for extended periods because we couldn't time travel very far into the future. We could see only about a day, maybe hours into the future, giving us no time to prepare. As a result, we had to always be prepared.

Part of our strategy was inefficient for most days but prevented catastrophic impacts in the rare instances when the worst happened.

A forecasting model pulls information from the future into the past. If I know a hurricane will hit me in three days, I change my behaviors three days earlier. I have more options for my daily behaviors and preparedness. I don't necessarily need to have a shelter in my home, for example.

Residents can evacuate at scale. Florida often evacuates millions of people. Atlanta once evacuated 2.5 million people in 3 days. We have options that are feasible today only because we pull knowledge from the future into the past.

That's a paradigm-changing capability. In a Sci-Fi show called *The Peripheral*, they use quantum tunneling to send information to and from the future. The connection works over a VR headset. Characters put it on and operate a robot in the future. People in the future can operate machines in the past using the same principles.

The show explores something interesting about the information exchange. When the future sends information back to the past, the future has been altered. Past me has knowledge I would not have had and will act differently.

We can think of a business this way. If my model predicts a hurricane, my business will board up the windows and put sandbags out front. I will close and send everybody home in enough time to leave the city.

I put proactive measures that prevent losses. Instead of destroying my business, I've altered the course of events. Without that knowledge, something different would have happened.

Highly accurate models take knowledge from the future back to the past. They change events. What would have happened without that knowledge will not happen anymore. That's an intriguing concept for business leaders. I use the hurricane example because it's tangible and visceral.

More mundane examples happen all the time. We react to weather reports, so ships reroute from the shortest course by distance to the course with the lower risk. Did they have to? No, but we assessed the loss due to travel time and fuel against the rare ship lost in a storm—the math pencils out in favor of rerouting the ship.

That's where we're going with predictive, descriptive, and diagnostic models. We want increasing knowledge and awareness of our complex business systems. CEOs need more certainty, especially now, and that's brought increasing focus on data, analytics, and advanced models.

Time Travel in the Real World

Nike failing to see how normalization in its supply chain would impact future inventory caused a loss in 2022. Data indicated that the business would have an overstock situation in a certain number of weeks, so it should have changed its orders.

Apple slowed down its orders in response to those changing conditions. About a week or two after the iPhone 14 launch, Apple told suppliers to slow production, so the company avoided overstock. It leveraged predictive models to prevent a loss.

Apple pulled information into the past and fixed a problem before experiencing significant impacts. Apple and Nike both had a bad inventory strategy. It was based on bad data, unreliable models, or a combination of the two.

The power of reliability is to understand where our models fail. Defining circumstances and situations that cause models to behave unpredictably is critical. When we encounter those situations, models shouldn't be trusted.

An assumption was flawed or failed to remain constant. We should be monitoring those specific data points corresponding to our assumptions. If one of them goes beyond the tolerances, action is required.

In Apple's case, it was probably a demand feature for the iPhone 14 that exceeded the model's set range. Culture plays a role. Information from one side of the business needed to be delivered to people in charge of ordering phones and working with suppliers.

This is a powerful cycle. Models pull knowledge from the future forward, and we can change outcomes. Tracking assumptions allows the data team to notify the business when an assumption has changed. A default can be implemented while the team works to improve or retrain the model. Once that's done, the data team can deliver the updated forecast and recommendations.

Again, I'm pulling information back (the model was about to fail) and fixing the problem sooner. The business learns faster, which is a critical piece of what data science does for strategy. If the company fixes problems faster than competitors, that capability creates an advantage. Over time, the business continuously improves faster than its competitors.

Data-Driven, Adaptive Strategy

Here's an example. You would have missed significant returns leveraging Warren Buffett's value-centric investing strategy from 2012 to 2019. The assumptions baked into value investing did not hold during that time, so it wasn't optimized for those 7 years.

His strategy avoids businesses with high risk and poor fundamentals. For 7 years, things like Bitcoin and unprofitable tech companies continually defied Buffett's investment strategy.

In 2021, the assumptions baked into Warren Buffet's strategy returned. Implementing his strategy in 2020 would have set your portfolio up for significant returns. Companies with high growth until 2021 are down as much as 90 percent.

Warren Buffet didn't pivot because he knew that fundamentals always return to the market. He didn't know when for sure, but he was confident that eventually, sanity would return. Tracking assumptions is an excellent way to play both sides.

Warren Buffet knows his strategy will be superior in the long run but misses out on significant gains by staying the course. His strategy is not dominant in some smaller timescales. There are periods when a high-risk portfolio becomes the dominant investing strategy.

Warren Buffett sticks to his single strategy because it outperforms others in the long run. However, if you have enough information to see assumptions faltering, you could surf from dominant strategy to dominant strategy. With reliable models and assumption tracking, we could adapt to changing conditions.

Getting Warren Buffet to trust a model enough to change from value investing to a high-risk strategy would be daunting. I don't know if it's possible to change his mind. That's the same challenge businesses face. People with significant experience have firmly held beliefs. How do we get them to listen to data that contradicts those beliefs?

Mercedes has a short timescale feedback mechanism. Making changes to its car on Thursday is usually days away from winning or losing the race on Sunday. The company gets quick feedback, and there's no arguing over the outcome because it's binary. The car wins or loses the race.

Immediate, clear feedback creates trust. Trust is why the company calls themselves a science-based business. Mercedes has realized the optimal strategy is to use scientific methodology. Mercedes AMG likely attempted the mid-steps and halfway measures, which did not work. Experts relied on their gut and experience. Data was used only when it supported conventional wisdom. The car didn't win more races or complete lap times faster than data and model-driven competitors.

Having so many races each year allowed them to try more of those partial approaches and learn from each mistake. Iterations that lead to a better outcome are kept. Failures are quickly abandoned.

What if you didn't need to run the track to get feedback? A simulator can predict the impact on lap time based on a change the team is evaluating. Effects can be measured faster, and responses can be deployed with greater certainty.

The ability to simulate the race and car becomes a competitive advantage for the team. That's why racing teams train on simulators. They run hundreds of races before ever taking to the track. The driver has the track memorized under multiple conditions and competitive scenarios.

The team can do the same thing with changes and modifications to the car. The simulation must become more granular with models for engine performance, tire wear, and dozens of other components. They all fit together and form a complex system.

Most companies cannot model something that complex, and there's no business need to justify the expense of maturing that far. For Mercedes AMG, they must. Waiting for race day to measure the impact of changes isn't a viable strategy. They would guess based on expertise but couldn't iterate as fast as needed without the simulation.

Predictive, prescriptive, and diagnostic models change how businesses react, impacting future outcomes. The models introduce new knowledge to the business and enable strategy planning to improve.

Transformation is continuous for products, operations, culture, and technology. It's iterative by nature, so the objective must be to increase the transformation or improvement rate. Data and models are powerful tools to increase that rate. In fact, they perform this function better than any other available technology. This is one way businesses *should* be using data and AI because there isn't a more efficient alternative.

What's Next?

Many organizations don't know which outcomes and metrics they should be measuring. In racing, it's painfully obvious. Did we win the race or run the track faster? It's not so simple in most businesses. Feedback comes from dozens of sources, and success has multiple potential definitions.

I make the joke with clients, "We need data to discover what data we need." That's one reason I start with experts. No matter what path I choose, version 1 will be flawed. Its only utility is as my baseline for improvement. I know people are flawed too, but most experts beat the version 1 model, so their heuristics are where I begin. It's another way to build trust, but I'm also setting an example.

My models are no different than the business and people. None of the three is perfect. There's always room for improvement, so there's no such thing as done. That breaks business culture. In the next chapter, I'll explain why and what to do about it.

Cultural change can be driven by necessity and demonstrated by feedback loops. No matter how powerful the framework, it will not come overnight or by the end of the quarter. There is no finish line.

4

Final vs. Evolutionary Decision Culture

If the business is to transform as a cohesive unit, a critical success factor for technical strategy, we need frameworks to manage the culture changes required to support transformation. We can bring data into the strategy planning process with new frameworks. However, most businesses aren't designed to support data and models. It's quite the opposite. Many current business constructs are built in a way that sets data up for failure.

Frameworks are a way of reconciling the two worlds, data and business. Once we introduce data science into the strategy planning process, it forces firms to address their cultural and strategic debt. The release of CNN+ is one of many cautionary tales that showcase the potential for brilliant people to seek data supporting their firmly held beliefs. That's just one kind of cultural debt built into the strategy planning process.

CNN+ was launched in a final decision culture. The choice had been made, and there was no way for leaders to walk away from the decision after a certain point. CNN+ hit a point of no return and launched in defiance of the best available evidence.

In this chapter, I'll explain how to break the business of its bad habits and set up incentivization structures to build new ones.

Implementing Change and Taking Back Control

Businesses must change the way that data is used and the ways decisions are made. Different technology waves are converging, so the company must continuously transform. Strategy must enable businesses to benefit from each wave and create short-term competitive advantages. A significant but not obvious challenge is centered on a foundational property of people's relationships with technology that I brought up in the previous chapter.

Ubiquitous high-speed connectivity, the cloud, and advanced digital applications enabled CNN+. It was built because it was technically feasible, even though the platform was not anchored to a significant value proposition. CNN+ disproved the notion that if we build it, people will flock to the new technology because it is unique. A massive body of evidence spanning back decades teaches the same lesson.

Technology's rate of advancement necessitates frameworks that allow leaders to drive technology with strategy. Value should come first and be the primary driver. Technology meets the business where it is, no matter how mature or immature.

When technology drives strategy, the company must be at a high level of technical maturity before realizing returns. Transformation must finish first; then, monetization can begin. That creates a significant up-front investment to accelerate the transformation and a lag from investment to returns.

When strategy drives technology, the business implements technology that matches its current maturity level. There's no waiting necessary before the business sees significant returns. Maturity progression happens incrementally, and value is returned at each phase. Transformation doesn't need to race ahead, so costs can be minimized and spread out.

Some businesses are not only technically immature but also strategically immature. Process discovery and mapping are attempts by the company to understand itself better. Many have started the process as part of their digital transformation initiatives. It's a common starting point that can help integrate data and AI strategy into the current transformation process.

Continuous transformation is the top-level framework to manage the complex technology systems evolving agnostic to and independent of the business. Continuous transformation allows nontechnical parts of the company to simplify the technical components of their roles so they can make high-quality decisions.

Their mental model is surfing from wave to wave and finding ways to leverage each wave to improve the business or their role. People in frontline positions can think about how these technologies interact and could enable competitive advantages. To do that, they'll need a framework for each technology too.

Top-level systems comprise smaller subsystems that can be broken down with more granularity. In this example, technical strategy is the top-level system. It can be broken down into sub-strategies for each technology the business uses to create and deliver customer value. The complexity of managing this across the enterprise is high.

Paying Off Cultural and Strategic Debt

What does data do? Data and machine learning models help us reduce uncertainty and manage complexity. Data products do that better than other technology-enabled products. There's an intersection because strategy planning follows a data science workflow.

In the past, strategy wasn't planned or even viewed that way. Strategy was tested in production with a broken process, as in the CNN+ anecdote. Leadership made some assumptions, found data to support their assumptions, and moved forward with those assumptions baked in. By the time it becomes evident that those assumptions must be reevaluated, it's too late.

The leaders at CNN+ knew they'd be fired for reversing course too late in the game, so there was only one option. They pushed harder to pull off the Hail Mary. Costs rise, and strategy moves ahead despite overwhelming evidence that it's time to change.

Business culture doesn't support admitting a mistake. Do it after an initial investment, and it's a black eye. Do it after significant work has been done, and it's grounds for termination. In both cases, the dominant strategy is to push forward and hope to make it work. It's a similar mentality to a gambler who keeps betting more to win it all back. They don't see the $20 as lost for good. It's in a limbo state of unrealized loss, and the only way to get it back is to keep playing.

Introduce data and models into the strategy planning process, and now we create evidentiary support for a proposed strategy to succeed. We can also introduce data into the strategy planning process to improve decision-making about when to change. As technology creates new disruptions, the business must adapt.

The introduction of data and models changes the decision-making process. With data and models, people don't make a one-time big decision that is treated as perfect. We know it's not.

Mark Zuckerberg pushed billions into the Metaverse. He had evidence to support making a dramatic move. Margins were under pressure, and ad spending was slowing down. What was once a greenfield of opportunity had become crowded with competitors fighting over a shrinking pie. The Metaverse held the promise of a new greenfield with higher margins.

Conditions changed, and the assumptions that supported Meta's moonshot didn't hold. Mark Zuckerberg tested a pivot and found support for a new direction. Meta slimmed down significantly and turned back to an earlier technology wave that it had already built best-in-class capabilities around, AI. Instead of clinging to a decision in the face of mounting headwinds, Mark Zuckerberg adapted. He walked away from a firmly held belief that he had invested billions in.

Every decision is based on a set of assumptions. The famous song from the musical *Annie* goes, "The sun will come out tomorrow." It's a safe assumption until the middle of winter in a city located at a very high or low latitude. In other words, a safe assumption in most places doesn't hold everywhere.

In the data-driven paradigm, we make decisions based on the best available data and most reliable models. Will we get better data later? Definitely, as we get closer and closer to the future that the decision was made to succeed in, events we were guessing about become more certain. As the business's data maturity grows, it will have access to higher-quality data and more accurate models. Decisions will be better informed tomorrow than they are today.

In this paradigm, we should continuously improve our decisions, which must be designed for that purpose. It's a process that stands in opposition to how businesses operate today. Rewarding "being right" enforces a culture that can't adopt data. We're working to transform this mindset when we teach data and model literacy.

A cultural change is necessary, and we must train the business to integrate data and models into their workflows. In many ways, we are reversing the old paradigm of thinking. In that mindset, if you're wrong, you could be fired. A bad decision is synonymous with the wrong answer, which is even worse.

Our educational system reinforces the paradigm. What happens if I don't have all the answers on a test? I fail the test and may not pass that class. I could be forced to repeat that class because I was wrong.

Playing Better Poker Means Folding Bad Hands

But that's not the way the world works. We are constantly making decisions under uncertainty. Annie Duke wrote two books, *Thinking in Bets* and, more recently, *Quit*. She's a former professional poker player and introduced a decision-making framework she used to make good decisions during tournaments.

When should she allocate her finite resources, poker chips, to a particular hand? As a poker player, she operated with incomplete information. Her realization was that uncertainty guaranteed she would make bad decisions. Given that some decisions will be wrong, how can she optimize her process to minimize the number of bad decisions?

She showed that people could not be quality poker players until they stopped fearing bad decisions. Once a poker player, or CEO, accepts that they will make mistakes, they can adopt a successful mindset. While they cling to the fear of failure, their decisions cannot be optimized.

In *Quit*, she explains an equally counterintuitive new paradigm. We need to quit. Quitting is considered bad, but nothing improves if we don't stop doing the wrong things. Quitting destructive behaviors is good, right? We must learn to change our decisions and actions based on new information.

For engineers, this thought process is built into our development life cycles. We assume defects will be introduced at every phase and put gates in place to catch defects as early in the process as possible. The earlier the problem is detected, the less expensive it is to fix. Even after the software is released, we still look for defects and update applications regularly to resolve them.

We should ship updates to our strategy as more information is gathered from the complex systems the business interacts with. We must change iteratively in a pattern that follows the continuous transformation paradigm. The business's decision-making process transforms, and individual decisions will too.

Strategy planning results in the best strategy leadership could come up with based on the best available information. It is made with the knowledge that our data and models will continuously improve. Today, if you ask C-level leaders whether they expect to modify their strategy in 3 to 5 years, most will say "yes." What if they are provided new data in 3 months?

The scenario played out in 2021 and 2022 for the US Federal Reserve. It evaluated the data around inflation and took the position that it was transitory. As a result, the Fed chose not to increase interest rates aggressively to manage inflation.

Six months later, the data proved that inflation was not behaving as it should if the thesis of transitory inflation was accurate. Economists, politicians, and investors clamored for a change in monetary policy. They said the Fed was moving too slowly and had its head in the sand.

The US Federal Reserve changed course and implemented a series of rate hikes. You would expect praise, but the same people who yelled for the change said the Fed had lost credibility. A few critics were appeased briefly, but they quickly returned to oppose the speed and magnitude of rate hikes.

The Fed was blamed for making the wrong decision based on uncertainty. It was blamed again for holding to it for too long. It was blamed a third time for listening to the data and changing course. Then when multiple banks failed, it was blamed a fourth time for raising rates too fast.

Which criticisms were valid, and which weren't? Using expert knowledge to assess the available data and conclude that inflation was transitory follows a solid process. Even though the Fed was wrong, smart people worked together to make the best decision based on their best available data.

The Fed should get some blame for taking too long to react to changing data. That's a valid criticism in a data-driven decision-making framework. The rate of improvement must be optimized so the business, or, in this case, the Federal Reserve, can detect errors and deploy an updated strategy as quickly as possible.

Changing course should not have been criticized. If responding to the evolving conditions is punished, no one will do it, and businesses will follow a bad strategy off a cliff. The change should have been a net positive for the Fed's credibility. Financial markets could trust them to be responsive to changing conditions even when the data contradicted their firmly held beliefs. That's how the process must work, and we should be incentivizing it.

Fixing the Culture to Reward Data-Driven Decision-Making Behaviors

The shift to data-driven decision-making behaviors is a cultural change. Being wrong is part of the process and always has been. We are simply being more honest with ourselves. In the case of the US Federal Reserve and most businesses, responding to changes in data isn't met with the correct response to make decision-makers more likely to do it again.

We are also far too forgiving of leaders who ignore the data altogether. During the 2023 banking crisis, basic exploratory data analysis would have revealed the instabilities banks would soon face. The US Federal Reserve was transparent in advance of their rate hikes. Banks knew this was coming, and the Federal Reserve advertised a target rate range in early 2022. Still, risks were not managed appropriately, and some banks failed as a result.

At what point does a lack of data literacy and willingness to be data driven become a sign of incompetence? When will investors come around to demanding more data and model literate business leaders?

The emphasis must shift from being right at all costs to revealing the strategic components that are working versus failing. Leaders must adapt and fix failures before the worst impacts occur. This is a different strategy planning paradigm. The faster problems are identified, the less it costs to fix them. The more accurately the fix addresses the root cause of the problem, the fewer fixes must be implemented.

When we introduce data and models into the strategy planning process, we've changed it. We don't have a static, monolithic "The Strategy" anymore. It should change as soon as the business is given a reason. It should be built knowing the business will have better information available in the future.

I watched a podcast recently about the implications of 5G, IoT, and our ability to use complex models to understand the data that these sensors will generate in real time. 5G makes it possible to communicate in near real time with various devices and sensors, even with large data sets. I learned the assumption that those use cases aren't feasible no longer holds.

Should I wait until the next major strategy planning cycle at the end of the year to start thinking about the opportunities they create? Should strategy adapt based on this new information, or does the existing strategy support integrating these opportunities?

Strategy must be redefined altogether. We need new frameworks to deal with the complexity that's always been there and the rapid change brought on by technology's shortening improvement cycle times.

Frameworks must be flexible enough that the constant emergence of new opportunities and threats enabled by technology fits into them instead of disrupting them. These frameworks run contrary to how businesses have planned their strategy in the past.

Strategy consulting companies used to, and sometimes still do, tell C-level leaders whatever they want to hear. Decisions have often already been made, as in the CNN+ example. The consulting company is brought in to figure out some way to justify and put a rubber stamp on those decisions. Data science has completely different objectives.

Data science aims to determine what is happening, what is most likely to happen next, and what should be done in response. While the starting point is the same (expert knowledge), the objective is to find improvement opportunities. The starting point is a baseline, and there's no assumption that it is right or the best. The purpose is to discover the best way to move forward.

Data is brought to bear to support and discover a better decision without a preset definition aside from the destination, goal, vision, or endpoint. Improvement is assumed to be continuous. This is central to the growth mindset, and that's what data science supports (a new mindset is required to manage the process; I'll cover that in the next chapter).

Decisions should be assumed to be flawed in some way, shape, or form. There is always room for improvement, and that's the purpose of adding data to the decision-making and strategy-planning processes. The better the data, the more accurate the models become. Decisions and the resulting strategy improve in lockstep, but only if the culture supports it.

The thought process is entirely different. Traditional strategy consulting brings people in to find the right decision. Data science is incremental. We introduced data, and people made the best decision based on the available information. The decision and data are expected to evolve constantly.

That creates an entirely different paradigm for making decisions. No decision is ever final. The plan is to adapt and evolve based on better data as it becomes available. The purpose of decision-makers is to constantly reevaluate data and the decisions they make based on it. The goal of data scientists is to continually review the data, improve their models, deliver more reliable inferences, and improve business outcomes.

A Changing Incentivization Structure

The culture changes when businesses take the approach of "the best available data and the best decision based on it." In a final decision-maker culture, people are punished for being wrong. In an evolutionary decision-maker culture, people are rewarded for continuously improving. That means being wrong is part of the process. Introducing data into the workflow achieves evolutionary decision-makers' objectives.

The purpose of decision-making in the evolutionary paradigm is to minimize loss, not to eliminate it. In the final decision-making culture, there is a flawed assumption that loss can be completely minimized. That's simply not the case. People make poor decisions because we're imperfect, data is incomplete, and we cannot wait for certainty before acting. The final decision-making culture denies reality.

The US Federal Reserve was faced with high complexity and uncertainty. The pandemic was unprecedented, and the impacts were difficult to predict because we lacked a historical data context. They gathered experts together and made the best decision based on the data they had. The process was imperfect, but there wasn't an alternative. This is the reality most businesses face; denying the level of uncertainty involved or the potential for failure is ridiculous.

In an evolutionary decision culture, the incentivization structure is also very different. Decision-makers are rewarded for the process of identifying loss and reducing it. Evolutionary decision culture admits our essential nature. Running a business is dealing with decision-making under extreme uncertainty. There will always be mistakes made. The purpose of data is to help the company understand those mistakes sooner. Data also helps evaluate the impacts of different fixes so that decision-makers can find the best one.

In an evolutionary decision culture, autonomy is maintained by decision-makers because they have absolute control over the decision. Data is there to support and improve. In a final decision culture, data is a threat. Data might reveal a flaw in decision-making. In that case, it contradicts the decision-maker and takes control from them. That's why data science can't succeed in traditional strategy planning or final decision paradigms.

What's Next?

This is innovative, and businesses don't manage that very well, either. In this chapter, I covered one aspect of the cultural change necessary for succeeding with data and models. In the next chapter, I'll explain how to make the business more innovative and open to experimentation.

5

The Disruptor's Mindset

Innovation can't happen all the time, even at companies like Google. When you are in that lucky position of leading innovation, managing the process, or participating in it, enjoy those times because they do not happen often. Innovations are typically incremental improvements. The business can be patenting, doing something in a new way, or applying a new technology, but it's a variation on a theme.

The bigger innovations build something that hasn't existed before; the artifacts are unique. It's rare to be part of true innovation. I've been fortunate to be a part of that amazing process. It comes and goes too quickly.

Innovation happens in a rare confluence of events when the business needs, can afford, and has the resources and talent to put it into practice. Conventional wisdom says that without innovation, the business will fail. That's insufficient and lacks the substance to develop a pragmatic culture of innovation.

Most companies aren't successful innovators because platitudes aren't actionable. A couple of books for people to read about innovation and an idea capture process result from platitude-driven process design. It's called *innovation* but has never successfully resulted in an innovation that the business monetized.

That's the litmus test. If the current process has not delivered anything to the market or internal users and generated revenues, then it's ineffective. In most businesses, the process must be developed from the ground up. If we can't innovate all the time, how does the business decide how much it should be innovating? That's what I'll explain in this chapter. I'll also introduce a new mindset that supports innovation in a domain knowledge–driven business.

The Innovation Mix

The innovation mix defines the number of resources the business should spend on innovation initiatives. Data professionals and engineers want an innovation process. We understand the need implicitly, but we must get the rest of the business on board with it too.

The financially minded people fear innovation will be a boondoggle. Money will be spent, and nothing will materialize. C-level leaders also fear that too much innovation distracts from supporting the core business. Resources will be transferred away from near-term opportunities, and the core business will suffer.

I will provide a few innovation mixes as general starting points. These are not fundamental laws or rigorously defined ranges. It's where I start my assessment. I will get into more detail on how to customize those values later in the chapter. These serve to set expectations and give you a baseline.

For most companies in competitive markets, 20 percent of initiatives should focus on innovation, and 80 percent should focus on supporting the core business with established technologies. These projects stick to the fundamentals and what the company traditionally excels at.

That mix won't work for every business. In a very conservative company, highly regulated industry, or where there's a monopoly/semi-monopoly, 90 percent core business and 10 percent innovation make more sense. It's still critical to create space for innovation initiatives.

For industry leaders, innovators, forward-looking companies, and those on the leading edge, as much as 60 percent standard and 40 percent innovation could be the right mix. Even in an innovative culture, most of the business's R&D resources should not be dedicated to innovative projects. Incremental change and improvements are critical for every business.

The first group to convince is finance, and the only approach that works is telling the ugly truth. The time and capital invested in innovation is a new cost of business in the modern competitive landscape. I say, "We're essentially throwing this money away more often than not. However, if we don't, the business doesn't survive."

It's a tough sell, so I have some explaining to do.

Exploration vs. Exploitation

Every business is facing different circumstances and needs to calculate the mix in a more granular way. The most significant factors are the amount of new revenue the business plans to generate and the opportunities it has to meet that goal. Innovation is a process of exploring and developing new opportunities. Standard initiatives and incremental innovation exploit existing opportunities.

The concepts of exploration versus exploitation help teams such as finance, which are numbers driven, come to terms with the need for innovation. Innovation mix becomes an optimization problem when it's framed in these terms. Like everything else in the business, it's not a fixed amount but should adapt to meet changing needs.

Exploitation optimizes what the business has already built to extract the greatest value from it. Exploration optimizes for the innovation process to produce new opportunities for the future. That often means the business throws money into nowhere because not every initiative will deliver results.

I use uncommonly stark terms because if I don't, at some point, everyone will come to that conclusion on their own. Why hide the reality? Investment in innovation initiatives is a tax on profitability, but the business eventually runs out of opportunities to exploit and fails without this function.

I use the metaphor of exploiting a mine. First, the easy ore is depleted, and we must work harder to extract the same amount of ore. Eventually, we run out altogether, or extraction gets so expensive that the unit economics no longer work out.

Similarly, there is always an end to even the largest total market. Competitors will deliver a better way of serving customers' needs, and those needs change over time. One way or the other, the business's current opportunities will run dry. Exploration allows the company to discover new mines.

Finance needs something more tangible than a metaphor, so I start with a question. How well are the business's current customers served? We need data to understand what needs are being met, which are underserved, and what customers are unserved all together.

If current products partially serve customer needs, the business has opportunities for growth within the current line. Incremental product improvements and additional features to support tangential needs haven't been fully explored. Opportunities exist to support more customers' workflows or improve how existing products support them. I will come back to the concept of workflows throughout the book.

The business faces a different future if the customer needs are well met. Multiple product alternatives in the marketplace, or an existing product that handles the entire customer workflow, are setups for slowing growth and eventually a contraction. Exploration makes more sense because the business will get diminishing returns from continuing to invest in exploitation initiatives.

The year after a new product line launches, the opportunities for exploitation should be the highest. During that time, the business should lean heavily toward standard initiatives. The company needs new growth opportunities when product lines mature and competitors saturate the market with alternatives.

What Happens with Too Much or Too Little Innovation?

Google presents a wonderful example of too much exploration but not enough exploitation. It has become notorious for this. Google releases a very innovative product, but customers aren't well served by the first versions. It barely suits their needs, but it's so innovative that some people adopt it and make it work.

Gmail is an excellent example of not enough exploitation. Google released it and has done little to disrupt email or take market share from competitors. When Microsoft was deep in its cloud-first turnaround strategy, Google had a window to take market share from Office, but it needed to invest in incremental innovation and serving customers in better ways.

Google had the earliest versions of GPT and built in-house productivity tools with it. It had a multiyear head start on

Microsoft's 365 Copilot functionality. Rather than exploit the opportunity, Google let it languish on the shelf until Microsoft and OpenAI beat them to market.

Google's productivity line languished due to a lack of focus. Its top talent was busy building the next significant innovation while less glamorous projects gathered dust. Gmail and its version of Microsoft's productivity suite could have enabled Google Cloud adoption if they had gotten more traction. I could spend a complete chapter talking about the missed opportunities.

If Google had innovated incrementally and exploited Gmail, it would have been a foot in the door to the enterprise. That's something Google is desperately trying to get today. Google exemplifies what happens when exploration is over-incentivized but exploitation is largely ignored.

The process must be a pendulum. The business sees slowing growth in its existing opportunities and starts the pendulum swinging toward more innovation initiatives. Those initiatives deliver a new line, and the pendulum swings back to take full advantage of the latest release.

Margin compression should trigger a swing to exploration. That's the leading indicator of a tapped market or opportunity, and it's time to innovate again. It's better to have always been doing 10 to 20 percent innovation. First, it can take several iterations to find an opportunity and successfully develop products.

Second, the business can fall out of the habit and forget the need for innovation altogether. When that happens, the company runs the risk of being caught flat-footed. The firm doesn't realize it needs to innovate until current opportunities dry up. The danger here is that the resources necessary to support innovation aren't available when the need becomes unavoidable.

Before Satya Nadella took over Microsoft, the company was flatlining, with nothing innovative delivered for almost 5 years. The company tried to drag growth from Visual Studio, SQL

Server, Windows, and Office. Azure was a product that lacked the attention needed to become a growth driver. Microsoft had been distracted by Zune and Surface failures, which emphasized novelty over customer value. Microsoft had forgotten why innovation is critical and lost its leadership position.

Azure was built like a loss leader to sell more Server OS licenses, and the company treated it like Microsoft's version of the Costco food court. It was unusable in the early days, so adoption was low. I worked at two businesses using the Microsoft development technology stack. Both evaluated Azure and decided not to adopt it. We were running an imperfect on-premises cloud with VMware and the hypervisor because the pain of maintaining it ourselves was lower than the pain of adopting Azure.

Nadella took over and restored innovation to Microsoft. The company went all in on the cloud and could do so only because Microsoft still had enough money. The company pivoted toward the cloud so late that catching up cost far more than it should have, and much of the market was firmly controlled by Amazon's cloud, AWS.

Innovate Before It's Too Late

Most companies don't realize the need for innovation until after their decline has cut deep into the business and depleted its resources. Companies pin their turnaround hopes on proven opportunities and core lines. Many companies will fail in the next 2 years by trying to revive obsolete products instead of moving on from them.

Companies that don't invest anything into innovation initiatives will have stagnant product lines and significant customer attrition rates. Competitors that allocate resources to innovation will have the advantage. Their innovation pipeline will deliver while other companies struggle to start the process.

In the middle of 2024, many firms will realize that their market share is declining because their products are no longer best in class. Some businesses will see the threat on the horizon and pivot to investing in innovation. Most will remain in wait-and-see mode, hesitating until the business impacts grow before responding.

The danger is that most companies will wait too long and pass a critical margin compression threshold. After that point, they don't have enough margin to invest in innovation. Margin compression is a call to action, and investment in innovation becomes critical to survival.

The death knells for current product lines are collapsing pricing power and an inability to differentiate. These both signal the need to do something innovative with that line or innovate in a new direction. Risk drives the fear that keeps businesses connected to lagging products.

Each business has a level of risk tolerance that dictates how much rope an innovation initiative gets before senior leadership pulls the plug. Risk tolerances also control how much profit the business will divert into the innovation money pit. Senior leaders are the most risk-tolerant when growth is easy, and money flows freely. The global economy exited that cycle in 2022.

Every business has spent the last 18 months reevaluating its risk tolerance, with most becoming more conservative. Innovation mixes were long overdue for a correction, which is a positive sign of maturity. Margins will continue to tighten, and revenue will fall for businesses with stagnating lines. The knee-jerk reaction will be to reduce spending on innovation even further, and that's the trap.

The more desperate the company becomes, the more risk-averse it becomes. Leadership will avoid the risk of investing in speculative innovation initiatives. The early parts of the margin compression cycle sap the business's will to support innovation. The mid-to-late stages sap the cash needed to invest. This cycle should be front of mind, but most C-level leaders have investors telling them to do the opposite.

When the business is profitable and still on top, leadership must imagine when the product line that can't lose today will start to fail. You can see the challenge in making that stick, making the innovation mix critical. Explaining margin compression and the cyclic nature of products helps frame the conversation.

EVs and Innovation Cycles

Electric vehicles competing against gas-powered cars set up the cycle in the auto industry. Gas-powered vehicles are facing a demand shift, and forward-looking companies saw the trend coming. Ford is taking factories that produce gas-powered engines offline. It invested billions in developing them for more than 30 years.

Ford made the tough call to idle them because the outcome would be even worse if it produced too many gas-powered vehicles. Ford is competing in a marketplace with reducing demand for gas-powered cars because customers are moving to electric vehicles (EVs).

A few car manufacturers are still charging into producing gas-powered vehicles. They're fighting economics and basic math. If the total number of gas-powered cars produced doesn't decline, margins will begin their downward spiral.

Forward-looking car manufacturers understood that they must innovate by investing in EVs, or they would die. It spurred them into batteries, new assembly lines, new plants, and walking away from investments in old product lines. They displayed the will to quit.

Quitting is an understated component of innovation. We must abandon the old, familiar, successful thing before it becomes the thing that kills the business.

The multibillion-dollar EV investment will no longer be possible once the cycle takes hold and margins spiral down rapidly. For a decade, companies could borrow their way back to competitive parity, but money is no longer cheap and flowing freely to declining businesses.

For innovation to succeed, companies must be forward-looking and begin exploration before margins dry up. The budget available for innovation should be a function of margins. A business with very low margins usually has a tiny innovation budget. However, innovation is the most critical in low-margin businesses, so spending runs contrary to margins.

Putting the Structure in Place for Innovation

The business needs someone who can say yes to innovation. That person needs a budget and an innovation mix guideline to align their decision-making with the business's needs and risk tolerance.

It's equally important to define innovation. Senior leadership must articulate the directions it is interested in innovating. The company must define what innovation looks like.

- New or existing customer segments to target
- Marketplaces to enter or new opportunities in current marketplaces to exploit

Undefined innovation makes it impossible to say "yes" and keep initiatives connected with business value. The process needs definition too.

- Who is involved in the innovation process?
- How does someone initiate the process?
- Who has oversight of the innovation process?
- Who reviews initiatives and keeps them connected to business value?

- Who ensures that innovation initiatives are technically feasible?
- Who green-lights the costs and approves the budget?

The business needs to create incentives for effort versus outcomes. Google is very good at this. It rewards people for the work they perform and what they complete versus the business outcome. Innovation fails more frequently than standard initiatives. If the business incentivizes based on results only, no one on an innovation team would put much effort into their initiatives.

Businesses need an incentivization structure to match the reality of innovation initiatives. Sometimes the only artifact is the work itself, and no measurable outcome exists. Rating innovation quality includes the initiative's viability. Did this have potential, and was it presented transparently from the start? Was there always a connection to business value?

The value at the other end of the equation could still be 0, so the business needs a way to evaluate and reward the work that went into 0. The effort must always be aligned with potential business value, even if it never materializes.

Did this follow the process? We can't reward people for going rogue, which is something that Google does not do very well. There are stories of Google engineers going off process everywhere. It seems like Google is challenged to drag people back on task.

I recommend connecting individual incentivization or employee reviews to the initiative review process.

- Was it followed?
- Were you an effective participant in that process?
- Were you transparent about progress, and did you effectively communicate it to the review team?

Building the Culture for Innovation

The business needs a new mindset to support data science, the Disruptor's mindset. The same way of thinking supports innovation too. The life cycles that produce high-value data science artifacts align closely with other innovation processes. I will cover managing research in later chapters and explain the relationship further.

Disruption and innovation are fuzzy, and the challenge is to manage the fuzzy thinking with a tangible, concrete framework. The most significant challenge is keeping innovation connected to business value.

The personalities and processes do not lend themselves to delivering something that fits on a product road map and delivers on a predictable timeline. The creation process is different because the output is disconnected from anything existing. Still, it must be connected to business needs.

Outcomes must be directed toward artifacts the business can monetize. Innovation in the business world differs from innovation in the social and academic spaces. We innovate at the government level for the nation's greater good, sometimes the greater good of the world. We innovate in academia to further the dissemination of knowledge and to discover it.

Businesses require a third type of innovation that's directed toward value and connected with needs. We cannot just implement any innovation. It must be something the business can monetize, or it doesn't matter how amazing the artifacts are.

The next challenge is avoiding ideation overload. Everyone has seen drop boxes or email addresses such as innovation@yourcompany.com where you can send your innovative idea. Those are horrible ideas and result in ideation overload.

Innovation rarely fails due to a lack of ideas. If you want crazy ideas, all you need to do is pull 50 people off the street, and you will get 50 crazy ideas. When we open the suggestion box to everyone, it gets filled with variations on existing themes. The business can get lost in minor improvements and miss the giant leaps.

The critical challenge is the dichotomy of connecting those two things, reality and fuzziness, together so innovation results in something tangible.

An Innovator's Way of Thinking

That leads me to the Disruptor's mindset. We know about growth and fixed mindsets. Innovators have something different, and it's why innovative personalities are so hard to deal with. Every interaction can feel like a verbal knife fight.

Innovators will not accept anything in front of them until it makes sense. Disruptors must be able to break ideas down on their terms. In a Disruptor's mindset, all views are welcome and under attack. A Disruptor proposes an idea not because they think it's real but because it might disrupt you. It's an attempt to jar your thinking and push you sideways, so you think differently about the problem or product you're looking at.

A Disruptor is not thinking in straight lines and says some absolute nonsense. Then they'll run it down because they're used to nonsense resulting in something. Nonsense is the way that their brain works things out.

They'll come up with an idea, and it becomes all-consuming. They found a flaw or an assumption they don't like. They found something that doesn't make sense anymore. Here's an example.

Data pipelines are engineered with the mentality that we deliver data to an application or traditional software, but we're not. We're delivering it to a model that doesn't use data like software. Models use data to learn about a complex system and create a simulation of it.

Models don't have a set behavior like applications do. The model architecture we're using is designed to understand the data. We hope the data represents the system we're trying to understand better, so it's generating the data set we need to focus on. The value data engineering delivers to the business is curating data for model training. Cleaning and transforming must be part of the data generation process, not an afterthought.

I removed the flawed assumption (we're delivering data to an application) to introduce a different endpoint and critical objective (delivering data to a model that learns the rules of a complex system). How does that change impact the data engineering role? That's a disruptor's question. The whole purpose is to get you to look at this role differently.

Disruptors begin at a spot we don't see, not because they have seen the path yet. They see something fuzzy, and they need to quantify or define it. It's like they are genuinely building a plane in midair, and the result is often a boat.

That's why innovation is so hard to manage. A necessary part of the process is being comfortable exploring a line of thought without a set of steps to define where the exploration will go. Innovators, much like data scientists, don't always see the full path or arc, so they'll end up with a finished product that may not match their original objective.

Managing Constant Change and Disruption

We can't always reach a consensus with disruptors because they don't have a set worldview. The connections between concepts in a disruptor's mind are not fixed. They reassemble the relationships between ideas, and by continually fighting with their understanding of reality, they can make leaps and discoveries that elude the rest of us. They break relationships and see what changes after thinking about the implications of something ridiculous to the rest of us.

We must change the need for consensus to support a data-driven culture too. We must look for flawed or changing assumptions for decisions to move from final to evolutionary. Our business views must be open to change and challenge.

You can look at a river and say it's frozen. I can look at a river and say no, it's flowing. What happens next? In a final decision-making culture, the person with the best title wins the argument. We can leverage the disruptor's mindset to be more data-driven and implement an evolutionary decision culture.

We can go down and poke a stick in the river. If the stick hits a hard surface, it's frozen. You're right. If it splashes, nope, it's liquid. I'm right. We've conducted an experiment and generated data to define the river's state.

For innovation to exist, we must let go of constant consensus. Not every interaction will result in us agreeing, so data gathering or generation becomes critical. We're used to pointing at historical precedents and our experience to support our firmly held beliefs. Data-driven culture requires constant reevaluation and openness to revisit what we thought we had proven.

The disruptor's mindset supports an evolutionary decision culture. Without the need for consensus, it's OK for people to have different views. Contradiction isn't conflict. It must become part of the process.

With the disruptor's mindset, a challenger may be unable to prove their perspective and refute the incumbents' perspective entirely. We must work together to support the challenger. That's the messy part about disruptive thinking and the disruptor's mindset.

I must be willing to quit my side, or I will never learn anything. We can't innovate if we hold to the same beliefs or make it challenging to introduce new ideas. The acceptance of constant challenges supports innovation but also enables a data-driven enterprise.

These minority views are critical because they bring new knowledge and information to the group. The purpose of data gathering and generation is to deliver new knowledge to the business.

When someone brings data or an experiment to validate or refute new ideas, the team must pursue that avenue of exploration. At the same time, a review process should be put in place to ensure the experiments we approve and the concepts they explore connect to the business. I talk about this more in the section on managing the research process.

What is the ROI for knowing the river is frozen versus flowing? Great data science starts with high-value business questions, which must be assessed before a question gets passed on to the data team.

Preventing Data-Driven and Innovation from Spiraling Out of Control

Assessing data gathering and experiments is critical because we need a gatekeeper who prevents chaos. The experimental outcomes must be valuable for the business, and there must be a path to monetization. Products that result from innovation or knowledge brought into the business through experiments must generate tangible returns.

Proving the consensus view wrong or developing a new product could have significant value, but we need a framework for evaluating uncertain outcomes. What if the business conducts the experiment and the consensus view is proven correct again? The money spent was thrown into thin air.

Chasing a very low-probability hand on a poker table can be lucrative, but the odds are I'm throwing my bet away, never to be seen again. I need one card to make a royal flush, but seeing that card will cost me $1,000. The odds aren't good, so I must consider my payout. I will win $500,000 for chasing a royal flush.

The one card with a low probability must be weighed against $500,000 in returns. It's never a simple odds-to-returns calculation. The statistically correct choice is to spend the $1,000 for a 2%+ chance of landing the $500,000. A business has more to consider.

How often will the business have the chance to make $500,000? If there are 10 options on the table and some have a better chance of success, the company must prioritize its experiments.

How much does $500,000 mean to the business? A small business making $5 million annually has a different perception of value than a large company making billions per year. Often the correct answer is to allocate people's scarce time to find opportunities with a magnitude of returns that are significant to the business's goals. The $500,000 could be the initiative that makes a small business's year, but it won't move the needle much for the larger business relative to their goals.

That's how businesses must evaluate data gathering and experiments. The value of being right is just as significant as the probability of being right, and probabilities are relative to returns.

The disruptor's mindset is critical because some data gathering will challenge firmly held beliefs. Experiments will discover patterns that contradict conventional wisdom. The business must transform culturally to support data-driven and science-driven paradigms.

The data team needs support from the C-level down for disruptive thinking. Otherwise, they can only present data supporting the business's current thoughts. Those initiatives are not innovative and will not give the business high-growth opportunities.

There's an important overlap between data science and innovation that requires a disruptor's mindset to support. In both, we're presenting something new to the business. Explaining an innovation or challenging a firmly held belief requires people to be prepared to change.

Adopting an innovative, data-driven culture needs a process and framework that allows people to evaluate challenger views. The disruptor's mindset is a method that helps people stop looking at a problem with the same biases and assumptions that prevented them from solving it in the first place. Disruptors challenge axioms and first principles. That's where the most significant new ideas and innovative products come from.

What's Next?

You're one step closer to implementing continuous transformation. You understand the sources of cultural and strategic debt. You have frameworks to implement a new mindset, decision-making process, and innovation mix. You know the value of introducing data into the strategy planning process to improve the business and stay ahead of competitors.

Next, I'll provide frameworks to tackle strategic debt, and those require a redefinition of strategy for the data and model-driven competitive marketplace. Why do we need a new definition of strategy? I'll explain.

6

A Data-Driven Definition of Strategy

The purpose of this chapter is to define business strategy with data and models as part of the process. Transformation is now continuous, which forces traditional strategy planning to adapt. Business culture must adapt to support the new paradigm. The foundation is there, and we need frameworks to develop the rest.

I promised to talk about systems and models too. This definition of strategy is a model that will explain the rules of the competitive marketplace or system. From there, the frameworks that come after will help your firm optimize for these rules and its desired outcomes.

Technology cannot be an external part of the strategy calculation or the core driver either. A new definition of strategy will help businesses to integrate technology into strategy. Like any other, it becomes a core pillar and needs its own strategy. Marketing, supply chains, and talent all have strategies, so developing one for technology is long overdue.

Technology is further reaching than most strategies. Data, analytics, and advanced models are cross-functional impact creators. Those products can be leveraged by HR, marketing, finance, and every other business unit. Customer-facing products can leverage technology to deliver significant value.

Technology can add value to every part of the business and operating models. It redefines strategy, but more than that, it redefines the business. In this chapter, I'll define strategy for the modern competitive marketplace. In the next chapter, I'll explain a top-level framework to manage technical strategy.

How Quickly the Innovators Became Laggards

IBM didn't change its strategy much from the 1960s through the 1980s and was enormously successful. It was a technology innovator in a time when technology didn't move very quickly. Then Microsoft showed up and took the PC business from them. How do they lose the PC business? They're IBM!

IBM went from innovator to laggard in a short time. It was building PCs and operating systems before Microsoft existed. The technology was there, and IBM was an innovator. *What was missing?*

IBM wasn't the first or last time we saw last generation's innovator become the next one's laggard. Mark Cuban came out of the dot-com bust. He sold his first business for a few million and did something clever with that exit. He used some of that money to buy Broadcast.com, a streaming audio service he helped transform into a streaming video service.

Yahoo realized streaming would become a huge business. Cuban and Broadcast.com had high-profile streaming events in the 1990s, like the Victoria's Secret runway show. He proved the concept and technology were viable before taking the business public.

Cuban sold Broadcast.com to Yahoo in 1999 for $5.7 billion. Yahoo shut down the business in 2002 in what's been called one of the worst technology acquisitions ever. The technology was there, and Yahoo was an innovator. *What was missing?*

Yahoo was sold to Verizon in 2017 for only $4.5 billion, $1.2 billion less than it had paid for Broadcast.com. Verizon combined AOL (a $4.4 billion acquisition) and Yahoo into a new company called Oath. In 2021, Oath sold for $5 billion. Fortunes are made and lost in technology in the blink of an eye.

What was a dominant technical competitive advantage one day can become obsolete the next. Yahoo owned an inside track to streaming content, e-commerce, search, and social media. The company lost each one to faster-moving startups.

Netflix was sending DVDs in the mail and competing with Blockbuster when it decided to pursue the streaming opportunity that Yahoo didn't have the vision for. Netflix leveraged the technology that Yahoo had in its hands for years. Today Blockbuster doesn't exist. Yahoo is a shadow of its former self. Netflix has become a giant. Why did this wave of startups succeed where better-positioned incumbents, even those seen as innovators of their time, failed?

Technology is a potent weapon, but only if the business understands how to wield it. It's time to deploy our technical arsenals with a strategy that amplifies their impact instead of constantly hamstringing them.

Many strategy discussions begin with the book *The Art of War*. There are overlaps in the nature of competition, but businesses and marketplaces are not comparable to warfare. I prefer to start with a different book on strategy and warfare. In *On War*, Carl von Clausewitz later made the connection between politics, civilization, society, community, and conflict. He explained what drives warfare is deeper than conflict at a physical and kinetic level.

The most critical concept that von Clausewitz introduced was that warfare or struggle continues until the cost of continuing to struggle is higher than the cost of submitting to another person's, country's, or business's law. That's powerful because he turned warfare into an equation that can be optimized.

Victory isn't achieved until resistance ends. On one side of the equation is the loss of submitting to change or transforming. On the other is the loss of continuing to resist change or transformation. The winning formula is to lower the transformation loss and increase the loss of not transforming.

Startups built on new technologies lack the resistance to change that incumbents have. Incumbents had to overcome that internal resistance before the business was ready to embrace the new technology and build its future in a new direction.

In companies like IBM and Yahoo, an internal war had to be fought and won before transformation could progress. Their industry leadership and incumbent status made the equation tip toward high resistance. *Why change what has worked for the business until now?*

In the era of continuous transformation, businesses cannot afford to be in a perpetual state of war with themselves.

Using Strategy to Balance the Scales

We're not just asking people to adopt something new. We are asking them to stop doing something comfortable and begin doing something uncomfortable. People believe change brings a ridiculous amount of effort, pain, and mental complexity. They see change as a threat to them and their way of life. Data and AI strategy must inform decision-making and enable change by reducing the loss, or it's worthless.

Data goes to war with people. Resistance is so strong because, across the business, people do not believe that data and models are here to help them. They believe data and models are here to help them end their careers. These are existential threats to legacy strategy and business culture. We are threatening firmly held beliefs with continuous transformation.

An MIT Boston Consulting Group study found that people view AI as a teammate, not a tool. A new teammate replaces someone. They didn't use to feel threatened by software tools or apps like Microsoft Word or Excel. GPT-4 and Copilot changed the perception. Jobs are clearly threatened, and for the first time, software engineers are feeling the threat.

Technical teams see data and AI products making users' lives better. Those internal users see a teammate and, eventually, a replacement. They will continue to resist until the loss of continuing resistance is greater than the loss, in their minds, of accepting this new law and culture.

Transformation will be easier with strategy because we provide everyone in the business with a decision-making framework. Now it isn't the data science team's law; it is the business's culture.

In warfare, strategy came into existence because we have very high stakes and complex decisions made under massive uncertainty. The stakes in business are very high. The business's survival and the success of everyone employed there hang in the balance. When strategy fails, people lose their jobs and livelihoods. Investors lose large sums of money.

Strategy informs decision-making to create a connection between actions and outcomes or investments and returns. Data and models can reduce uncertainty and improve decision outcomes. But first, we need to redefine strategy so it can be optimized.

Redefining Strategy

Strategy is a statement of why that forms a thesis for action. It's a larger construct that helps us select what we should do. It acknowledges that we are faced with multiple alternatives. Each alternative or opportunity has potential but also hides risks.

Strategy must be actionable and inform decision-making, turning it into a unifying force. Alignment can be built by giving the enterprise a single framework for decision-making about technology. This is one of the primary purposes of data and AI strategy.

At the top level, strategy is the study of leverage and advantage in competitive zero-sum games. This definition fits the data and AI-driven competitive landscape because it's expressed in game theory terms.

The first concept is leverage, and it's best to think about it just like a physical lever. A lever is a tool that allows us to lift more than we could without it. In business, leverage follows the same paradigm. Technology creates leverage for the company. It will enable the business to create and deliver value better than competitors.

Once a company has that lever and advantage, it can take more resources than its competitors. The firm uses the lever to create an advantage and become more successful. Opportunity discovery is focused on finding levers that the business will use to perform better in the marketplace.

What is a zero-sum game? It means there are winners and losers. Competition is forced by finite resources and multiple players having overlapping objectives.

In the Internet age, it's hard to think of anything as finite or limited. Meta's market size, the total number of customers they could potentially service, is massive but finite. Something as vast as everyone with an Internet connection is still limited. In this case, they're in a fight for attention. Meta's competition ranges from video games to streaming content to other social media companies.

There are only so many people who can spend time on Facebook. We have only so many hours in the day to dedicate to a social media platform or any entertainment content. That creates an upper bound on the total amount of time Meta can get people to spend on its platforms.

Those limits have a direct connection to revenue. Meta can serve only a limited number of ads to each person. It needs levers to create an advantage over its competition in the battle for attention. As large as that seems, the resources are still finite, so it's still a zero-sum game, and strategy is necessary.

The zero-sum game reveals the less obvious types of competition that are going on. Facebook and a video game like GTA are competitors, but it's not immediately apparent. However, breaking the marketplace down to first principles makes it evident that the two compete for the same finite resource. Customers are deciding whether they play a video game or spend more time on Facebook. Each business in the attention economy needs to find a lever that gives it an advantage over its competitors in an attempt to get more of that finite resource.

Scale has changed the nature of competition, and technology alters the competitive landscape. With complex technical platforms and Internet scale reach, companies can now expand to such an incredible size that they fight for resources like the attention of Earth's population.

That's an enormous marketplace. In it, social media, gaming, streaming services, all forms of entertainment, and even educational content fight for hours. The most precious resource for many companies is our attention. They need levers to help them gain some of that precious time and attention.

This book competes against Meta or a video game. You could be doing anything right now and giving your attention to many other platforms. I appreciate you reading this book because I understand the myriad of choices you have. I must admit, I'm also a little proud that I can win the competition against a Titan like Meta.

Resistance and Autonomy

Technology enables competition at scale and allows businesses to deploy levers for advantage at scale. Companies can leverage data and AI to see complex patterns emerging in the competitive landscape. Businesses can study leverage and evaluate the efficiency of one lever versus another. The lever's strength in an individual market can be quantified. If broken down appropriately, this becomes a data science problem.

Once we understand strategy in data science terms, we can break it down into a problem space, connect it with a data space, and define a solution space. Strategy is also a data science workflow; we evaluate both strategy and data science in much the same way. What's even more powerful is what we can do once we leverage data and advanced models to learn the competitive zero-sum game's rules.

Through the process of transformation, we will encounter resistance. One primary motivator that gets people to pick up books like this is they're encountering significant resistance to data and AI. This points directly back to constructs of warfare. Why do people resist change, even when it is obviously in their best interests?

They don't want to submit to someone else's law or the zero-sum game's rules. One side doesn't like the other telling them what to do. This creates an existential threat because transformation and adoption attack people's autonomy. Data in AI could be prioritized above other technologies. The budget for those technical resources could be prioritized over other organizations. That inherently leads to conflict.

We're back to the competitive zero-sum game and internal warfare over scarce resources. People will resist change. When we introduce data into people's workflows, we ask them to change. We're saying, "Quit the old and adopt the new." This seems like an easy, no-brainer from the data team's perspective.

However, we're telling people to stop doing what they're doing and learn something new. If those people have an approach or methodology that works today, their question is, "Why? Why should I change?"

This creates two opposing sides. On one side, the data team says, "Just use this report or this new automation." On the other side, there is heavy resistance because people are working and succeeding now with what they have. As a result, there's no value proposition in changing. Again, we need a strategy to help inform decision-making so people understand the value.

Data and AI strategy succeeds within the enterprise only if we understand why people resist change and how to reduce their resistance. The original framework is that resistance will continue until the pain of continuing to resist is greater than the pain of submitting to someone else's law. In this case, they are submitting to using reporting or automation. Across the business, it feels like these applications are slowly creeping in and making other organizations submit to the rule of the data.

There's a threat to autonomy that technical teams fail to acknowledge when we talk about change and transformation. We're giving people a new way of doing things. To us, it feels like progress, but to them, it feels like a loss of autonomy. It is perceived as work and often feels like accepting someone else's law.

Most people don't change on their own. They don't always see the benefit of adopting new technology or solutions, even if that solution is obviously better than what they already have. We must prove that they are being given a better way to do their jobs. We must make the connection back to them, but more importantly, to value.

Strategy informs decision-making, and one critical question is, "Why are we changing?" As someone adopting technology, you want to know why you should do something different than you've always done. The business's data and AI strategy must inform that decision. We must make a connection between the technology, the solutions we deliver, and something valuable to the people being asked to change. We must justify that this thing we're giving them performs better than an alternative.

Buy-in is challenging, and adoption is so slow because people don't see the value or impact on them. Without a strategy, data and AI don't have a chance. Nearly every framework in this book targets getting people to adopt, be on board, buy in, invest, use, purchase, and prioritize. All of these are critical and central to why we need a strategy. We must realize that we are overcoming inertia and resistance.

The Cost of Resisting Change

We're seeing now that even disruptors can be disrupted. Google was once seen as an innovator, and the company was recently caught flat-footed. We're entering an era where businesses can be snapped out of their leadership position. The rate of change is coming for entire business models and industries.

Before Apple delivered the iPhone, BlackBerry, Nokia, and Motorola owned the mobile phone market. Then the iPhone showed up and disrupted the entire industry. The App Store was the major innovation, and we're still building business models around it even now.

What most people forget is the digital camera marketplace. It used to be thriving with companies like Kodak and Fuji. As soon as Apple put cameras on its iPhones, it was the end for traditional camera manufacturers who had transitioned to digital cameras.

Apple didn't even realize it was pushing a business model aside. The company had no idea those companies were in the way. It was not Apple's objective to disrupt the digital camera industry. It simply happened.

GPT-4 and Bard have been integrated into search products, and we're seeing the same types of disruptions play out again. Bing and Google have eliminated several industries without even realizing it in the battle for search ad revenue. Changes in user workflows have plowed under content categories and even media companies.

With the camera on a cell phone, we no longer needed a digital camera. It was an easy replacement because it targeted a challenge in the workflow, a point of friction. There were hundreds of daily opportunities to get pictures we would love to keep with us.

However, it wasn't convenient to always have our digital camera handy. There were multiple steps to get the camera out, get ready to take the picture, and then take it. Sharing photos with people who weren't physically next to us was difficult.

The cell phone changed that workflow because now you have a high-quality camera in your pocket. The mobile storage device for those digital images was also connected to the Internet. It became easier to take pictures whenever we wanted to. It became feasible to share photos precisely when we took them. Digital cameras never had a chance.

It's the same pattern emerging again for many legacy content providers. Our search workflow has changed. Instead of assembling a complex search string and evaluating several options, I now ask a question. An intelligent agent provides me with a summary of multiple website results. I get those in a single pane and no longer need to click through to get the answers to many questions. Reading content across sites has been made redundant. Without thinking, Microsoft and Google have altered several marketplaces, especially in content.

Competition is happening in new ways. When two AI-first titans go at each other, entire industries can be casualties. They will provide services for free in their attempt to gain a top-level market share. Those services used to compose small businesses, entire business models, and product lines. Over the next five years, companies will disappear.

The cost of resistance is higher than the cost of submitting to transformation. The business transforms, or it fails. People adapt, or their jobs are lost. The equation is tilted toward transformation and adopting data and AI. Resistance used to be futile. Now it's fatal.

What's Next?

There's also a significant danger here. It's tempting to run the business's strategy using technology. If data and AI are such amazing things, why wouldn't we do that? When technology runs strategy, the result is more technology.

Businesses exist to create and deliver value to customers, and strategy drives that. The risk is getting too much into the technology and allowing it to drive strategy.

It may feel like the whole point of business is creating more technology. However, we still need something that connects the technology that the company creates to the value customers expect. A strategy must drive technology, or the business will fail to succeed in its core objectives.

The connection is critical because the one thing that hasn't changed about strategy is that it must be the driver for the business. It's vital to remember that the true nature of technology is to serve and perpetuate itself. The company must rely on strategy to leverage technology to serve the business. In the next chapter, I introduce the framework to make that happen.

The Monolith—Technical Strategy

What does a data-driven business look like? How does transformation change the business and operating models? C-level leaders need a top-level strategic construct to make decisions about technology from a value-centric perspective. That includes technologies they don't completely understand.

The technology model and technical strategy frameworks reduce the complexity of those decisions. Business goals should be the guiding principles behind how the business decides to leverage data and AI. Monetization and competitive advantages are locked in the data team. The technology model begins the process of unlocking both.

In this chapter, I'll define business and operating models for those new to the concepts. I explain how data and AI transform both, creating opportunities and threats. This supports the need for technical strategists and the technology model, which I cover in greater detail.

The Business Model

Most companies have one or more business models, and most don't understand them. Why? Legacy business models don't generate data. Exploring business and operating models reveal the oceans of data contained in and continuously generated by businesses. Almost none of it is being captured. All the data businesses gather is only a fraction of what's there.

The business model is a statement of value creation. It explains what the business monetizes, which, most times, is what it sells, and explains why the business exists. At the heart of every business model is a truth about strategy. Companies do not have to continue to do the same things repeatedly. Businesses can change; they just rarely do.

Strategy planning is a process of continuously evaluating the business model. There are alternatives to explore. Opportunity discovery is the process of assessing and sometimes uncovering opportunities for the business to consider.

In the past, opportunities were discovered through best guesses or expert knowledge. The business must adopt a data-driven opportunity discovery process to improve on that original design. Opportunity feeds strategy. During the planning process, C-level leaders decide which opportunities to pursue. The business model talks about opportunities and makes connections to products. What should the business produce, and which customers should the business produce it for?

A Few Examples of Business Models

Amazon has Prime, which is an e-commerce business model. When Amazon bought Whole Foods, it acquired a brick-and-mortar retail component. The two were complementary, so the acquisition made sense.

What is McDonald's business model? McDonald's is a fast-food business selling cheeseburgers, but that's not its business model. McDonald's has a franchise business model. It sells businesses in a box. At some point, McDonald's leadership realized it had perfected the fast-food business.

The most valuable thing it sold was no longer food. The company sells a business-in-a-box to franchisees and takes a percentage of profits. That business model allows them to scale faster than they could in the past.

Amazon made a similar pivot. When it built the infrastructure under Prime, Amazon saw a new opportunity and realized it could sell that infrastructure. Amazon's most valuable capability was no longer the e-commerce store itself. Inadvertently, it had built an entirely new business model, selling the hardware, the infrastructure, and all of the knowledge it had used to scale out Prime. That's how AWS began and grew into the dominant player in the cloud space.

McDonald's perfected a process and quickly realized it was more valuable than the individual products it sold. Amazon perfected the process of developing the infrastructure to run a large-scale digital business. AWS resources have become more profitable than the products that Amazon Prime sells. AWS is a consumption-based business model. It sells access to scale and charges based on how much scale a customer needs.

Staffing firms used to do something very similar. They provided access to talent so that businesses could scale. Many companies have a seasonality to their business. During the holiday season, for example, retailers need new people. Staffing firms rose to the occasion and provided people on demand so companies could scale up and down more efficiently.

These examples are variations of a theme. Many physical business models have digital equivalents, revealing an interesting opportunity for strategy planning. Businesses can now evaluate what opportunities technology creates, and that's what Amazon did. They say the cloud is just someone else's PC, and, for most of the world, it's now Amazon's PC. Without a strategy and the continuous evaluation of opportunities, it would have played out differently.

The Need for Technical Strategists

Technology enables new business models. It creates new opportunities, and as data and AI strategists, that's one of our critical roles. We introduce opportunities during the discovery phase that the technology we are experts in creates for businesses. We reveal new ways of creating and delivering value to customers.

Doing this up front is essential because changes to the business model may be necessary to monetize data, analytics, and more advanced models. If one of the technical teams charges ahead with a new product line, the business may be structurally incapable of generating revenue from it.

That's why it's critical to introduce technology into the opportunity discovery and strategy planning processes. Data strategists help the business to improve its business model iteratively. The hybrid capability set is critical here. We see the strategic implications of this new data and AI-driven business.

In the next 5 years, being a C-level leader without a significant background in technology will become an enormous challenge. How can you run a technology-first business without a background in the technology that your company is dependent upon?

Satya Nadella is a technical strategist. Whether you love or hate him, Elon Musk is also a technical strategist. Jeff Bezos is another example. The minds behind Google, Uber, and many of the most successful technology companies worldwide are technical strategists.

Again, Google gives a great example of what happens when innovation runs the shop. In the business model paradigm, Google is leaning heavily toward opportunity discovery. The business is built for innovation and discovering new opportunities enabled by leading-edge technologies.

However, Google is not set up to monetize the opportunities that it discovers. Amazon, on the other hand, is. I would argue that Amazon's opportunity discovery process is far less mature than Google's. However, Amazon is significantly more successful because it is very good at monetization.

If you look at new leaders like Andy Jassy, the question immediately arises, why were they brought in? Tim Cook replaced Steve Jobs. Why him? It's because they're very good at monetizing opportunities. After the innovators, we need someone to come in and handle the operational side.

Jassy and Cook are excellent at making the connection from innovation to the business model. They understand how to exploit opportunities and maximize the revenue from existing innovations. That's why you see people like Bezos step aside. Amazon is no longer in opportunity discovery mode. It's in the optimization and maximization of profitability.

Microsoft, Google, Amazon, and many other companies have spent the last 10 years innovating around AI. The partnership between Microsoft and Open AI and the products that have resulted from it shows the shift in focus from innovation to exploitation. It's time to seize those technologies and bring products to market. The largest tech companies will be the first to move in this direction, but others will follow quickly.

The timing for data and AI strategists is excellent. Traditional businesses and industries are forced to do something they haven't ever truly excelled at. They need a new type of talent to help guide the opportunity discovery process.

This is one way technical strategists get their foot in the door and a seat at the strategy planning table. We bring opportunities to C-level leaders, make the connection to the business model, and demonstrate how to monetize the technology. Most strategy planning processes lack and sorely need that.

Hybrid capabilities set technical strategists apart. More traditional roles have either one or the other side of the fence, but we need both. Being all technical misses the business connections, and seeing just the business misses the technological innovations and opportunities. Too much of one or the other results in either a failure to monetize or a failure to discover.

The Operating Model

The operating model explains how the business creates value for customers. It explains why the company leverages its particular value-creation process. For McDonald's, it answers a range of questions. Why do McDonald's produce hamburgers in the way that they do? Why put eight on a grill? We could make the grill bigger and put 40 of them on. Who would flip 40 burgers at a time? Should we use a person, or is there the potential to introduce mechanical automation into the process?

McDonald's has evaluated completely automating the internals of its restaurants. Its CEO said the unit economics simply do not work. It has piloted a few fully autonomous stores, but even in them, people still run the kitchen and work behind the scenes.

It's the same story in Amazon's fully automated retail locations. While many roles have been eliminated, people still work in the stores. It appears we humans are not wholly obsolete quite yet. However, the slow creep of automation reveals a deeper trend for the operating model.

McDonald's could automate 100 percent of its stores. Its CEO said the unit economics didn't work out, not that it was impossible. The technology is there, ready, feasible, and likely functional. However, automation is still more expensive than people.

We are in a race to the bottom on price with AI. It's a fairly dystopian-sounding future. One goal of a technical strategy is to wrestle the business and operating models back from AI. Companies will depend on data, analytics, and models for success, but technical strategy reveals the necessity for people.

For C-level leaders to implement the technology model construct, we need technically literate people as part of the strategy planning process. We are constantly evaluating opportunities to go from physical-, labor-, and location-dependent to a technology-dependent operating model.

We must help define the process for transferring pieces from the operating model into the technology model. As technical strategists, one of our primary roles is to define the technology model and help the business make these sorts of decisions as part of the strategy planning process.

Why are we moving parts of the operating model into the technology model? Amazon made a mark in the business world in 2020. The pandemic flared up, and suddenly everyone was locked down. Amazon's demand went through the roof. It was as if Black Friday built up over two months and never ended. In a brick-and-mortar store, this would have been impossible to manage.

Think about what would have happened in a store like Walmart, which is labor-intensive and physical location dependent. Transitioning from servicing 1,000 customers an hour to 2,500 or 3,000 customers an hour would have been an enormous challenge. The traditional retail operating model has a limited ability to scale and handle sudden increases in demand.

The only equivalent to what happened to Amazon Prime is the holiday season for retail. On Black Friday, anywhere between 3 and 10 times the number of customers can go through a store. Retailers spend months ramping up in preparation for the 8 weeks between mid-November and the beginning of January. They bring in seasonal help and plan their supply chain around having merchandise in stock.

Amazon scaled and didn't miss a beat. Over the course of a few weeks, it went from handling average demand to handling Black Fridays every day for months. That had to be absolutely terrifying to the rest of the retail world.

A company as large as Walmart could blink out of existence, and Amazon would scale to pick up the demand. A retail giant that large could fall off the face of Earth, and another company would just step in and pick it up.

During the pandemic, the most significant impact on Amazon Prime was that some deliveries took three or four days. That was it. Think about the enormity of the challenge that any other traditional retailer would face with handling that sort of overnight surge. Demand showed up, but the Amazon Prime website was resilient.

Compare that to how Twitter worked in the early days. We all knew what the "fail whale" looked like because Twitter went down quite a bit as it scaled to handle overwhelming demand. Niantic, the company behind Pokémon Go, was another example of runaway demand crashing an application. Those glitches and outages would have doomed their product if the game hadn't been so enjoyable and had such a loyal fan base.

Amazon, on the other hand, scaled overnight with no glitches, no website outages, and no problems. It kept up with its five 9s (99.999 percent uptime) availability. The most significant disruptions resulted in Amazon apologizing for being a few days late on its two-day delivery guarantee. That's the power of shifting parts of the operating model into a technology model.

In later chapters, I will cover a framework called *core-rim*. The core-rim framework allows the business to decide what parts should be transferred into the technology model and which it will keep in the hands of people. It's a decision framework that helps C-level leaders understand and make more informed decisions without managing the technology components.

The central theme is that when you push workflows into the core, automating and reducing the complexity of operating the business, the core eventually becomes a platform. Amazon Prime's e-commerce core became AWS.

Scale to Infinity and Super Platforms

Elon Musk has aspirations to turn Twitter into a super platform. WeChat is the closest comparison to his vision for what Twitter could become. Customers and users can live their digital lives, for the most part, on WeChat. A super platform intends to provide so much functionality that you never need to leave. That is what Musk is trying to build from Twitter. It will be interesting to see precisely how close he gets.

The United States and the European Union have laws and regulations that make it more challenging to create a super platform. It wanders dangerously close to monopoly territory. Google, Amazon, and many others are regulated in a legacy paradigm, and current guidelines fail to address this new type of technical monopoly.

Our concept of "being too big to fail" is evolving. In the past, a company like Sears going out of business would have resulted in some bailout. Sears failed, and nobody noticed. It could be the same with Walmart. Now think about what would happen if Microsoft failed. Much of the business world would stop functioning because it depends on Microsoft's software and infrastructure.

It would take time to return to normalcy after a Microsoft failure. The same would be true if Amazon went under tomorrow. That's the power of these businesses. Their operating models allow them to scale and become ubiquitous quickly. They integrate their products into so many parts of our lives that it is impossible to function the same way without them. We would struggle to extract all our connections to a company such as Amazon, Microsoft, or Google.

Some banks and financial institutions got bailouts during the last financial crisis and the recent regional banking crisis. They were too big to fail because the entire economy would suffer if they did. So much sat on top of these financial titans that the world could not afford to let them fall. Now the global economy sits on digital and AI-first titans.

Amazon is increasing its efforts to move more of its operating model into its technology model. It is pushing the limits of automation. Amazon has increased its reliance on robotics and automation to pick products and fill packages. They are attempting to use self-driving cars to automate the last mile of shipping deliveries. However, they're running into feasibility limits.

Scale becomes a challenge and a drag on progress. An automated drone can have 99.99 percent reliability. That means only 1/100th of a percent of flights will have some issue. Is that good enough? If they do 100,000 deliveries per day by drone, how many fall out of the sky with even 99.99 percent reliability? The answer is more than we are willing to accept.

Suppose an autonomous vehicle can run for 100,000 miles before its first crash. Is that an acceptable level of reliability? Considering the hundreds of thousands of miles that Amazon vehicles drive daily, probably not.

Switching from a manual operating model to a technology model increases reliability requirements. It's not as if people are better drivers or drone operators. We are simply given more leeway than automation and machine learning models.

We aren't expected to have 99.99 percent uptime. People get sick. We get tired, and we go home. We need vacations. We have families that we would like to spend time with. We're not five 9s (99.999 percent) reliable.

Hardware, on the other hand, is. Websites are expected to be up and running five 9s. One benefit of moving operations to the core is increased reliability. The business's ability to rapidly scale and service customers improves. The company also reduces its reliance on people to change.

The Implications of an Automated Operating Model

As I discussed in earlier chapters, people are hesitant to change and resist adopting new ways of completing their workflows. If I automate a workflow entirely, I no longer need to worry about retraining a person when I improve the workflow. I retrain the machine learning model and redeploy it. That's it. If I improve an automated pricing model, no people training is required. I push it to production, and the improvement is deployed with it.

People's rate of change and adaptability for simple tasks and repetitive work show how fast the business can improve. People's questioning and continuous reevaluation of complex tasks speed up the business's rate of improvement.

Another implication of moving from the manual operating model to the technology model is speed. Those automated operations that live at the core can be continuously improved faster. That frees people up to focus on high-skill work.

Transferring from the manual operating model to the technology model means those parts of the workflow now generate data. People don't frequently save their brains and what they know to a database. On the other hand, automated processes save anything and everything we program them to. We can log with increasing granularity, which is not always good. These logging data sets can grow to be enormous, and not all of that data is useful.

This introduces the concept of transparency and opacity. Opacity and a lack of data generation are the main reasons businesses do not understand their business and operating models. The transition from opacity to transparency requires a deeper understanding of workflows. I'll explain both in a later chapter.

Building data products can start with simple logic and expert systems. Rather than relying on data, we can ask intelligent people how a particular workflow should be handled. Smart people are usually better than version 1 models, so why not start there? The business has experts who are worth listening to no matter how much data we have.

Improvement begins from this baseline, so initiatives focus on what people don't do well instead of replicating what they are most capable of managing. Another framework I'll explain throughout this book is the data and model-supported product maturity framework. The simplest data products, at level 0, are indistinguishable from digital software.

The framework's power is intentionally evaluating the workflow and introducing technology that gathers data in a very targeted way. It gives technical strategists a longer-term view into the life cycle of a digital product that turns into a data, analytics, and eventually AI-supported product.

The Technology Model

These are the foundational concepts behind a technology model. We need it because anything that makes the business money requires a strategy. That's the thesis behind needing a data and AI strategy but not the end. There are other technologies, so businesses need a digital, cloud, data, AI, and, someday, a quantum strategy. In the framework of continuous transformation, it never ends.

That's the new paradigm. If the business turns its back on technology waves, it will be smacked by one of them and pushed under. Now that competition is back, this is how laggards will begin their slow run to failure. Without continuous transformation, one of these technology waves will be leveraged by a competitor to put them out of business. We are firmly in adapt-or-die territory.

Parts of the business that resist change or that refuse transformation can become exceptionally dangerous. Failure to adapt and transform is a risk to business survival. As technical strategists, we must make the gains and losses of adopting new technology evident to people across the business.

Some companies are stuck in the early phases of transformation. As they watch competitors move ahead, they feel a sense of urgency. They want to jump ahead and move directly from digital to AI. With operating system models like GPT, that's now possible for some use cases but not all.

Waves of change are necessary. Transformation is continuous, and we must think of it that way. Without the cloud, it's tough to support machine learning workflows. That means the cloud is an enabling technology for data science and machine learning.

Without digital technology in workflows, it's tough to introduce or gather data in the first place. Without a digital platform, delivering value to customers and introducing it into their workflows would be impossible. In my story about cloud transformation, I explained how much technical debt we accrued by denying the reality of cloud migration. Businesses continue to make the same mistakes repeatedly with each wave.

This is where a technical strategy and the technology model can add significant value. Strategy informs decision-making. A continuous transformation strategy informs decisions not only today but for the future. A business with a longer-term view sees the necessity of moving from wave to wave.

Business decisions made today must support future transformation waves. The best approach to decision-making is no longer simply short-term with the goal of meeting immediate needs. Companies must look longer term to set up for success across multiple waves. To be sustainable, decisions today must deliver near-term value and amplify subsequent technology waves.

Previous frameworks failed because they tried to drag C-level leaders into managing technology. That brings value-focused people into a very tactical workflow-based role. If we drag C-level leaders out of their comfort zone, we make them far less effective. Leadership needs a framework to manage technology from the value creation standpoint.

The technology model represents all the technical capabilities that the business currently has. It represents the sum of the technical opportunities discovered during the strategy planning process and opportunity discovery, which I'll discuss later. Leaders can now decide which opportunities the business should go after. It allows for an evaluation of trade-offs, not at the technology level but at the business level.

C-level leaders regain control over the business and value creation. It allows senior leaders to make conscious decisions about what technology should and should not do. Senior leaders can determine which ports of value creation will continue to be managed by people and which will be handed over to technology. They can decide how technology will enable them to deliver value to customers. It also allows them to determine what parts of value delivery the business and its people will maintain.

C-level leaders now decide what part of the business and operating models will be transferred into the technology model. During the strategy planning process, C-level leaders can evaluate trade-offs of keeping aspects of the business and operating models out versus in the technology model. They can consider whether moving a piece into the technology model aligns with the core strategy. Leaders can evaluate how effectively that move will help the business achieve its larger strategic goals.

It reframes products too. If the business decides to develop a new data or AI-supported product, they understand the support required to move it out of the business model and into the technology model. This has been the missing piece for a very long time. Companies have solved the technology problem but never had visibility into the business challenges that come with it.

The technology model allows senior leaders to evaluate the entire landscape. They can see the implications of moving parts of the product or operations into the technology model. The motivation and value proposition come first, and the technology required to do it is secondary.

Technical decisions happen one layer down and are part of what technical strategists do. Technical strategy is also an evaluation of trade-offs. It's time to understand which technology enables that transition best after making a decision.

The Best Tool for the Job

We often say data science or AI shouldn't be the first tool used. That's because it's typically the most expensive. If a transformation can be managed by a less expensive technology, digital, for example, it should be. The technology model and technical strategy give us a framework to evaluate the trade-offs of one technology versus another. We can look at it as a cost analysis.

Technical strategists act as advisers to help senior leaders understand what each technology does best. One side of the role is revealing opportunities created by technology. The other is assisting leaders in understanding which technologies will manage that transformation from business and operating model to technology model.

We've given C-level leaders a tool to evaluate the trade-offs of continuing to do things the way the business always has or adopting a new way of creating value. They can assess whether transformation is beneficial from a value creation and delivery standpoint.

This framework reverses the transformation process and control flow by giving the business a framework to decide what should change. It becomes part of the strategic planning process. Now leadership decides what gets transferred from the business and operating models into the technology model.

The technology model is a top-level strategic construct. It explains why the business uses technology to create and deliver customer value. If it's possible to use software or advanced models, which is the right business decision? Since software is typically cheaper than developing, deploying, and supporting models, these new features should be done with software.

What are the fundamental benefits of data and AI versus other technologies? Data and advanced models manage complexity and reduce uncertainty better than any technology.

In later chapters, I'll break down data product strategy and explain these concepts more concretely. For now, it's enough to understand that data and AI can do things that no other technology before them could.

However, they add value in a tiny number of use cases. It's counterintuitive, but the business will not use advanced AI for most applications. Digital technology performs just fine. Here again, in the strategic evaluation of trade-offs, we're looking for opportunities where data and AI are the only technologies that can deliver. Businesses become much more selective about the initiatives they move forward with once they fully understand the decision and the trade-offs.

Data and AI are expensive and time-consuming to develop. The returns of the initiative must scale faster than the costs of the technology. We can use that framework with C-level leaders to help them understand which opportunities are possible and feasible from a business standpoint. It's not enough for the technology to be ready. The business and opportunity must fit too.

Immediately behind transformation strategy and continuous transformation is the technology model. Continuous transformation drives a top-line business decision. How much of the business and operating models will we transfer into the technology model?

That connects product and internal efficiency initiatives to core business value. It also shows what additional work is required on the business side to support product launches.

Each technology under the technology model has its own individual strategy. The strategies define how each technology creates value in a new or different way than alternatives. A major purpose of the technology model is to simplify interaction with this process.

C-level leadership and nontechnical parts of the business don't need to understand the technology side of the equation.

It's unnecessary to assign an initiative to a technology at this phase. That happens one level down and remains connected to the core business strategy.

Making the Connection to Value from the Start

This is how we begin to connect technology initiatives with business strategy. The whole point of moving something into the technology model is to capitalize on an opportunity. Those fall around specific categories such as delivering new value and value more efficiently or effectively to customers. C-level leaders see the top level of the technology model only.

They also know there are technical strategies underneath it. This framework provides support for decision-making about each technology from a value-creation standpoint. It gives the business a way to evaluate trade-offs for technology during the strategy planning process and understand the opportunities created or enabled by each one of the technologies. With all that information, strategy planning can deliver a road map for taking parts out of the business and operating models and transferring them into the technology model.

Once senior leaders decide, it goes into the technology model. Now, data strategists, data product managers, the data team, digital product managers, software and cloud strategists, and everyone else who is part of the next level down take over. Strategy planning and opportunity discovery are completed. Now it's time to implement the strategy.

Data and AI strategists take over at this point. We defined the move into the technology model. Each initiative supporting that move transforms from one technology to the next. The team makes decisions about how the initiative should be shaped. Which technologies should be leveraged? How will each technology get to break even and achieve profitability?

The initial digital product deployment should have some value creation associated with it. If a data gathering or generation component is added, we've added a data product, and that should have some value creation. This leverages the product maturity framework. Incremental improvement or transformation should deliver incremental returns. Each wave must be self-sustaining from a revenue standpoint, or the process becomes too expensive.

With continuous transformation, we have altered the one-time generational investment paradigm. Continuous transformation and the compression of technical cycles mean that businesses are investing in transformation more often. The time to generate returns before the business must invest again is shorter—each transformation must be self-sustaining.

Every product must have near, mid, and long-term returns. Without this continuous transformation framework, where incremental delivery and value creation are coupled into the long-term vision for where the enterprise is going, the entire initiative is unsustainable. The business cannot afford to continue to invest and reinvest in transformation wave after transformation wave hoping for big returns a long way down the road.

This is a different way of thinking about transformation. The business will invest $25 in each of these waves. Before it must invest its next $25, the business must have generated more than $25. The first technology wave or product maturity level must generate that return. Without this paradigm, it's just an endless, continuous investment of $25 in hopes that something will come back someday. $25 turns into $50. $50 turns into $75 and $100. When do the returns materialize?

Each phase must get to break even and begin to generate returns. This starts with small initiatives and simple technologies. Using the continuous transformation paradigm, I will include a small data-gathering component when I deliver a new digital product. I'm making a decision today that sets up the next iteration.

However, that first implementation, the stand-alone digital solution, must have some return on investment. The data gathering must also generate positive returns, so I must find ways to monetize the data set. The great thing about data is that it can be monetized multiple times.

This is the construct of incremental improvements and incremental returns. It is the only way improving technology makes sense to the business. The framework also addresses one of the largest challenges that data and AI strategy have: costs. When viewed alone, the costs of data and AI initiatives are typically too high to justify. If we take a long-term-only approach, returns don't materialize fast enough.

Some companies decide that they want to go directly to AI, but in reality, that's impossible. There's always a platform that needs to be put in place first to deliver value to customers. Another platform is necessary for internal users to leverage everything from reporting to automation. Every data product will have some digital side to it. Even initiatives targeted at a longer-term goal still need to mature incrementally. As technical strategists, we hold on to each initiative's vision and maturity model. Even when the business doesn't care, we have to. Planning a successful initiative means understanding how the product will mature from phase to phase alongside the business.

What's Next?

Do data and AI move forward endlessly like water reclaiming the land? People are critical for the business no matter how advanced technology becomes. Large models like ChatGPT won't 10 times everyone overnight or completely replace people in the business.

An amateur with ChatGPT will still produce amateur work. They'll just do it 10 times as fast and with 10 times more complex tools. GPT-4 automates mindless clicking and keyboard-pounding tasks. Not the thinking required to do them. What parts of your job would remain if I took your keyboard and mouse away?

Writing SQL queries can be automated. Knowing which queries will deliver insights to stakeholders can't be.

Writing code can be automated. Knowing which functionality will meet your customers' highest value needs can't be.

Building, training, and validating models can be automated. Aligning business metrics with model metrics, experiment/study design, review, results validation, and delivering reliable business solutions can't be.

Large operating system models like GPT-4 may have all the answers, but they still don't know what questions to ask. That's the future of work. In the next chapter, I explain who survives disruption and who doesn't.

8

Who Survives Disruption?

This chapter introduces the core-rim framework, which can handle part of the technology model decision-making process. Technical strategy addresses the value creation aspects of moving parts of the business and operating models into the technology model. If data and models followed a digital paradigm, that would be enough.

Models don't work the way software does. I write code, and the computer executes the instructions I give it. There's no variance from the behavior I describe in the code. There are defects, and complex applications can perform unpredictably, but everything traces back to the instructions I wrote.

Models learn from data sets and feedback. Once trained, they are no longer rules-based like software is. Core-rim handles this unique aspect of data and AI products. C-level leaders need this framework to make decisions about reliability.

Automation taking over workflows moves parts of the operating model into the core, the business's technology platform.

From a value standpoint, everything that's cost-effective and technically feasible should be moved into the core. Some complexity is irreducible because, even though the models can be built, they are not reliable enough to take on that complexity.

That's where core-rim comes into play.

Using Frameworks to Maintain Autonomy

You could be forgiven for thinking this all sounds horrifically dystopian. There's a euphemism hiding in transferring from the operating model to the technology model. It means replacing people with technology, and jobs will be lost.

As I begin to discuss the core-rim framework, it can feel like the core is the slow creep of progress taking over jobs that people used to do. It immediately brings to mind the manufacturing automation boom of the 1980s and 1990s. Manufacturing jobs never recovered. Solid middle-class incomes were disrupted. The losses from that wave are still being felt.

Will people continue to play a critical role in businesses? Yes, but obviously, there will be significant differences. I think it's essential to admit there will be massive job disruptions. Some workers who are challenged by this disruption and the resulting transformation will be displaced. History will repeat itself, and some roles will never recover.

Waves of layoffs have hit HR and marketing especially hard, and these jobs are probably gone for good. When demand returns, automation will enable teams to scale without additional headcount.

However, the power of the technology model is putting control back in the hands of people. People will decide who is disrupted. Bottom-up opportunity discovery enables people at the frontline to choose what parts of their workflows are up for automation.

The real fear isn't the loss of jobs but the loss of control to technology. People must maintain autonomy not only of their workflows but also of the business. These frameworks return autonomy to people. When technology drives strategy, we surrender an unacceptably large level of autonomy. Leaders lose control of the company. Workers lose control of their jobs.

When strategy controls technology, we remain in control of both. That's critical for a future where technology is a partner. If technology is viewed as a replacement for people, it will not succeed in the business. Not all tasks should be done by technology. We simply shouldn't trust it in every case or every role.

Reducing Complexity While Maintaining Autonomy

The purpose of AI-supported automation is to reduce the complexity of the business. However, some complexity will always be irreducible. Those parts of the business live at the rim. In the core are parts of the operating model that people should never have been doing in the first place. So much of the menial, repetitive, low-skill work should be pushed to automation.

Most of that work was soul-sucking and terrible. No one truly wanted to be doing any of those tasks in the first place. As we replace them, I don't think anyone will mourn their disappearance.

At the same time, some parts of our jobs are uniquely human. We don't trust machines to lead us. This is one of the three people groups that survive disruption. Our leaders will always be human because they are the most effective at leading other people.

Leaders make the team more productive than a collection of individuals. They are mentors, and the best leaders create deeply personal connections with their teams. People are willing to go further and deliver higher-quality work for exceptional leaders.

Complexity exists in the leadership role that should not be reduced.

A computer can be an adequate manager and administrator. However, leadership is something significantly more important. It's an intelligent process.

A logical process is something that we can write up the steps for. It follows a mapped sequence of events. The decision-making is simplistic and rote. It doesn't require much creativity or synthesizing knowledge for novel situations.

Think of logical processes like the manual, repetitive tasks performed on an assembly line. Having humans take a part off an assembly line and put it into a box is unnecessary. That is something that should be automated.

It frees people to utilize their minds. We should be working primarily on intelligent processes and workflows. An intelligent process requires us to generalize our knowledge to novel situations. These defy being defined by a simple set of steps or logical flow. The decisions associated with many steps are too complex to map out.

This is where most people thrive. We consider this work to be challenging. Succeeding in intelligent processes is very rewarding. AI products present a challenge to our supremacy over intelligent workflows.

AI, as it is today, has knowledge but not actual intelligence. Models are showing the early signs of understanding, but intelligence is a long way off.

Highly reliable models can take over small parts or simplistic intelligent workflows. With the technology model, we remain in control of deciding which intelligent workflows are handled by automation. Just because it's possible and feasible doesn't mean we should do it. This calculation is often missing from data science.

Technology Cannot Solve All Our Problems

Projects are evaluated backward, and technology is sold as a solution to all problems. In the engineer or data scientist's mind, if it can be done, it should be built. The decision-making process must be more complex than that.

Businesses and data scientists can find themselves in significant ethical peril by making decisions backward. Much of the data privacy mess we find ourselves in results from selecting projects because they were feasible versus practical. The equation changes when we look at these decisions as business and human-centric. We need frameworks that put people first.

I worked for a startup that automated part of the recruiting workflow. Our models handled intelligent processes. In this case, those were the evaluation and screening of the mountain of résumés that would be submitted for each job posting. Some jobs got hundreds of résumés.

Reading through each of those was a time-consuming and soul-sucking task. Most applicants weren't qualified, so their résumés weren't worth reading. That recruiter could spend hours parsing résumés for people who shouldn't be brought in for an interview. These types of workflows are perfect for intelligent automation.

We developed the system to do something remarkably simple. The model parsed through each résumé's text and classified key phrases by type, skills, experience, education, and certifications. Each type got a different color of highlighting on the screen. Now, instead of reading the entire résumé, recruiters could skim the crucial bits based on the highlighting. The time it took them to review a résumé and get the complete picture went from minutes to seconds.

We had moved part of the résumé screening process to the core. When potential customers (large recruiting agencies) evaluated our software, they unknowingly decided to move part of their operating model into the technology model. You can see how making this decision carelessly can have significant consequences. That's why the technology model and the process of moving things from the rim to the core are critical.

We must think about intentionally moving parts of an individual's job to automation. There are implications to consider. In the case of a recruiter, is it ethical to allow a model to evaluate an individual's résumé at this level? That was an essential piece of the feature design equation for us to consider.

We spent months talking about exactly how much of the workflow should be managed by automation. At this small startup, we intentionally chose what amount of control to give to the model versus the recruiter. Based on early feedback, we decided to provide the recruiter with as much autonomy as possible. The model would be an assistant but not take any autonomy from the recruiter in the decision-making process.

This seemingly small decision was a critical success factor for the product. Customer adoption was very high compared with alternatives because recruiters felt completely in control. We chose not to hide any résumés unless we were explicitly told to by the recruiter. We did not eliminate anyone from the search results.

By targeting a tiny part of the workflow and providing high-value automation, we successfully created an initial product that recruiters enjoyed using. It wasn't until a few years later when I reflected on exactly why the product was so popular that I realized we had intentionally made a decision using the core-rim model. It would have taken us significantly less time had we had a framework in place.

Making Decisions with Core-Rim and the Technology Model

Customers for other HR automation vendors weren't so fortunate. Many automated applicant tracking systems took too much autonomy away from recruiters. Ethical issues arose everywhere. It was a clear case displaying that not everything should be moved to the core. Even when automation is employed, a person still needs to be in charge of some decisions.

The threat of algorithmic bias in hiring decisions is simply too high. The data sets we work with are filled with different forms of bias. No matter how much work we put into debiasing the data and evaluating the model, it will still creep in. That means we can make the process simpler and faster. However, at the end of the day, the recruiter must maintain autonomy over the final decision. Intelligent automation cannot remove any aspect of choice in that case.

People at all levels of the company can make decisions about moving parts of the business to the technology model. They choose to reduce the complexity of the business but don't realize they must also evaluate all of the implications that the decision brings. Using the technology model, our customers would have decided something like this.

During opportunity discovery, the change would be brought forward. Highly reliable models presented an opportunity to automate résumé screening at different levels of functionality. The question would have been posed: will this provide significant value to the business? For most recruiters, the answer would be yes.

At the C level, the decision would be made to move parts of the résumé screening process into the technology model. The secondary question is precisely how much the business should move. This is a central question revolving around autonomy. There are systems out there that promise to automate the entire end-to-end screening process. With those systems, the recruiter is shown only the top five or ten candidates based on their résumés.

At the other end of the spectrum are systems like the one I helped develop. It highlighted key capabilities within each résumé, making it easier for recruiters to screen a large number of résumés in a short amount of time. It ranked candidates based on the information in their résumés compared to the job description's requirements. Every candidate was still displayed. The system just showed the best ones first.

No candidates were excluded from the results set because they didn't have every capability listed in the job opportunity. Lower match scores were shown later in the results set. The recruiter was free to continue the search for as long as they felt was necessary to find high-quality candidates. We designed the system to allow recruiters to maintain complete autonomy. The intelligent processes that were automated were meant to improve their efficiency.

Using the core-rim framework, senior leaders can decide how much autonomy should remain in the hands of people. They can specify criteria for the software to meet without getting dragged into the technology itself. The conversation isn't about the model accuracies or approaches. The specifications are based on a business decision and domain expertise. Technology barely comes up in the conversation.

This is how the technology model and core-rim help senior leaders leverage strategy to drive technology. Technology decisions are made from a business and value-centric perspective. In the recruiter use case, the usage of models was secondary. It didn't really matter if it was a digital, data, analytics, or AI use case. The final decision would be the same no matter what technology hides under the hood.

Defining the Value Proposition

I have gotten ahead of myself a little bit. A question needs to be answered before we even get to this point. Why should the business reduce complexity and leverage technology? Why automate anything in the first place?

The knee-jerk response is that we will save money. It's essential not just to assume this will happen. Many technical boondoggles have started with the assumption that technology and automation equal cost savings. That's not always the case.

Remember, the McDonald's CEO said the company could automate restaurants. The company decided not to continue because the unit economics did not work. That means we can't dive into these initiatives blindly, assuming that AI will always be the less expensive option—far from it. In many cases, it is more expensive.

AI is often the most expensive technology available to the business. If there is a less expensive technology, digital, for example, that can be leveraged, it should be. We shouldn't use data science for most use cases.

Justifying why we use data, analytics, and AI is critical. Just like everything else in strategy, it is an evaluation of trade-offs. There are other technologies available.

At the same time, I've already detailed some benefits of moving parts of the operating model into the technology model. I've discussed the significant opportunities to deliver value to customers with new AI-powered products. We see a new example of a company making significant gains with a novel AI product every week. The opportunities are proven, so when *should* we use AI?

That's a legitimate question, one that more businesses must stop being scared of asking. I may be the last person you'd expect to advise this route. However, I firmly believe that AI must sing for its supper. That's why the technology model is so critical. AI must be a strategic driver of growth and advantage. It must prove itself worthy as a lever. Otherwise, what's the point?

Technical strategists must provide forward-looking, actionable information for C-level leaders to make sound strategic decisions. Evaluating technology with a strategic lens means a lot of businesses will think the best thing to do is to sit on the sidelines. As much as I am advising caution, the worst thing a company can do is sit on the sidelines and wait for others to prove opportunities.

Fast follower used to be a viable strategy. In many cases, it was actually the preferred strategy. Why dive head first into an unproven technology or unverified market? Let an early innovator do all the work, and then we'll sweep in once they're done.

In the past, being a second mover could be an advantage. Standing back and watching allowed companies to learn from others' mistakes. First movers would build entire marketplaces and prepare customers for this new product. When technology advanced slowly, there was enough time to enter the market with a substitute before any first mover gained a majority of the market.

In the past, disruption was not a quick process. Businesses did not scale fast enough to seize a massive new opportunity. That meant second movers had time to evaluate and decide to enter the market later. Standing on the sidelines was a good strategy when disruption moved slowly.

Amazon took advantage of legacy thinking and caught retailers off guard. Companies like Walmart sat off to the side and waited to see how e-commerce played out. They weren't used to an online business's rate of scale. That's why Amazon Prime could come in and so quickly mop up market share from companies who had dominated that area for so long.

An automated core creates a competitive advantage when it comes to rapidly taking a large amount of market share. Competitors with automated cores make it challenging to be a second mover. The justification for intelligent automation is the competitive advantage it creates and the threats it mitigates.

An automated core is also an advantage when it comes to margins. In the past, scaling a business meant buying more physical locations and hiring more talent. The more digital and intelligent a company is, the less reliant it is on physical sites and talent. That makes scale not only faster but less expensive. Bringing each customer on board costs less.

The fast follower and second mover strategies used to be viable because it took time to build those physical locations and hire all those people. Demand typically outstripped the business's ability to service it. That left a significant amount of the market on the table for competitors to swoop in and take. An automated core changes that.

How Technology First-Businesses Scale

Tesla had to scale between 2016 and 2019 to take advantage of the massive EV market it had helped to create. They couldn't make cars fast enough, and Elon calls this time their supply chain and logistics hell. Tesla almost didn't make it because trying to scale anything manufacturing, especially advanced manufacturing, is extremely difficult.

With Tesla, we're also talking about novel technologies thrown into the mix. Batteries had to be researched and continuously improved. Rare Earth materials had to be sourced. Assembly lines needed to be built, and people had to be hired to work on those lines.

I live in Reno, Nevada, just a few miles from one of their massive gigafactories. The scale of the building is staggering. It feels like it took a long time to build, but really it didn't. Fifteen years ago, it probably would have taken two to three times that long to get going.

Tesla succeeded. It went from a startup to capabilities that rivaled some of the largest automakers in the world in about 4 years. It overcame significant challenges that companies in the past have been challenged with. It cost billions.

It was burning through cash quickly. In the past, that would not have been feasible for a company to do. Ford and GM didn't have the luxury of VC investors. Before the venture capital model, it was unthinkable for a company that wasn't profitable yet to burn through billions.

Under the old paradigm, Tesla would have been forced to scale slowly. Competitors would have had plenty of time to build their product lines and bring their EV lines to market, all before Tesla could fully satisfy the customers it had built.

In the modern competitive environment, a company can come to market, gather significant market share, and create substantial barriers for other competitors. They can create a moat around their business model and seize much of the opportunity. There's little left for competitors to swoop in and take. Being a second-mover or fast follower is not always feasible in the modern competitive landscape.

Can We Be Confident That Business Units Won't Be Completely Erased?

The way I approach this takes a page from Accenture's accounting automation initiative. Accenture implemented significant machine learning–based automation across accounting workflows. It didn't have to hire more for these teams as Accenture grew.

There are two sides to keeping the promise of augmentation versus job losses. If the business must scale to handle more business, it's difficult to justify cutting people. On one side, AI makes the business more efficient and people more productive. On the other side, the new opportunities and growth that AI delivers create more business. That means more work to be done.

We should have more customers to service and a greater need to scale the business. At the same time, a company with a more automated operating model should scale faster and at a lower cost. The result should be handling scale without having to hire more people. Margins will increase alongside revenue. This is the theory behind returns scaling faster than costs to justify more advanced methods.

If the technical strategy is built properly, the business will leverage technology to create new opportunities and better exploit the opportunities in front of it. Without data and AI-supported automation, the company would need more people, and scaling would slow while hiring ramped up.

With core-rim, existing staff focus on new workflows or different parts of their workflows. People are still necessary at the same levels, even though we continue to augment and make them more efficient. That's the promise.

Will we always meet that promise? That's harder to say, especially with something like customer service. I don't believe that all businesses will be committed enough to innovation, applied research, or partnerships to grow the pie and increase the need for scaling the business. In those companies, the focus will be on cost-cutting and eliminating business units like customer service.

There's a huge danger there. Businesses with that mindset don't realize how many customers a bad implementation will cost them. Poor customer support is one of the leading reasons for churn. If a customer has a bad experience with an automated bot, they're leaving in higher numbers than someone who had a good customer experience.

If the company can't leverage AI for growth, it's doubtful they can execute on cost savings either. Laggards will use large models indiscriminately. The implementations will be substandard. These companies will lose customers, not gain them by becoming more efficient or improving service levels.

Successful companies won't ignore the growth opportunities and simply focus on cost savings. Companies that don't believe in their ability to execute for growth won't succeed with cost savings either. Those companies will be disrupted and probably fail.

Losing 5 to 10 percent of their customer base every year due to poor service levels won't sustain a laggard for very long. Margins will be compressed by more successful competitors that leverage data and AI for competitive advantage. In my view, businesses that can't keep their promises to employees won't keep their doors open for long.

What's Next?

Businesses must continuously innovate around their operating model to be adaptive and move quickly. The decisions around transformation must be made from a business and strategic perspective. Otherwise, technology runs away with the company.

The role of the CEO is to preserve the rim of the business. Companies can't lose what makes them excellent in the race for new technologies and advantages. CEOs are the protectors of what made the business great in the first place. Technology will become a partner. However, the best parts of a company are still driven by people.

CEOs must hold on to that, even under the slow encroachment of intelligent automation. Customers don't connect with machines. They connect with companies and brands that have people at the center. Even though I call automation the core of the business, the heart will always be the people who handle the irreducible complexity.

That's the final facet of deciding what should be moved from the rim to the core. Will that movement make the business forfeit what made it exceptional in the first place? People will remain a business's greatest competitive advantage.

9

Data—The Business's Hidden Giant

The modern competitive marketplace hasn't seen the bigger data picture yet, but it has awakened to the realization that there is a much bigger data picture to be uncovered. Workflow mapping is where I'll open the next layer of this onion, but let's spend a moment thinking about something before we move on. Data is being generated all the time by the systems that surround us.

The amount of data exchanged between a breeze and a tree moved by it is astounding. That is a simple system we can observe and make immediate high-level sense of. The movement of branches doesn't seem very mysterious until you're tasked with predicting which way a branch will move next. Then the enormity of the data-generating power of trees in the breeze hits home. Businesses are hundreds of times more complex than a tree, and the breezes they move in are too.

Few parts of the business operate transparently. Most work is done in the dark. Most customer value is delivered without a trace. The majority of a business's internal and external work-flows are opaque. That's a huge risk and opportunity for modern businesses.

Does the Business Really Understand Itself?

Most businesses don't understand their business and operating models. There's a firmly held belief that they do. Ask C-level leaders how well they understand their business, and you'll get a resounding, "Exceptionally well!" Ask more granular questions, and the cracks begin to expose themselves.

A customer walks into a retail store location. They spend 5 minutes in the store before leaving without purchasing anything. This is a common customer workflow that retailers want to understand better. Why did the customer leave without buying? What could salespeople have done differently to get the customer to have made a purchase that day? What motivated the customer to come into the store in the first place?

All three questions can't be answered. This customer work-flow is entirely opaque to the business. However, ask the CEO of this retail business how well the company understands customers, and you'll get a resounding, "Excellently!"

A customer walks into a car dealership and purchases a vehicle. They drive it for two years, and it has almost 30,000 miles when they trade it. However, their next vehicle is a different brand. Why didn't the customer remain loyal? Was there an event that caused them to abandon the brand? What was the decision-making process that led them to a different brand?

All three questions cannot be answered because this work-flow is also utterly opaque to the business. Customers come and go all the time. Most companies don't understand why.

A retail company's best-performing location converts 70 per-cent of the customers who walk in their doors. No other store performs above 40 percent. Why the difference? What happens at the top location that causes a significantly higher closing rate? What is it that employees are doing differently?

Again, all three questions cannot be answered. The cause could be hidden in any number of different workflows. This location has figured out a secret formula, but it is completely opaque to the rest of the business.

The only way other stores can benefit from their exceptional performance is to go to that location. Someone must spend time at the store trying to determine what they're doing differently. It's a manual process that could involve surveys or observation. It's a forensic initiative to decipher the secret formula this one location has discovered.

The retailer could send the store's management on training trips to other locations. They could have the management and sales associates create manuals for every other store to follow. Should everything the top store is doing be replicated across the company and all locations? It's hard to say. It requires us to understand what causes this higher level of customer satisfaction.

Dig down into the actual business workings, and you'll find that the business doesn't understand itself very well. Moreover, there is significant motivation in high-value use cases to better understand parts of the business. The common thread along each one of these examples is that none of them is generating data.

Moving from Opaque to Transparent

For early data maturity businesses, moving parts of the business and operating models into the technology model creates opportunities for data gathering. Until technology is introduced, that part of the business or customer workflow is opaque. The company struggles to understand any part of itself that doesn't generate data.

If the retail location were an e-commerce website, things would be different. A customer coming to the website generates data as soon as they arrive. Every part of their time and journey through the website can be tracked. Items they put into their shopping cart but eventually abandon or failed product search attempts can be logged.

This is the power of platforms. Anytime technology is introduced into a workflow, it becomes possible to gather data. Platforms are data-generating dynamos. In traditional businesses, very little lives on a platform.

Technology isn't part of every workflow in traditional business and operating models. Most workflows have no space to introduce technology, making data gathering either a manual process or impossible.

We've already seen the power of mapping workflows and processes in digital transformation. Documenting how the business does everything it does can be time-consuming. Technology and data provide a shortcut, but only if the process or workflow leverages technology in a way that allows the business to gather data. When digital technology is absent, we have no way to move forward with data products.

Now begin to think of the enormous amount of data the business generates but has not captured. Every customer greeted or failing to be greeted at a retail location is data generated.

However, it's rarely captured. A business that wants to understand the connection between greeting customers as soon as they enter the store and the purchase rate can't. There's no data on that.

Many have resorted to gimmicky sensors that track when a customer enters and leaves. That data is connected to the total number of sales made that day and gets crafted into a janky metric, sales divided by customer entry. The data being gathered isn't granular enough to make any sort of decision. The data team's job is to provide actionable information and bring new knowledge into the business. The sensor data alone doesn't meet that standard.

Getting Deeper into Workflows and Experiments

The cause of a customer leaving without making a purchase is buried deeper within their workflow. The fact that they came and went without a purchase is not actionable information. For the business to improve something, it must know why. It's possible to see a store with low performance and ask them to implement some treatment or intervention. Both are fundamental terms in experimentation and study design.

The treatment or intervention is the policy or change we introduce because we believe there is a causal relationship to be measured. Suppose a low-performing store is required to greet every customer within 5 seconds of entry. The treatment is the greeting and time frame. The assumption is that there is a causal relationship between greetings and higher purchase rates. Is this a valid experiment?

If customer purchase rates decrease, does that mean greeting customers within 5 seconds causes fewer sales? If success rates rise, does it mean that greeting causes more sales? With this specific experiment, we have no idea. Businesses implement policies all the time based on flawed experiments. The reason is they don't have enough access to the customer's workflow to do the experiment they really want to.

We want to get deeper into the customer's workflow and understand what they did throughout their journey. Businesses need to understand this at scale. It's simple enough to survey or even surveil a single customer (survey design challenges aside). Attempting to scale up to handle hundreds or thousands of customer journeys is a significantly more complex proposition involving a lot more labor. Is there an opportunity to introduce technology into this workflow?

Most retail locations have camera systems. It is possible to use cameras with basic computer vision models to understand a customer's journey throughout the store. We can map where they walk, where they go, and where they pause. We could try to find relationships across multiple customer journeys that ended without a sale. Now we've introduced technology more deeply into the workflow, and we better understand what customers are doing.

We could posit a new hypothesis based on new data. Customers who spend 2 minutes in a store without finding what they're looking for are more likely to leave without making a purchase. Our new treatment is to wait 90 seconds before greeting customers and asking if they're having trouble finding what they're looking for.

This is a more specific treatment. It is targeted to a particular behavior that we've observed and believe is related to people leaving. Will we learn anything from this experiment? Probably not. To really understand what's going on, we would have to know whether the store had what they were looking for in the first place.

We could infer that, if after speaking with the salesperson, they left immediately, the store didn't have what they were looking for. In this case, we've introduced some confounding. What if the greeting itself was the reason that they left the store? It is possible that being approached by a salesperson is viewed as a negative. For some groups, this will lead to a higher rate of leaving without making a purchase. It isn't easy to differentiate between people who left because we didn't have an item in stock and people who left because the greeting put them off.

We could rely on the sales associates to write down this information. That is a messy and unreliable process. In a high-volume situation, they probably don't have enough time and may not remember after the fact. If there are negative consequences for a customer leaving after being greeted, sales associates might be incentivized not to report them accurately.

Again, we need to get deeper into the customer workflow to get data and make a more informed decision. However, there are limits to how much data can be gathered. Parts of a shopping experience aren't accessible for experimentation or even data gathering. We will always be limited in what we can collect and how deep we can get. There's a thin line between being helpful and creepy. This applies to salespeople and data gathering.

Data Gathering and Business Transparency

Multiple steps are involved in moving from opaque to transparent and delivering value to the business simultaneously. Data must be gathered intentionally to be used in model training. It must be connected with the workflow to maintain its business or customer context. It must be used enough to generate data in the required quantity for model training.

The digital product that is introduced first must have some value or utility. Otherwise, it won't be adopted. No adoption means no opportunity to gather data, so the very early initiative to introduce digital technology into an internal or customer-facing workflow must have a value proposition. Phase 1 of our data-gathering expedition must return value.

Phase 2 is integrating data gathering, and the digital product needs a data-gathering component. High-quality data is gathered when we understand what parts of the workflow the business is most interested in tracking. Data professionals are extremely good at figuring out creative ways to get data. This is what happens at this next layer under the technology model. Each individual technical strategy reveals the power and the advantage of using its technology.

In this case, data gathering is doing something that digital technologies can't. Even though we enable data gathering with digital technology, we are still developing a data product. In the case of the surveillance camera, it already has value. Surveillance is being done for store security and theft prevention. That means the early initiative has already returned value. Adding a data product on top of that is a matter of gathering the data collected by the camera.

Data gathering must be done deliberately. We shouldn't pull in every part of the video if we don't have to. No one's concerned about the empty parts of the stores for this use case. The workflow that we're interested in is customers walking around the store.

We're also not interested in the raw video itself. What we need to keep is a route map. We will also compile data about how long they were in the store and where they stopped. Outside of that, we don't need to keep anything else.

Breaking initiatives down this way reduces costs. The temptation in many businesses is to over-gather data. The company will save a significant amount of money by processing but not sending video data when customers are not in the store.

Workloads can be pushed to the edge. Video can be processed on-site with only the necessary data sent to a centralized repository. This saves on bandwidth and storage. In this use case, multiple technical strategies come together to save money. Each implementation emphasizes the strength of the technology with the goal of producing value.

Solutions are limited when initiatives are seen in connection with a single technology. Few data teams think like a CIO who worries about bandwidth and storage costs. Decentralizing part of the architecture and optimizing it to run on low-power hardware should be part of the initial design. Usually, it's an update delivered after the bills start rolling in.

Understanding the Workflow

The critical component of keeping AI products connected to value is staying close to workflows. No one buys AI or technology. They buy an outcome or an experience. Customers buy to meet a need. The closest we can get to that need is their workflow.

Workflows are the set of steps a person completes and decisions they make (alone or with the help of technology) to achieve a desired outcome. A workflow can be any process comprised of actions and decisions with measurable results. All workflows generate data, but not all of that data is or can be captured digitally.

What will people be doing with this product, and how does it improve their workflow? The improvement represents the value delivered to internal users and customers. Staying close to and thinking in terms of workflows keep data and AI products connected to value. If the product improves the workflow, it serves the customer and meets a need. The higher the workflow's value and improvement to it, the more valuable the product.

Workflows are how we keep technology connected with what people want to use it for. They are how we get increasingly granular and break initiatives down by value. Workflows are a powerful concept. Anytime we introduce technology into a workflow, we create the opportunity to gather the data generated all the time.

That data tells us how people use products or do work. Without that knowledge, there is opacity into critical parts of the business. Without that information, the business cannot make decisions with much certainty.

Gathering data intentionally based on workflows is how the business moves pieces of itself from opaque to transparent. Once a workflow is transparent, the business can decide how it should improve or if it should at all. Advanced models can be brought to bear to help automate or understand the business better. The amount of inefficiency hiding in the opaque parts of the company is astonishing.

The opaque parts of the business model also hide customer interactions with products. The moments where they interact with the business, brand, or products that aren't captured are filled with missed opportunities.

This revisits the continuous transformation concept. The business will continuously transform parts of workflows from opaque to transparent. In the past, this was done without a framework, so it had no direction. Today, businesses of all revenue levels and sizes are at the earliest stages of capabilities maturity. Technology is still used unintentionally, even in mature digital transformation initiatives.

These frameworks are meant to change that. Introducing technology into workflows in a targeted way will improve how users and customers experience technology. It will make technology initiatives more valuable and impactful. Resources will be used more efficiently.

The point-of-sale system was an excellent example of introducing technology into retail workflows. I worked in retail, selling shoes in the early 90s. It helped me get through college and keep a struggling business afloat.

Even in the mid-1990s, we had reporting. They came in these long, long reams of printed sheets. One report showed total sales. Another broke down sales by associate. Still, another gave sales per hour. There were inventory reports, too.

Data is not a new development. We've had reporting for more than 30 years. It's much easier to gather and serve than it used to be. I leveraged these reports to help me become the top salesperson for my department.

At first, my co-workers despised me for it, but eventually, they asked how I did it. I gave them my system. I broke it down like the engineer I was learning to become. To make $150 in daily commission, I had to make just over $1,500 in sales. On days when the company wasn't running promotions, I had an average selling price of around $80 per ticket. On promotional sales days, it was closer to $60. However, on sales days, we had more customer volume.

On nonsales days I had to ring up 20 sales to make my quota. My closing rate was just under 50 percent. That means I had to have 40 customers try on shoes to make 20 sales for the day. There was one more step in my process, but I never gave that one out.

I learned it was all about greeting customers and staying close without being creepy. I worked to perfect my greeting and follow-up. I think my follow-ups were what really got me to reach my quotas. The shoe floor constantly needed to be cleaned and rearranged. I would initially greet customers and then give them a few minutes to walk around.

After greeting them, I would grab something to clean with or put away a set of display shoes. That would give me an excuse to walk past them a minute or two later and ask, "Are you still doing OK?" I would do it almost over my shoulder as I was on my way to a destination. It made me look busy. Still, even being busy, I was willing to see if they needed help. Theatricality is a powerful tool in sales.

Over the few years I worked on that shoe sales floor, I picked up many of these small tricks. I broke my previous record every year because of minor improvements to my process. I've just outlined a simplistic workflow for a salesperson to get more follow-ups after the initial greeting. The objective is to improve the number of customers who go from being greeted to eventually trying on a pair of shoes.

The rest of the business had no idea about my experimentation and optimization. That part of the workflow was completely opaque, even to the people around me. As a result, my domain expertise and ability to improve that part of the sale were never passed on to the rest of the business. Thousands of sales associates across a large retailer could have benefited. However, at that time, gathering data at that level of granularity was impossible.

The business knew I was the top salesperson at this location and department. They didn't realize that it was my process that set me apart. The point-of-sales system could gather only so much information about my workflow. More technology and access to my workflow would have been required to understand why. The business also needed the culture to support that sort of investigation. Neither was present.

Improving Workflows with Data

That doesn't mean they weren't working to make improvements to different parts of the sales workflow. One particularly painful part was when we had to tell customers we were out of stock.

Savvy customers would ask a question that all of us dreaded. "Can you call around and see if another store has that?"

This process was called a charge send. It sometimes involved an hour or more of calling other locations, sitting on hold, and waiting until someone checked to see if the shoe was available. We had no idea which store in the chain might have the shoe and size we needed. It was a guessing game based on intuition and prior success. We started with the biggest stores first, which had the most inventory. From there, the guessing game began.

We were disincentivized from doing the charge send. Each salesperson worked on commission, so every minute we were not on the sales floor was a minute we lost money. Most of us put little to no effort into finding shoes from other locations.

For the store, that resulted in a significant loss of revenue. The lack of incentivization and inefficient process combined to make it almost impossible for these charge sends to succeed. Inventory languished on the shelves at some stores, where it could have sold in others.

Finally, the company added functionality to the point-of-sale system. We could look up inventory by location. The point-of-sales system was the initial introduction of technology into our workflow. Improving the charge send process was the opportunity. There was new revenue to be made by saving sales. The costs of markdowns and inventory taking up space in the back was also a factor.

Data handled this workflow better than any alternative technology. Without data about inventory levels at other stores, we wouldn't have been able to improve the charge send process successfully.

Our workflow didn't change. I still called the store and asked them to find a shoe for me. The sales associate on the other end of the phone still went into the back, pulled the shoe off the shelf, and got the customer's information. The decision-making process was the improvement.

Instead of guessing and facing massive uncertainty, I could now rely on the data to tell me exactly which stores had the shoe in stock. With that data, I made a better decision. The improvement in decision-making resulted in better customer and business outcomes. I completed the sale while the customer was still in the store.

Automation isn't always targeted at physical work. In this case, we were using data to reduce uncertainty. The uncertainty was where a particular shoe might still be in stock. With uncertainty, it took me a significant amount of time to find it. Using data to replace my guessing, I could complete the process in a much shorter time.

It took the business multiple years to fix this problem. Why? Most people in the corporate office didn't realize it was such a significant problem. They, too, were dealing with uncertainty. What technology initiatives should they select? They, too, were guessing.

Designing a Better Framework

Introducing technology into a workflow allows the business to start tracking inefficiencies like this one. Had there been data gathering about the charged send process, the problems would have been obvious much sooner. Without data, the business guesses in the dark about the best initiatives. Technology initiatives are selected by people who are often detached from the processes and products they are designed to improve.

Using the technology model, the C-level decision would have been significantly simpler. Data would have identified the part of the operating model which was currently inefficient. That begs the question, can we use technology to optimize this workflow? Technical strategists would have been able to come back with a yes. Is the data reliable enough to support this decision? Again, we could return with a positive answer. The initiative would have been selected based on its value and the data's ability to meet the salesperson's reliability requirements.

At the next level, technical strategists would have decided which technology could be leveraged to deliver the optimization best. C-level leaders make a business decision based on the opportunity size. The technology part of the initiative is handled at a completely different level.

The final piece of the puzzle is measuring outcomes. Part of the initiative needed to track the improvement or change to charge sends. If the feature accomplishes its goal, we should see an increase in charge sends completed. This is my first example of feedback loops.

A data feedback loop measures the actual impact of a technology initiative. This piece has been missing for a long time at many businesses. Today, the bar for technical teams is simply delivering what the company asks. In the modern competitive landscape, the bar needs to be delivering the outcome that the business needs. After introducing technology, the connection between a baseline and the new outcome provides an easy way to calculate ROI.

Workflow mapping helps teams who deliver solutions stay close to business value by measuring outcomes. Outcomes answer two questions. Did we successfully provide the expected value? Are there still opportunities to incrementally improve the value that we're delivering? Technology isn't a static entity. Businesses should reevaluate their opportunities to improve how current technology delivers value to the business and customers.

Data and AI provide opportunities to improve traditional digital solutions. Which ones should the business go after first? With the technology model, that decision gets abstracted from the technical details. It helps create a prioritization framework for the data team's work. Opportunities are selected not only by technical

feasibility but also by the magnitude of the opportunity and solution reliability. This is the alignment most businesses are
missing.

What's Next?

The hidden giant reveals the complexity that's been there all
along. Businesses need lightweight frameworks to manage alignment across business units, capabilities, and products. In the next
chapter, I explain the first three maturity models.

The goal is to reduce the cost and complexity of continuous
transformation at the implementation and execution levels.
Strategy without execution is the slowest road to success. The
maturity models make the connection between these top-level
constructs and frontline implementations.

10

The AI Maturity Model

Over the next two years, companies will make the same mistake over and over again. As AI hype continues to grow, companies will start looking for shortcuts to go straight to AI, like a race car going from 0 to 100.

With a race car, you'll hear it go through gears, revving the engine and then powering down. On the outside, all we see is a car flying forward. If we were trying to reverse engineer the motor, we might never understand the power of gears just by watching it drive.

It's the same thing with going from digital to AI. There are few shortcuts, and even those require a framework. Every business, product, and initiative goes through a maturity model. In past iterations, startups have had the advantage of not being bogged down by an existing solution. Even startups building from the ground up still have to go through a progression to get from digital to AI.

It's a common mistake. Startup founders want to build machine learning solutions because they are cutting-edge. They'll call in a data scientist to evaluate the potential. Most of us have been through something like this. We've all devised creative ways of explaining that without data, there's no way to build a machine learning solution.

First, the startup needs access to something that generates data. Without a version 1 digital product, the startup doesn't have a way forward to gather data and build a model. Without that original digital product, the startup doesn't even have someplace to put the model. There's no way to deliver a model's value to customers.

In this chapter, I explain how to progress through the maturity phases and align all the moving pieces.

Capabilities Maturity Model

Businesses all begin at early levels of technical capability. Most companies can move a digital solution to production. Some have evolved to support the cloud. Others have sophisticated data-gathering apparatuses. A tiny few even have AI capabilities. AI-first companies may want you to think they were always AI-first, but that's not really true. Even AI-first companies must start with a simple digital solution. How else would they get access to data?

In the previous chapter, I talked about my experience selling shoes and my system for improving sales. Over the course of a year, I became somewhat of an expert. The approach I designed fits under the paradigm of expert systems. These digital solutions are coded based on a domain expert's workflow.

Experts are still the best place to start, even in the AI-driven marketplace. I've never seen a version 1 model that outperformed an expert. I've also never seen an amateur become an expert just because they had access to data or analytics. People are smart, and when data scientists begin to build from smart people, the result is a better solution.

I call this level 0 maturity. At this level, the objective is to introduce technology into the workflow. For this to fit into the continuous transformation framework, the purpose cannot be data gathering alone. The point-of-sale (POS) system and McDonald's big-screen TV menus are great examples.

The digital solution serves a purpose and returns value immediately. It pays for itself and justifies the initial investment. McDonald's TV menus saved time by eliminating the need to change the drive-through menus manually.

A POS system completes sales more efficiently and facilitates digital payments seamlessly. Few remember when credit card sales were completed by taking an impression of the card and having the customer sign a physical receipt. POS systems automated this process, and an Internet connection made the funds verification process more accurate.

In the AI-driven marketplace, digital solutions will not be entirely forgotten. They are an enabling technology for data and models. The models handle the application's behavior, and the digital solution supports the user's behavior.

The original version of ChatGPT had a simple, digital front end: a single text field and a start button. Google, Yahoo, and AltaVista launched Internet search with the same digital solution we still use today. The evolution of that interface is only now happening. Search is being integrated into an increasing number of products. Additional context can be pulled from our workflow at the precise moment we need to search.

None of that would be possible if it weren't for the original digital solution. ChatGPT would have remained a novelty without that familiar interface. Level 0 maturity is the ultimate expression of meeting the business where it is. What technology does the company currently leverage? What opportunities does that technology afford us to introduce data into the workflow or gather data from workflows? These are where simple yet very high-value initiatives can come from.

Data Gathering, Serving, and Experimentation

Once technology has been introduced into the workflow, level 1 is possible. Level 1 is focused entirely on data gathering. Before data gathering in level 0, the business is very opaque. Level 1 brings a move toward transparency. The more data the company is capable of gathering, the more transparent its customer and internal user workflows become.

The point-of-sale system affords retailers the opportunity to gather sales data. Companies like McDonald's have a treasure trove of customer data from decades of sales. Their big-screen TV menus provide an opportunity to move to level 2. At level 2, we can reintroduce data into the workflow. McDonald's uses the TV menus to serve recommendations.

An apple pie or chocolate milkshake is a good recommendation if the customer doesn't order a dessert. If it's early in the morning, a good recommendation could be a cup of coffee or orange juice. The margin of the item can drive recommendations. If done properly, recommending high-margin food items should increase the average margin per ticket. The recommendation is an experiment, and by measuring the margin per ticket, we can connect an intervention to an outcome.

That's the power of introducing data into a workflow. I had a baseline of what customers were ordering before I presented recommendations. After making recommendations for six weeks, I can take another measurement. Have these recommendations met our initial assumption of higher margins per ticket?

These simple experiments open up the path to level 3. The business can perform basic experiments and deliver more reliable models at this maturity phase. Early models are descriptive, which means they describe the data. There's a critical differentiation that I need to make before we move forward.

The data that point-of-sale systems gather comes from thousands to tens of millions of customer purchases. Transaction data describes a rich system and marketplace. There are patterns in this data that are obvious. Most descriptive models give what I call Captain Obvious insights.

One Captain Obvious insight is that customers prefer coffee in the mornings. An expert could have told us that without the machine learning model or reporting system. It's an insight that a child or amateur would bring to senior leadership.

In data science, we're often guilty of presenting Captain Obvious insights. It's novel to us in the data team, and we assume it will be novel to the rest of the business, but it rarely is. What analytics should focus on is the unknown and opaque. Descriptive models should surface patterns that are not obvious and bring new information to the business.

Starting with Experts

That's the purpose of data gathering. If the data doesn't contain any new information, then it is not worth keeping. I recommend starting with experts because most data reveal obvious patterns. An expert system is a baseline that represents existing business knowledge. By starting with experts, we use the best available business knowledge. Just like with everything else in the continuous transformation paradigm, that will change.

Gathering data aims to improve the best available business knowledge. Starting with expert systems prevents us from reinventing the wheel and rediscovering the known. Data teams waste significant time and money doing that in early-maturity businesses.

Expert systems reveal what is known and what could be valuable to know. A core tenet of the opacity and transparency framework is to connect value with transparency into parts of the business and operating models. Data should be gathered to make high-value workflows more transparent and support initiatives that follow the maturity model.

Experts in the business can even provide a sanity check for the solutions data teams develop. They could help data teams understand if they've surfaced a novel insight or something that seems nonsensical. If it's the latter, we need to do more work because the barrier of proof is higher. We are contradicting experts. We should always treat that with the gravity it deserves, no matter how much data we have.

Starting with experts builds a relationship based on trust. The technology team trusts experts enough to create the version 1 system to their specifications. In level 0, we are capturing existing business knowledge. We use it to decide what could be helpful to gather in level 1.

For businesses, this is a novel construct. I call this intentional data gathering. If experts in the business already know something, there's no point in going out and proving it again unless a disruptive thinker enters the conversation. A challenge to a firmly held belief can make it worth reevaluating existing expert or domain knowledge.

That's another reason disruptors are so powerful and valuable to the business. We should trust experts until we have a reason not to. Disruptors give us cause to challenge strongly held beliefs and the existing status quo. They can point out assumptions to help us decide if it's time to gather data around a workflow we previously thought was well understood.

The disruptor is calling out that something we thought was transparent might have another opaque layer. In that case, it's time to gather new data and validate or refute the firmly held belief. It could even be time to experiment.

The goal of level 1 and data gathering is to help experts be better experts. By gathering data, we can either make them more certain or improve their domain knowledge. Intelligent people are the baseline, and data gathering aims to improve performance over the baseline. Data gathering that doesn't meet that standard isn't worth doing.

Once we introduce data or descriptive models into the workflow, we have a new baseline. The improved outcome becomes the new standard. Anything we do needs to represent a significant improvement above that standard. Justifying an initiative means justifying cost versus the improvement's expected return.

A Race Against Complexity and Rising Costs

An important concept to understand is that costs rise quickly once you go from level 2 to 3. Most models are not expensive to build. Data typically doesn't cost very much to gather. Levels 3 and eventually 4 are so expensive because describing the data is no longer sufficient. The goal of level 3 and 4 capabilities is to describe the process or system that generates the data.

In the top capability maturity levels, model development is only the beginning. Initiatives must progress into a second phase. The model becomes a hypothesis. Data scientists must develop experiments to verify or refute the hypothesis put forward by their models.

Once a model is developed, we must leverage it to create a hypothesis. Explainability methods must be brought into our approach. Data scientists need to turn what could be a very complex model into something they can explain, so experiments can be designed to verify or refute. The process can be quite time-consuming.

Not all experiments are feasible. Some run over very long time spans, possibly even several months. As the reliability requirements rise, so too do the costs. Returns must scale faster than costs do for an initiative to be justified. Most stop at level 2 because there's just not enough ROI to justify it.

In level 2, we use descriptive models, which are faster to build and less expensive. In levels 3 and 4, we use predictive, diagnostic, and prescriptive models. The models are rarely expensive to build, however, the validation component is where costs balloon.

The five-level model connects back to a C-level decision. How far should the business take each initiative or any opportunity? Level 0 is where most legacy businesses are today. At level 2, the business will be at parity with its competitors. I call this competitive maintenance. While these initiatives will break even and provide returns from a marketplace standpoint, the business is treading water.

A level 3 initiative gives businesses a competitive advantage. Today, most companies do not have the capabilities to build anything beyond descriptive models. They lack the frameworks to manage research and deploy experiments at scale. As a result, moving to level 3 provides a significant barrier to entry against competitors that have not developed their capabilities to this level. Many businesses are not even aware that there are more capabilities to be developed beyond descriptive models.

Level 3 initiatives can be significant revenue generators or cost savers. In products, level 3 features provide functionality that competitors can rarely match. It's these cases where a fast-follower strategy is often impractical. It can take too long for a competitor to catch up and produce a substitute, especially if that business is at a level 0 on the capabilities maturity model. By the time the competing product made it to market, it would be too late to get much market share.

Internal efficiency projects and initiatives provide a competitive advantage by preserving margins. This is one of the major benefits of the core-rim framework. The business scales faster and serves customers at lower costs. Operations can also continuously improve more quickly. Competitors without level 3 capabilities have difficulty competing in a pricing war because their operating models are less efficient.

Level 4 capabilities and initiatives push the company into innovator territory. Those businesses become industry leaders when their products deliver best-in-class functionality to customers. They operate with the highest efficiency levels and lowest costs of scale. These advantages give innovators pricing power and the ability to rapidly take market share from competitors.

At level 0, workflows are opaque. By level 2, they've become transparent. Businesses can continuously improve transparent workflows faster. Just like in the charge send example, companies can more easily find workflow issues and have more options to improve them. Another reason many initiatives end at Level 2 is the law of diminishing returns. At level 2, the cost of finding and fixing new issues becomes higher than the returns.

Even with the ability to deliver advanced models to production, the goal is still not perfection. It sounds strange, but a certain amount of imperfection is acceptable. At the end of the day, the cost of a few errors is often lower than the costs of the processes and workflow changes necessary to prevent them entirely.

The higher the maturity level, the fewer use cases it supports. Levels 3 and 4 are feasible for many use cases from the technology perspective. However, the value proposition simply isn't there. This is yet another reason to repeat the mantra, "Don't use AI for everything."

Each initiative the data team takes on comes at the expense of other initiatives that could have been done. The data team's resources are finite. Prioritization should be driven by the highest value work that can be done at the time. Squeezing incremental returns out of initiatives is rarely the best way to utilize the data team's time.

Three other frameworks run in parallel to the AI capabilities maturity model. Remember, strategy informs decision-making across the business. To support that end, frameworks need to run in parallel to each other, supporting different parts of each initiative.

The business chooses the capabilities level it develops based on the opportunities it has before it. Initiatives are designed to capitalize on these opportunities. Each initiative leverages the capabilities that align best with returns and C-level leadership's strategic goals (competitive maintenance, competitive advantage, or industry innovator/leader).

Initiatives lead to products. Products require data to support them. People within the business work with technology and products to create and deliver customer value. That requires frameworks for all three.

The Product Maturity Model

The product life-cycle maturity model also has five levels. Each corresponds to a level on the AI capability maturity model. Level 0 businesses use technology in an unmonitored way. Digital systems are deployed to support internal business needs and customer workflows. However, as we've already established, this is done unintentionally.

It is especially unintentional when it comes to workflows. Typically the workflow a technology supports is not well mapped. It generates data, but data is not being gathered intentionally.

The data being collected isn't connected with the workflow or any concept of value creation. As a result, it's missing business context and has very little value for model training or insight generation.

At level 1, the business intentionally introduces technology into the workflow. Level 0 represents an opaque workflow that may have digital technology already incorporated into it. Level 1 is the transition between opaque and transparent. Technology is introduced into the workflow to add value, whether that's to internal users, through productivity and efficiency products, or externally to customers.

At level 0, the business sees limited returns from its digital technology. Level 1 improves the returns and provides a way to gather data about the workflow. At level 0, the business invests in building level 1. At level 1, it realizes returns based on its investment in the digital technology (level 0 product). The company decides to reinvest some of those returns into collecting data and moving to a level 2 initiative.

Level 2 is where the business can monetize data. Data is reintroduced into the workflow using basic descriptive models. In the charge send example, level 2 introduced visibility into other stores' inventory levels. Shoe size availability data improved the quality of workflow and outcomes. It took sales associates less time to make these new sales.

Level 2 provides a return on level 1's reinvestment. We're faced again with the decision, should we reinvest returns into a level 3 initiative? At level 3, basic models are introduced into the workflow. At level 2, we can measure the improvement from the level 0 expert systems baseline. The process went from taking an hour or more to less than 5 minutes. The number of charge sends done and sales saved increased significantly.

Is there value in reducing the time the workflow takes further? Can the business justify a more expensive approach to reduce the time from 5 minutes to 2? Probably not. Introducing even basic models into the workflow can't be justified by a 3-minute time savings. Charge sends simply aren't done often enough. Costs will scale faster than returns.

If we lived in an alternate reality where charge sends were far more frequent, then it's possible that returns would scale faster than costs for the 5- to 2-minute improvement. I estimate the charge sends were less than 5 percent of the total sales I did on any given day. The ROI calculation would change significantly if that number were more like 60 percent.

In the charge sends case, it simply would not be worth improving efficiency further. Slightly inefficient people are more cost-effective than highly efficient models. Businesses will come to this decision a surprising number of times. While AI is the future, that doesn't mean its place is ubiquitous. We're still several years away from that happening.

At level 4, we go to high-reliability models being introduced into the workflow. A minimal number of use cases fit the need. At level 3, costs scale quickly, but at level 4, they accelerate unbelievably fast. The experiments here are more complex. The need for massive data sets and the compute power to process them is exceptionally high.

This is where the largest AI-first companies will play in the long run. Most businesses will partner with those world-class innovative AI companies or buy access to these models from them. I explain that paradigm in Chapters 14 and 15, on Large Model Monetization Strategies.

Level 0 represents a legacy business. Level 2, again, provides competitive maintenance. Level 3 creates competitive advantages, and level 4 puts the business in an industry-leading innovator position.

From a workflow perspective, level 1 begins to optimize the workflow. However, no changes are made to these steps.

The same is true for level 2. In the charge send example, my actions didn't change. Introducing data into my workflow reduced the number of iterations it took for me to be successful. That's where the time savings came in.

At level 3, workflows begin to change. Internal users and customers still maintain autonomy over the workflow, but the model has made changes to the workflow to improve it. At level 4, workflows change, and people begin to hand over limited autonomy to the model. This creates the connection to the human-machine paradigms I will get to in the next chapter.

The Data Generation Maturity Model

The next maturity framework centers around data generation. Everything the business does to create value and everything customers do with products generate data. In the earliest stages of maturity, the business is opaque because it is not collecting much of this data. Ironically, it could be collecting terabytes worth of data today, but since it isn't doing it intentionally, there is nothing new inside of that data. The purpose of data is to bring new knowledge into the business, and not all data meets that standard.

Data gathering is completely undirected at level 0 in the data generation maturity model. Data generation is happening throughout the business at all times, but the gathering processes are not well understood. Traditional data engineering is focused on building pipelines and transforming, cleaning, storing, and serving data. When this is the focus, the collected data is rarely high quality enough to build reliable models, even descriptive ones.

At level 1, we introduced the concept of mapping workflows or processes. They generate data, and when the business intentionally gathers data, it maintains the connection or business context between the workflow and the data set. The goal is to get a better understanding of the workflow.

At level 1, data is generated by workflows and gathered intentionally. Workflows can be internal user or external customer. In either case, this is a transition step between opacity and transparency. The business should decide to move forward with an initiative only if significant value is associated with that data set.

In level 2 of the product maturity model, we introduce data back into workflows. This corresponds with the data generation maturity model's level 2. Changes to workflows now generate data. This is where we begin to create the feedback loop and connection to outcomes.

Level 2 is where we do our earliest experimentation. The initiative puts forward a hypothesis: if we introduce a specific type of data or change into a workflow, it will result in an improvement. At level 2, we are beginning to control the processes that generate data.

In level 3, we integrate more complex experiments. Now the business and data team are beginning to develop new data generation processes intentionally. Experiments generate data that lead to more reliable models.

At level 4, we reintroduced the construct of the ontology. An ontology can represent a business's domain knowledge and expertise. The new data-generating process is the changes to these ontologies. What business outcomes result from changes to the ontology? These are the most complex experiments, and I won't dive too deeply into them in this book.

The result is causal knowledge. At level 3, the data team is interested in measuring the strength of the relationships between variables. In level 4, the data team is interested in measuring the strength of the causal relationships between variables. This gives you a bit more insight into why it is so expensive to go from level 3 to 4. Causal methods are never cheap.

The business has no documented domain expertise at levels 0 and 1 of the data generation maturity model. The knowledge trapped in experts' heads is uncollected. This is a significant contributor to the business's opaqueness. How the company operates and customers use products are siloed in their workflows. What's happening during those workflows? Only customers and employees know.

Level 1 and the process of workflow mapping begins ontology generation. This is a lengthy process, but it's worth noting that it starts even in early maturity phases. At this stage, the business is focused on documenting and validating current business and domain knowledge.

In level 2, data becomes exceptionally valuable and distinguishes itself as a novel asset class. The purpose of data gathering at level 2 finally achieves its potential, introducing new information into the business.

At levels 3 and 4, the business is now at the top end of the maturity model. This represents a significant competitive advantage or positioning the business as an industry innovator. In previous maturity levels, the ontology was an informal construct. The business introduces new business and domain knowledge captured in the ontology.

Even though levels 3 and 4 are forward-looking today, they won't be for much longer. In the framework of continuous transformation, these maturity levels are inevitable. All businesses should be building today with the knowledge that domain expertise being developed into ontologies is where they are going. This will connect with causal methods and become a dominant strategy for businesses.

What's Next?

These frameworks have explained maturity with respect to the business, data, and products. The final piece of the puzzle is far more complex. The way people work with models matures. Just like with every other part of continuous transformation, there are two sides. On one side, the technical capabilities and maturity develop. On the other side, people must develop a new relationship with technology.

Building this relationship is most efficient when both sides amplify each other. Products must be created intentionally to fit into a paradigm. People must be prepared, sometimes trained, to interface with this new product paradigm. Both sides evolve in lockstep, or this doesn't work. The value of data no one uses is 0. The value of the most advanced AI product that no one adopts is the same. As with everything else, it's not the technology that changes the most.

In the next chapter, I'll explain the human-machine maturity model.

11

The Human-Machine Maturity Model

A primary challenge with AI products is how they interact with people. You might be thinking, "Wait, did he just say that backward?" No. AI products interact with people just as much as people interact with them.

AI products are a novel paradigm for many reasons. The one most relevant to this chapter is their adaptability. As new training data is introduced or feedback is given, they update themselves. Models are designed to retrain and continuously improve.

Retraining a model is the process of introducing new information to the model. In many applicant tracking systems, if a recruiter rejects a candidate who was considered qualified, the weights used to decide what qualified means are changed based on the feedback. These feedback cycles are standard with machine learning–supported features and AI products.

With the original version of ChatGPT, you could correct the model. If it said something wrong, you got an apology, and it updated future responses based on your feedback. This paradigm is entirely different. People are used to adapting to technology. Many are not ready for technology to adapt to them.

In this chapter, I'll cover the most misunderstood aspect of data, analytics, and advanced models. They work with people in new ways, and the implications won't become obvious until models begin to behave unpredictably. Models work exceptionally well while the assumptions they're built on hold. When they fail, there's no warning from the model that it's become unreliable. We need another maturity model.

What Happens When Technology Adapts to Us?

Content recommendation systems are another example of adaptive models. Companies such as TikTok have become masters at quickly curating a feed for new users that keeps them engaged and on the platform. Some have estimated that they need as little as 12 pieces of feedback to create a highly personalized content feed.

Over the last few years, a backlash has grown over social media's content recommendation algorithms. Data scientists and AI professionals often wondered what the big deal was. Why, only recently, are people so concerned with the functionality of these algorithms? They have been with us for almost a decade.

This reveals an interesting truth about how people interact with models and inference. Users and customers don't know AI is there. They don't have the native sense and background to realize they're dealing with an advanced model that adapts its behavior in response to theirs.

An MIT Boston Consulting Group survey asked people whether they used AI as part of their jobs. More than 60 percent answered not at all or very infrequently. The researchers then explained what AI was and gave examples of products that integrated it into their functionality. Forty-three percent now said yes, they used AI somewhat frequently or frequently as part of their jobs.

Our users and customers don't know they're interacting with models. Most people don't understand how much of their online experiences are influenced by models. Data and AI products surround us daily, but there's very low awareness of that fact outside the tech bubble. Most people still think they're using more traditional digital products even when they're not.

Digital products and features have stable functionality. They don't change very often, and it's easy to see changes in functionality after the company behind the product makes code changes. In those cases, it's obvious. The new feature appears or changes its functionality overnight.

Models change more slowly. Through continuous retraining, model functionality changes incrementally. With data and AI-supported products, the changes and improvements happen so gradually that people often don't notice. AI adapts to users' preferences and optimizes to personalize their experiences, but that's not advertised by an update or new version. They don't know the changes are happening.

In some ways, that's a good thing. It means data scientists and product engineers are doing their jobs. Technology no one notices is the best kind. It typically indicates a high-quality user experience and excellent integration into workflows.

However, the hidden components of AI hide the true need for a different usability paradigm. When people interact with models but don't understand them, unintended consequences often come to life. The same is true when businesses design AI products but use digital paradigms. Those products typically do not end up meeting users' needs.

The Human Machine Maturity Model

The purpose of the human-machine maturity model is to help businesses intentionally design products for this new paradigm. It's also intended to reveal the changes and transformations necessary to support those products. Internal users and customers need training to be prepared for how model-supported features will work with them. People must adapt to the models that are continuously adapting to them. They must provide feedback in new ways. They need to articulate their requirements differently.

Without this new paradigm and the general awareness that it brings, users are often unaware that they need to make any changes. They assume every product is a digital product. As I said earlier, that doesn't end well.

At level 0, the human-machine paradigm is uncharacterized. Unintentional use of technology doesn't have a structured interaction paradigm. Before introducing the construct of expert systems, human-machine interaction isn't planned for. Workflows provide the connection between the machine and how it needs to function to service people.

There's a common complaint that's as old as digital products and software itself. The application works but doesn't work how users need it to. It's not very user-friendly. What hides behind that assessment is the level of effort required by users to actually use the software.

The changes they're forced to make leech more value than the application delivers. Poorly designed applications are difficult to use, and in the end, it can take more time to complete a task with the application than without. Connecting products with workflows enables a more seamless integration into user workflows.

Expert systems introduce the construct of the workflow to the application's design. Business and domain knowledge are built-in because experts are part of the design process. The resulting products are designed to be as easy to use as possible by people with an expert understanding of the workflow the product supports. Steps and unnecessary actions are pulled out of the application's functionality.

Expert systems represent level 1 for the human-machine paradigm. This is called *human-machine tooling*. People work with the application like it's a tool. The hammer is a similar construct in the physical world.

Before hammers, we had to hit a nail with a rock. Hammers introduced a better design and made it easier to drive nails home. When people used hammers, they became more efficient at driving nails. Still, the steps completed are exactly the same whether you're using a hammer or a rock.

In the charge send example, the data provided by the point of sale system was also a tool. It worked much the same as a hammer would have. Salespeople with inventory data are more efficient at this workflow. However, the actual steps completed did not change. We did the same things, but we could do it better with data.

In all the other maturity models, levels 1 and 2 represent a human-machine tooling paradigm. You can think of data like a nail gun. My workflow hasn't changed, but my hammer has become much more efficient. It requires less physical effort, so I don't need to be as strong to wield it.

Hidden Changes as Models Take Over

To this point, the objective has been to optimize the workflow but not alter it. At level 3, we introduce human-machine teaming. The primary difference is the change in the workflow. In the social media content recommender example, this is where the problem started.

People consuming information on social media didn't realize that their workflow had changed. They thought they still had autonomy and control over the content that they saw. Many people believed that posts were shown chronologically and would only see posts and content from people they followed. That wasn't the case.

In the background, the recommender algorithm had taken over. Social media companies realize an uncomfortable truth about how we consume content. People don't always know what they want. Sometimes they aren't very up front about it either. As a result, people leave social media platforms earlier than they would if someone else was taking control of content curation. In this case, the someone else became the algorithm or content recommendation model.

On social media, our feeds are curated based on what's most likely to keep us on the platform and engaged. Behind the scenes, our workflow had changed. When the CEO of TikTok testified before the US Congress in March 2023, he touted their new limits for children and parental control features. If they simply turned off the content personalization and recommendation models for users under 18, the problem would be addressed more effectively.

Take the advanced model out of the workflow, and autonomy returns to the user. TikTok would revert to a tool, and users would be more in control of their usage. While the model retains autonomy over content curation, the addictive nature of the social media platform will remain.

In the hammer example, human-machine teaming replaces the tool with something the employee works with more like a teammate. Robotic arms wielding hammers would fit this new paradigm. The more advanced technology changes the employee's workflow. Rather than doing the hammering themselves, an employee would be in charge of a series of robotic arms all hammering away. If the job were to install a new roof, an employee would oversee multiple arms hammering nails across the rooftop.

They wouldn't give over any autonomy. The worker would still completely control when and where each nail was driven in. The introduction of multiple arms would make that one employee more efficient, depending on how many robots they could manage simultaneously.

In the social media example, people unknowingly gave over autonomy. Social media users expected to have complete control over what content they saw based on who they followed. In reality, the algorithm was taking an increasing amount of autonomy away from people. Chronological order was replaced by one that was driven by the algorithm. It showed social media users what was most likely to keep them on the platform.

Human-Machine Collaboration Is a New Paradigm

This is a danger inherent in level 4. Human-machine collaboration is where the workflow changes and people hand over some autonomy. As we've seen with the backlash against social media algorithms, their reactions are severe if people don't realize they are turning over autonomy.

In our hammer example, it would no longer be the employee controlling a series of arms. More sophisticated robots would roam the construction site. They would be given a task like building a roof. The construction worker would oversee the entire process of the roof being built. There would still be a human in the loop, but most of the autonomy would rest with the robot.

Each level requires an increasing amount of trust. Handing over a piece of the workflow means a person trusts the model or algorithm to do that task as well or better than they could. Handing over a piece of autonomy means they trust the model or algorithm to make good decisions independently.

There's a massive jump in trust there. I have complete control of a hammer, so it doesn't require a whole lot of trust. I must believe it is well made and won't break as I try to do the job. The robotic arms require the next level of trust.

I need to see that robot drive in a ton of nails before I turn the hammer over. I need to know that I won't be cleaning up behind it. I don't want to pull a ton of nails from the roof and redo them myself. That wouldn't be a very good user experience. It would result in me altering my workflow and doing more than I was without the robot.

In the social media content recommendation model example, if my feed were filled with videos I didn't enjoy, it would make my experience worse. The model would make it more difficult to find content I enjoy, and I would quickly abandon the platform. On Twitter, I have the option to turn the content recommendations off and see a timeline of content from people I follow in chronological order. That puts the control in my hands, and I can choose to let the model take over or retain my autonomy.

In human-machine teaming, the robotic arm is still entirely under my control. I told it where to put the nails and when to do it. The machine doesn't need to make any decisions. The robotic arm just needs to be proficient at swinging a hammer and putting a nail into a roof.

Turning over autonomy is another thing altogether. I need to trust that the robot understands all the variations that it could be presented with. Hammering a nail seems like a simple thing, but deciding where nails need to go so that your roof stays on is more complex. Again, I don't want to spend my days fixing poorly built roofs completed by a robotic roofing crew.

Holding Machines and Models to a Higher Standard

The human-machine collaboration paradigm is almost exactly like having a team. I don't want a single team member to become a problem for the rest of us. We don't have to worry about laziness with robots, but we must still deal with incompetence. If you have ever worked on a construction site, you know the thing everyone hates the most. The workers have no idea what they're doing and make more work for everyone else. That's the fastest way to get fired.

It's the same with turning over our autonomy to our robotic crew. For me to trust this set of robots to do my job, I'm going to need them to perform a type of job interview. This brings up an interesting perception that people have with robots. We expect them to actually perform better than people before we turn over autonomy to them. And not just a little better.

People are unforgiving when it comes to AI-supported automation. ChatGPT gives us another case study. People are wrong on the Internet all the time. If I run a Google search for a complex concept, I will be presented with a series of high-quality and low-quality results. It's on me to parse through the good and the bad to figure out which one has the answer that I need.

ChatGPT hallucinates. It often provides the correct answer, but the more complex the questions asked, the less reliably ChatGPT performs. When I use it for search, it's about as reliable as your average website. However, people have judged it far less kindly. They abuse ChatGPT and expect it to perform well. If we did the same to a person, they wouldn't meet our human-machine teaming and collaboration standards.

The concept of reliability is critical to understanding human-machine paradigms and model or AI-supported products. With digital products, we articulate our needs for their functionality.

With data and AI-supported products, we need to articulate something new: reliability requirements. This is yet another contributor to the high cost of levels 3 and 4 maturity. It's the reason why describing the data is no longer sufficient.

For an individual to turn over pieces of their workflow, there needs to be some evidentiary support that the model can handle that part of our work. For us to turn over autonomy, there is an even higher bar. The model must demonstrate the ability to make rational decisions under a myriad of different conditions.

We see this challenge playing out in autonomous vehicles. Tesla crashes while on autopilot have gotten significant coverage over the last two years. Questions are growing as to its true level of capability. At the same time, companies like Mercedes and Hyundai are releasing level 3 capable autonomous vehicles. Those still require a driver. However, the driver is not required to be attentive at all times.

That was the promise of Tesla's autonomous driving functionality. At least, it was in the general public's perception. Most of us who are familiar with machine learning models' functionality were far less trusting. I bought a car with level 2 autonomous driving functionality. Before giving it any control at all, I tested it thoroughly.

It performs very badly on lengthy turns. It's unreliable in traffic or when the lane lines are unclear. On city streets, it is entirely unusable. It does perform very well in light traffic situations on freeways.

During long drives between Reno and San Francisco, I'll often turn on the autonomous functionality for a bit of a break. One hand stays firmly on the wheel, and I pay attention the whole time. Still, it's not the same level of focus as I would have to pay with traditional cruise control. I can sneak in a drink of water or stretch.

Many people did not do the same level of validation for their Teslas. Drivers did some things that were ill-advised while on autopilot because they put too much trust in the car. Regulators are now more heavily involved in auditing these types of autonomous functionality.

Understanding Reliability Requirements

The gap here is a framework for elaborating reliability requirements. Auto buyers don't know they must articulate reliability requirements or evaluate how well solutions meet their needs. If it functions most of the time, they assume the autonomous features will continue to function in the same way.

Vehicle manufacturers haven't done a great job up until now of disclosing the conditions that autonomous features will handle with high reliability and which ones they won't. We are still in the Wild West of autonomous functionality.

The same lack of awareness and transparency about reliability had led to wild overestimations of large language models' capabilities. Some people claim that GPT-4 can make complex decisions and have the chats to back them up. However, there's no warning before the model begins to hallucinate. GPT-4 can make those complex decisions with very low reliability.

That doesn't mean those models are useless, far from it. They are exceptionally valuable for most human-machine tooling and some teaming use cases. With retraining, the human-machine teaming use cases these models can handle increase to include high-value workflows.

Most businesses are rushing head first into building with large models but not considering the reliability requirements. Products will work well, be released, and only after they are adopted will the problems surface. Rapid adoption will turn to rapid attrition, and many products will snap out of existence.

The high rate of data science initiative failures businesses have experienced also connects back to reliability. Small pilots are quickly built to meet simple workflow needs. As those pilots attempt to scale and handle more complex workflows, the methods used to deliver pilots don't meet the reliability requirements. Products fail in production environments, and users abandon them.

This leads back to the C-level decision. What parts of the business and operating model should be transferred to the technology model? Another point to consider is the reliability requirements for the use case. Is the company, or are customers ready to trust autonomous functionality to do this part of their workflow? Again, just because something is feasible from a technology standpoint doesn't mean it is feasible from a business standpoint.

Focusing on the workflow gives us a way to bypass the technical details. Each time we decide to move something from the business or operating model into the technology model, we have a simple question set. Will this optimize the workflow without changing it? If the answer is yes, it falls into the human-machine tooling paradigm.

Will this optimize and change the workflow but not require the user to turn over any autonomy? This falls into the human-machine teaming paradigm. Reliability requirements increase significantly.

Will this optimize and change the workflow and require the user to turn over autonomy? This falls into the human-machine collaboration paradigm. Reliability requirements scale massively. Proceed with caution.

What's Next?

I've been talking about opportunities for several chapters. Now it's time to turn our attention to frameworks for discovering opportunities. Why wait so long?

Businesses need a significant amount of background information before moving forward with opportunity discovery.

In my process, I'm typically about three-fourths of the way through my initial assessment before I begin the first opportunity discovery sessions and workshops. It's tempting to dive straight in, start looking for opportunities, and then move forward.

That's one of our most significant data and AI strategy pitfalls. Once opportunity discovery starts, optimism and enthusiasm overwhelm people. Common sense and basic judgment can often go out the window. The business needs to understand all the context to discover high-value opportunities. I call this the big picture. In these first chapters, you've started to see the big picture.

Developing a vision for data and AI across the enterprise is critical. The big picture and continuous transformation views allow planners to see what they're starting and where it goes. Strategy should be forward-looking and prescriptive. All this context enables us to be forward-looking and prescriptive about the initiatives and opportunities we choose.

In the Marvel movie *Doctor Strange*, the main character jokes that the warnings come after the spells. They really should come first. In this book, you'll find the warnings and the context you need to make informed decisions will always come first. Even when that means taking the long way to end up at the beginning.

12

A Vision for AI Opportunities

Companies sat on the sidelines waiting for a signal to start the race into AI, but few companies knew what to look for. The last decade has been littered with AI failure cases. Meta has public failures with ad tracking and its research-driven open-source tools. Amazon pushed an automated résumé screening and recruiting app that was quickly pulled due to bias. IBM Watson shipped to hospitals, and those customers rapidly put a "return to sender" sticker on it and sent Watson back.

After e-commerce's disruptive waves flooded retail, businesses began paying closer attention to the risks and opportunities that technology drives. There was consensus that AI will disrupt, but when?

Then ChatGPT changed everything. It demonstrated a massive opportunity like no AI product before it. It also made clear the risks that businesses faced. AI was no longer something on the distant horizon. It has matured into a team member writers use to be more productive. Students cheat on exams with it.

Researchers use it to pass exams students spent their 4-year college degree program preparing for.

Three months changed everything because OpenAI did what no one before them had. ChatGPT was easy to use and presented an ocean of potential applications. Microsoft implemented it rapidly and offered paid tiers after short trial periods. It powered several features in their existing product suite. Everything Microsoft did demonstrates a new focus on monetization.

I'll explain how this plays out over the next two years in this chapter. This will help you guide opportunity discovery and develop your own vision for what's next. I will also introduce the first of two opportunity discovery frameworks.

The Zero-Sum Game: Winners and Losers

We can learn a lot from synthesizing what the winners in the AI arena do to our own businesses. What will a winner look like from the outside? What will the winners focus on versus the losers? How can we tell a good story from a business poised to seize the opportunities before them?

In the next two years, we will see a lot more talking about AI than actually doing it. That's no different than what's happened over the last 10 years. In Google's first demonstration of Bard, the company focused more on talking about it than on results driven by doing it. Based on one shaky demo, outside investors began questioning the company's AI credibility. Many switched from believing in Google's growth and innovation stories to punishing the stock for not delivering.

The big question was, "How can a company spend so much money on AI innovation yet be unable to produce results?" It was a head-scratcher.

The trend that hit Google will play out across industries over the next 2 years. Every industry will be disrupted; it's just a matter of when. Data and AI products will enter marketplaces and compete directly for customers. Opportunity discovery is a critical component of mounting a response to competitors.

The questions investors asked Google will be asked of countless other companies. Investors will look for a response when a competitor enters the marketplace with an AI-supported product. They'll ask the hard question. "If you've spent all this money to build AI-supported capabilities, why can't you deliver?"

In the past, businesses have been able to invest without much justification or returns. Now the focus is firmly on results. What we saw happen early in 2023 to Google's stock is proof. Investors abandon ship when the story doesn't match the results.

Starting the process of opportunity discovery is evaluating near and midterm opportunities. This is part of the technical strategist's role. We must be forward-looking and prescriptive. The vision for implementing AI across the enterprise is useless unless it's actionable.

Near- and Mid-Term Opportunities

In the near and midterms, the opportunities for AI products will follow the cloud cycle for the very biggest models. Developing products like ChatGPT or Anthropic's Claude will be the domain of the largest companies. Titans will dominate the large and highly functional model space.

This will shake out much like the cloud has over the last 10 years. There's a small number of massive providers at the very top. There's space in the middle for best-in-class or best-in-breed providers.

Most businesses will partner with or purchase from the top or middle tier. Developing a large language model is simply too expensive, and there's not enough monetization potential. This is an excellent space to evaluate opportunities to work with one of these large providers or an emerging startup. However, looking at opportunities to develop your own version of one of these top-tier models is typically a waste of time.

The top-tier companies will offer holistic end-to-end solutions. Each will have its own big model platform. They'll provide services that ease the integration of their large models into customers' existing product offerings. They'll have frameworks that simplify developing new products on top of these large models.

The top- and middle-tier providers will allow businesses the option of training the model with their own data. This retraining will enable large and midsize models to generalize across more specific use cases. Companies will still be able to create a competitive advantage based on the quality of their data.

A tools ecosystem will develop around each one of the large model platforms. Development, integration, and operations tools will help reduce the costs and knowledge required to support integrations. Solving the problems of training large models or reducing the complexity of developing these models will be a valuable business model over the next 5 years.

The tools ecosystem will help small and midsize businesses overcome the talent gap. Most companies don't have access to enough talent to develop large-scale models. An ecosystem of tools, vendors, and service providers will help bridge the gap.

The purpose of top- and middle-tier providers will be to reduce the cost of owning and developing AI products. This will bring down the barriers to developing models and AI products. More companies will rush in, and the race will be on in earnest.

Just like many businesses run a hybrid cloud, there will also be hybrid AI. It'll be similar to the adoption arc for the cloud. Much of the business's workloads are getting offloaded into the cloud, but some are still on-premises. In the same way, there will still be some models built and maintained internally.

Most of the very large machine learning initiatives will be partnerships with these top- or middle-tier players. Businesses will move onto their platforms, adopt their tools, and use their ecosystem. Still, there will also be an on-premises AI.

Best-in-Breed Solutions

The AI version of on-premises will build best-in-breed solutions for specific workflows. There will be a few winners in each category. A few critical success factors exist for companies in this best-in-breed workflow-focused model arena. The greater the business's access to the workflow and the more usage the model gets, the better their model product will become.

The advantage here comes from the speed of iteration and improvement. The more of the workflow the business has access to, the greater the range of functionality the AI product can support. The more people using the model and each part of the workflow, the better the feedback will be. Remember, people using the model generates data. Their feedback is some of the highest-quality training and retraining data you can get.

Integrating models into the workflow will also be critical. This represents the usability side of AI-supported products. Higher usability or deeper integration into workflows will lead to greater success because adoption will be higher.

There will be winners and losers in this best-in-breed marketplace. The losers will have an amazing story. Those companies will focus on talking about how innovative they are. They'll talk about using all these different leading-edge models and frameworks. They will point to research and some publications. Maybe even a few partnerships.

They will continue to point at all the potential in their new AI product pipeline. They'll have evangelists and influencers talking about the upcoming amazing things. Most companies will also point to their transformation road map and explain how it will move the business forward. They'll tell investors everything will improve, and products will soon start rolling out.

The problems will be uncovered when the questions begin. When investors ask what innovations have been monetized, the company will discuss minor, incremental improvements and features. When investors ask how much money AI products have made, there won't be much behind them. The story starts falling apart when investors expect results.

Microsoft went the other way with its AI product rollouts. They weren't telling much of a story at the end of 2022 and early 2023. They were shipping products to market, running demos, and selling subscriptions. Microsoft's products and the people who rapidly adopted them told the story.

Microsoft isn't bragging about the potential of what's in its pipeline; they're just showing it to people. They're incrementally rolling out new functionality across their platforms and suite of applications. Their subsidiaries, like GitHub, have been doing the same for more than a year.

Preparing Products for Transformation

Microsoft has been preparing its products for AI-supported features for a long time. It has been building products knowing that, eventually, each app will incorporate data-driven and AI-driven features. Microsoft has its own version of continuous transformation and AI maturity.

What may surprise you is something that I've speculated about for months. If you had asked when ChatGPT would be ready in early 2022, I don't think anyone would have been able to give you a date. If you had challenged Satya Nadella to tell you when the new Bing search would be rolled out, I don't believe he could have told you the precise timing. This is the nature of AI products and research.

Microsoft built up existing platforms and products, knowing that at some point in the future, it would adopt ChatGPT functionality. Even without a specific deliverable date, Microsoft decided to make integration simpler and seamless no matter when it was ready.

Now that these model capabilities are available, Microsoft can integrate them quickly into the workflows and spaces it has been making all along. Microsoft waited until the functionality was ready and shipped it instead of discussing it. You'll see winners in this space follow the same paradigm repeatedly.

Winners will talk about how they're developing their pipeline and building it out to make it deeper. This follows the construct of opportunity discovery and is one of the big reasons companies need it. The lack of talk is rooted in companies not having hard dates for when models may deliver.

That's one of the challenges of managing data science and advanced research projects. It's on a road map, but the business isn't 100 percent sure when it will be complete. Research and model development don't always run according to a schedule. It's iterative and painful.

Companies will have plans for where models will integrate once they are complete. However, making promises they may not be able to keep is a recipe to set investors up for disappointment.

Winners will talk about adoption once products are released. That'll be a huge focus. Microsoft has been slowly leaking the OpenAI and ChatGPT adoption story. Microsoft's Bing went from #14 in the App Store to #2 in the productivity category. After the initial demo and reveal of exclusive access, Bing went viral. Those words contained in the same sentence were unthinkable just six months earlier.

Then came the revenue. On earnings calls, Nadella teased earnings growth from ChatGPT-enabled functionality. He talked about how improvements to individual products and apps improved adoption and led to significant revenue growth.

This paints a picture of what data teams will be expected to deliver over the next 24 months. It's the new bar. Opportunity discovery is designed to build and develop the pipeline. Strategy runs on opportunities, and products won't succeed without them.

Businesses will have all these initiatives and opportunities in the pipeline, but they won't be sure when each will appear. That's why winners will focus on pipeline depth. Some AI products will deliver sooner than businesses expect, but most will deliver later than they hoped. That's the concept of a pipeline versus a road map. Road maps have solid deliverable dates. Pipelines don't.

Opportunity Discovery Gets the Business Off the Sidelines

Worry and optimism drive business questions. When do businesses need to start taking AI seriously? Is your business moving fast enough? Today, the answers are more evident than they were 12 months ago. It's time to start taking AI products seriously, and, no, your business probably isn't moving fast enough.

The problematic question is, when will it be too late? This should be the focus because, in every technology cycle, there are milestones defined by technical capabilities. Any business that hasn't developed or matured to meet the milestone is so far behind competitors that it will never catch up.

Barriers to entry have fallen across industries. Technology enables a handful of people with minimal capital to bring a product to market. Technology gives them access to distribution and a low-cost way to scale to meet rapidly growing demand.

A startup can self-assemble, develop an innovative product, deliver it to customers, and quickly take market share from incumbents.

By the time Microsoft saw Internet search's massive potential, Google had built technical and community dominance. Bing failed to thrive. Even technology-first incumbents can fall so far behind that they will never catch up. However, each wave provides a fresh opportunity to leapfrog competitors and rapidly take market share.

As a quick aside, Nadella oversaw Bing when Google asserted its dominance and brushed the aspiring challenger aside. As ChatGPT-powered Bing launched, he told Google to remember who had made them dance. Nadella had seen competitors brush Microsoft aside from a first-mover position too. He knew it was possible to leverage a disruptive technology wave to regain industry leadership. Nadella has been plotting this for a very long time.

Remember Zune, a digital media device and subscription service? It was first to market, but failed to see the opportunity's bigger picture, what I call the *arc of disruption*. The iPod stepped in and took over. I had a BlackBerry in the early 2000s and loved it, but it was another company that did not see the arc. The iPhone stepped in and took over. The iPad has market dominance that Google and Microsoft have failed to dethrone. Even titans fail when they cannot see the arc.

Incumbents can resurrect themselves by taking advantage of a new technology wave. They can innovate their way back to market dominance. Microsoft did that with Azure. The company went all in on the cloud and turned around a company struggling to remain relevant.

IBM didn't see the arc when Microsoft disrupted the PC market and took over the OS segment. With AI and Watson, IBM attempted to innovate its way back and failed because it was too early. IBM overpromised with Watson before the technology was ready for prime time. Innovation is not enough. There's another facet to the arc.

Technology waves have always been part of businesses' rise and fall. IBM, Microsoft, Google, Apple, and many others have shown that too early or too late is a recipe for failure. How can the amorphous concept of timing the market become actionable?

Technology must be feasible and monetizable with access to distribution or a path to scale. The whole arc of disruption is as follows:

1. Technology introduction.
2. Monetization.
3. Early adopters.
4. Distribution and scale.
5. Market dominance = too late.

Top-Down Opportunity Discovery

The arc defines actionable characteristics to look for when businesses decide it's time to get off the sidelines and get into the game. Top-down opportunity discovery leverages the arc of disruption framework to find large opportunities. This is typically part of strategy planning and a C-level exercise.

There are four stages to the arc:

- Is the technology ready? Point to implementations being used today.
- Is the business model ready? Point to businesses making money with the technology.

- Is it feasible? Point to the internal capabilities, data, monetization path, infrastructure, and prepared customers/users.

- Are we too late? Point to unserved or underserved customers, unmet needs, and value associated with meeting those needs.

C-level leaders need a framework to assess what's feasible versus what's smoke and conference-driven development. Hype is one of our biggest enemies. Without a framework, asking C-level leaders for opportunities can lead to fairly wacky answers.

The influencers and futurists have been whispering about GPT 8. Elon Musk got up on stage with a robot that did some impressive things. That's not what we need.

Most businesses aren't there yet because most industries and marketplaces don't live on the bleeding edge of technology. Those applications make for exciting theater but not reliable foundations for products. Top-down opportunity discovery must be forward-looking and prescriptive but tempered with pragmatism.

Part of a technical strategist's job is to be a voice of reason. We teach the rest of the business how to discover realistic and down-to-Earth opportunities. Everything we build must have near and long-term potential. Ten years ago, a good story about returns coming over the next 5 years was sufficient. Today, most businesses can't wait more than 6 months to start seeing some impact from initiatives.

The arc of disruption is the framework to find realistic opportunities. It returns autonomy to C-level leaders. They regain control over the direction their business will be taking to develop leading-edge technology. It puts strategy first and technology second.

The first question in the arc of disruption is, is the technology ready? The easiest way to answer that is to point at real-world implementations. It's one thing to present a product at a conference and quite another thing to put it into public use. That separates vaporware from feasible products.

Underpinning technologies and methods must be ready for prime time. Just because it can be built doesn't mean it can be turned into a product. The two are entirely different.

McDonald's has done extensive piloting with completely autonomous restaurants. If I were a competitor like Jack in the Box or Burger King, I would point to those pilots as proof the technology is ready. Those early pilots point to the second critical question in the arc of disruption.

Monetization Assessment

Is the business model ready? This question is the AI hype killer. Many companies have released AI products but never made a dollar. There's a big difference between technically feasible and feasible for the business.

The second question looks for implementations of the technology with evaluation criteria around profitability. Technologies and implementations must be mature enough to be monetized. At the second stage of top-down opportunity discovery, we're attempting to determine if we can profit from this. Is it just cool technology, or is there potential here for monetization?

The purpose of most businesses isn't publishing papers. Companies are in business to make near- and long-term profits. Investors are expecting growth, not a great story. If no one's figured out the monetization, the technology is not ready.

Amazon's Alexa unit was recently disclosed to be losing $10 billion annually. The product works. It's installed in millions of homes and has just as many satisfied customers. At the same time, Amazon hasn't figured out anything aside from monetizing the hardware. Alexa's intelligent assistant functionality isn't monetized.

The lack of a recurring revenue model is problematic. That's why Alexa is losing so much money. If Amazon made $0.10 every time I turned on a light, it would have a home run on its hands. Unfortunately, the things people use Alexa for the most are the things Alexa doesn't get paid for. The smart part of smart home isn't producing a whole lot of money.

As a result, anyone who proposes a smart home AI application during opportunity discovery must support it with a viable monetization model. In the arc of disruption, that's the bar to starting innovation initiatives. It's perfectly fine to bring new ideas to the table. The pragmatic side is ensuring a monetization model behind the technology. That's how innovation is connected to ROI.

C-level leaders are willing to fund innovation only after people make a specific case for monetization. Sometimes the business model is just as innovative as the technology. Companies that can figure out how to combine the two have home runs on their hands. When someone in the company can figure out how to make money with a novel technology, you get something like ChatGPT.

That's where Microsoft hit a home run. GPT models have been around for a long time. Strategists at Microsoft were able to innovate business models around AI products. The combination is why ChatGPT went from zero to 100,000,000 users faster than any other product in history.

Just Because It Can Be Built. . .

The third question involves feasibility. This evaluation happens at the next layer down. Technical strategists, data product managers, and data teams work together to determine whether the business has the capabilities, data monetization path, infrastructure, and prepared customers or users.

The arc of disruption can feel like the setup for a fast-follower strategy. That's why looking outside the business's current marketplace and industry is critical. Looking at the innovators in big tech can provide forward-looking information and a bit of a glimpse into the future.

I'll return to Amazon Prime's search recommendations as an example. Reducing it to first principles, the machine learning behind Prime's search manages the complexity of its product catalog. Data and advanced models are the only way to facilitate this use case. The logical workflow is too complex to map or display in a user-friendly way.

The monetization is there as well. Most customers wouldn't buy from Amazon Prime if the search results were terrible. Again, it's easier to understand at a workflow level. Users would scroll through two pages and just give up. Customers would leave and find their products elsewhere at a site with a better experience.

Amazon Prime makes more sales because its search is effective. That's a measurable value proposition too. If a customer selects one of the first five search results the model serves and eventually buys it, that's a high-quality search result. If a customer leaves after scrolling through 2 pages, that's the opposite, a bad search result. A simple workflow-based evaluation is often all that's necessary to make a case for an AI product or improvement.

That same problem space's characteristics could overlap with the business's current problems and challenges. The company doesn't have to be Amazon to have issues with complexity. Are there any opportunities to help customers find or discover what they need? Once top-down opportunity discovery has surfaced a feasible and monetizable technology, it's time to look for overlaps with the business.

I call this use *case geometry*. The use case differs, but you find significant overlaps when you break it into its fundamental components. It's a different use case, but the shape is similar. This comes back to reducing complexity and managing uncertainty.

It is the central theme in any potential application you're evaluating. What kind of complexity was managed? What type of uncertainty was reduced? Does the business have the same sort of complexity or uncertainty? Do customers view either one of those as valuable?

When we get down to that level, we can think about technology in a way that generalizes to businesses that aren't Amazon. The focus is still on use cases and workflows that have monetization potential. This avoids doing the pie-in-the-sky type exercises.

It creates a more straightforward presentation framework.

- Use case and opportunity for the business
- Example of what another company has built that's similar to it
- How they're making money with it

Outline the capabilities, data, monetization, path, infrastructure, and user or customer base required to support it. Compare it to how much the business currently has and what it costs to bridge the gaps.

This is everything C-level leaders need from a strategy standpoint to identify technology-based opportunities. Notice that in the presentation, we're barely scratching the surface of the technology itself. The focus is on utility versus a technical breakdown.

The final question is, are we too late? Businesses have a narrow window to follow existing solutions to market. Being a second mover is only a viable strategy for a short amount of time. How can the business evaluate if there's still opportunity left to be taken advantage of?

This is also a simple presentation that's based on the workflow. We need to point to unserved or underserved customers. Using the workflow, we should detail their unmet needs and explain what about their workflow is unserved or underserved.

The last piece is putting a value that the customer or user associates with meeting those needs. Top-down opportunity discovery overlaps with product management at this stage.

The arc of disruption is a framework for evaluating proven use cases to find the first principles that connect them. Opportunities follow the maturity arc to become increasingly functional products. Recommendations make it more convenient, and in some cases make it possible to begin with, for users to access a complex catalog of offerings. How can a business find opportunities along the same lines?

What's Next?

Top-down opportunity discovery has a counterpart, bottom-up. These opportunities are smaller, incremental improvements to existing products. They are easier to implement than what is typically discovered in top-down opportunity discovery.

Some companies call this low-hanging fruit, but it's not right in front of the data team. We need partners across business units to surface the needs they're closest to. The best people to discover and define unmet internal and external needs work at the frontlines. They need a framework, or competitors will capture these opportunities.

13

Discovering AI Treasure

Businesses have been promised treasure, but how do they find it? I often joke about a three-slide presentation companies use to sell AI. Slide 1 is all about AI and its potential. It's filled with stunning futuristic images.

Slide 2 is entirely blank.

Slide 3 is filled with massive numbers under the header "Profit." That's what businesses are given to develop strategy with. There is a wealth of information about the potential for the technology to generate profits. There's next to nothing explaining how to go from slide 1 to slide 3. This book is slide 2.

Opportunity discovery is where initiatives should begin. When they don't, the business quickly loses faith in data science. There's no connection between business strategy and initiatives without an opportunity discovery process. With that gap in the process, data teams are set up to fail.

In too many businesses, data teams are traveling around trying to find work. They bring opportunities to the business, and
the results are mixed. Our constant theme of staying close to the
workflows is broken when the data team is the primary source of
opportunity discovery. The data team is close only to the data
science workflow. For the rest of the business and customers,
they are outsiders.

Data teams have accessed so much data that they feel like
domain experts after a while. However, most of that data has
been gathered unintentionally. It isn't reflective of the workflows
behind it. There isn't enough context to understand the processes that generate the data. As a result, we sift through all that
data. We think we have found some fantastic opportunities.
Unfortunately, that's rarely the case.

In this chapter, I explain the second opportunity discovery
framework that manages the bottom-up process. It gets the data
team out of the opportunity discovery driver's seat.

Bottom-Up Opportunity Discovery

Opportunity discovery must be a collaborative process, and
frontline workers must have a way to be involved. When that
doesn't happen, data teams struggle to deliver value independently.

In bottom-up opportunity discovery, technical strategists
and data product managers work with frontline teams to find
opportunities based on existing products and internal workflows. This is yet another example of starting where the
business is.

McDonald's recently released a new strategy called "Accelerating the Arches." I'm using McDonald's as an example because
this is about as hard as opportunity discovery gets. McDonald's is
a franchise business model centered on restaurants. It sells food,

not software. There is no way to introduce data, analytics, or advanced models into your cheeseburger.

At a company like McDonald's, bottom-up opportunity discovery is more critical than anywhere else. The less obvious the connection between data or AI and value is, the more critical this framework becomes.

One of McDonald's growth pillars is doubling down on the 4Ds. Those are delivery, digital, drive-through, and development. Development is a recent addition that refers to developing new stores and opening them in partnership with McDonald's franchisees. If I were a technical strategist at McDonald's, that's precisely where I would begin.

The McDonald's CEO has made it clear that opening new restaurants is its most significant growth driver. For the next few years, that's what C-level leaders see bringing the increase in revenue that investors expect. The goals that C-level leaders care most about are the same ones that the data team should also put at the top of their list.

What workflows around restaurant development could I target to deliver value to McDonald's? That question would be taped to my monitor. At a Level 0 maturity company, I need to ask the question, 'What data about those workflows do I have access to today?' I need to find experts on the process of developing a new restaurant. Documents about the process would be even better.

Technical strategists and data product managers must live with our customers. The process starts by getting closer to the workflow. The better I understand how new restaurants are developed, the better I'll be able to support the strategic goal.

I'm also going to leverage the strength of data and AI. They reduce uncertainty and manage complexity. As I evaluate the workflow, I look for uncertainty and complexity. The first thing that comes to mind is the workflow to become a franchisee.

I would spend time talking to experts about this process within McDonald's. I should be listening for areas that are time-consuming or expensive. I need to ask questions about friction. What parts of the process do people walk away from? Are there parts of the process that hold up the application? Does any part of the workflow cost a lot to complete? Costs can be in hours or actual dollars.

How much of the workflow leverages technology? The answer to this question helps me evaluate the data being gathered versus generated. Level 1 maturity opportunities are focused on the gap between gathered and generated. Is there high-value data that is currently not being gathered? To answer this question, I evaluate the cost or value created by each step in the workflow. The higher either of those variables is, the more likely the data will be equally valuable.

How much of the workflow leverages data? I am looking for use cases that are currently supported by data. I also want to understand what level of value the current data provides. It's critical to measure a baseline for performance. This is where the earliest experiments begin.

What opportunities exist to introduce or improve data in the workflow? This is an evaluation of how well data currently serves customer needs. I'm looking for opportunities to improve the service level or begin to serve previously unmet needs. This represents a level 2 maturity initiative.

At most businesses, this is the extent of available opportunities. They lack the talent and infrastructure to deliver levels 3 and 4. The incremental steps to get to those levels have yet to be undertaken. Bottom-up opportunity discovery is focused on evaluating where the business is today and what opportunities the company has for the near term.

Using these breakdowns, it's possible to estimate the size of the opportunity and costs. The opportunity can be broken down into smaller initiatives that follow the maturity models. Opportunity discovery should flow seamlessly into those processes.

Giving Frontline Teams a Framework to Leverage Data and AI

John Deere introduced AI-supported features into its tractors. It began by adding sensors to gather everything from data about the tractor's position to its usage. At the next level, the company reintroduced data into the workflow. It provided tractor owners with access to detailed reporting. Finally, it offered semi-autonomous functionality so tractors could run primarily unattended. This sounds like a great opportunity discovery success case.

In reality, John Deere customers, for the most part, did not want any of these features. They were utterly unwilling to pay for them. A secondary market for used vehicles that didn't have any of this data or AI-supported sensor technology was created almost overnight. Customers preferred to buy used instead of new.

When companies don't have a good bottom-up opportunity discovery process, ideas that sound great to the business or data team don't necessarily meet customer needs. That's because the people in charge of selecting these more incremental improvements are often disconnected from the workflows they intended to improve. The closer opportunity discovery happens to the need, the more valuable the opportunities that surface will be.

Bottom-up, opportunity discovery is a process driven by frontline workers. Teams interacting with customers daily are most keenly aware of how they currently use products. Frontline workers and teams are the best people to bring opportunities to the data team. So why don't they?

Bottom-up opportunity discovery was missing in the McDonald's story. One of the inefficiencies that McDonald's CEO lamented was the fact that it had 260 different chicken sandwiches. One was performing amazingly well in Asia. The CEO's question to the business was, "Why don't we just do that one everywhere?"

It seems unimaginable that you would reach the point where 260 different chicken sandwiches were deployed across all McDonald's locations. Wouldn't you have some data or report to raise a red flag when you reached, say, 11?

The whole point of data is to prevent this sort of repetition from ever happening in the first place. I'd bet someone at the frontline knew the problem. They lacked a process to surface their needs for reporting around the number of different variants for each type of product offering. The McDonald's Chicken Sandwich report would have taken a few days to develop. Who knows how much money it would have saved?

Even for small initiatives, the business needs a way to monetize and manage value creation. Building every idea that surfaces is a setup for failure. AI product governance provides a framework to evaluate and prioritize these bottom-up initiatives.

Frontline employees know best which opportunities exist to introduce data into their workflows and improve how they deliver customer value. The people closest to customer workflows know how to do the same thing to enhance existing products and services. They're also best positioned to articulate the reliability requirements based on the workflow and use cases supported.

The AI Product Governance Framework

The AI product governance framework has three components—monetization, commercialization, and productization. Frontline workers will surface the opportunities. Those are passed on to data and AI product managers.

The first determination is whether this is a data science problem or a digital problem. In the early phases of AI product governance implementation, most of the opportunities that get surfaced are digital. That's the paradigm everyone's used to. Part of those early education processes is teaching frontline users the difference between digital and data problems.

There's a new construct that must be surfaced along with the opportunity. In traditional bottom-up opportunity discovery processes, the functional requirements are specified. That's still important, but there's a new component that data and AI products add. The business needs to collect reliability requirements. Reliability requirements will help us understand where on the maturity model this initiative will fall.

Data and AI product managers handle the commercialization piece. Commercialization is focused on going to market. At the product manager level, opportunities are estimated. Costs are considered. The initiative is broken up based on the four maturity models.

Reliability requirements are again at the center. Commercialization focuses on the last mile and getting models out of the lab and into the real world. Models built in labs work only in the lab environment. The real world has completely different conditions, and customers have different expectations. Getting close to the workflows the model will support is critical for bridging the gap.

Most customers don't understand the model paradigm. That's why we see such a wide variety of responses to the original ChatGPT. User opinions ranged from "This is trash" to "This is the greatest thing in the world" and every flavor in between.

Tesla provides a great real-world example of failing to prepare customers to use AI products. People do fairly ridiculous things while their cars are running on autopilot. For people in the data field, these are head-scratching. As I mentioned earlier, most people lack the background to understand that intuitively.

The challenge is Tesla hasn't done a great job explaining how reliable its autonomous driving capabilities are and when they will behave unpredictably. This is a marketing problem as much as anything else. In pharmaceutical advertising, a long string of potential side effects is listed in every commercial. We need something similar with AI products. In this case, it would be a list of conditions where the autonomous driving features will perform unpredictably.

Most of Tesla's autopilot accidents result from people misusing the functionality, and only a tiny minority result from the model going rogue. Reliability requirements must be communicated well, or people will abandon model-supported products. This is the core concept of preparing users or customers.

Productization is the next phase. Once a model is trained, it must be developed into a product. The model isn't ready for market until it has been integrated into customer or internal user workflows.

Models are novel asset classes because they can be monetized in multiple ways. OpenAI's partnership with Microsoft is showcasing this unique property. In one example, GitHub leverages GPT in its Copilot for code generation. The primary value creator is the model because it handles Copilot's core functionality.

In Copilot, no one would adopt the raw model alone. It would be exceptionally cumbersome to use as it is built. GitHub has succeeded with Copilot because it integrated the model's functionality into the developer's workflow. Microsoft followed that up with integrations into VS Code. Again, the central theme is integrating it into an existing developer workflow.

That is a critical piece of productization. The integration leverages a digital front end to manage the user's behavior.

It creates the experience users adopt. The better it integrates into their current workflow, the higher the adoption.

A good opportunity must become a valuable product for customers. Getting people to pay for inference is more complex than gathering data and just building a model.

The third component of AI product governance is monetization. This can be managed by the sea level or a committee of stakeholders with the assistance of data or AI product managers. As I'm fond of saying, the AI last-mile problem is really a first-mile problem.

Before anything moves forward, all the information gathered by frontline workers, data and AI product managers, and the data team is evaluated. This paints a complete picture of monetization. C-level leaders or the committee can assess every piece of the initiative and how it advances along maturity. The decision to move forward should be made with all this information. This is the final hurdle before the initiatives are given the green light.

What Happens if No One Brings Opportunities Forward?

Sometimes, the business is not ready to bring opportunities forward. Technical strategists and data product managers may need to lead the process and teach people across the business how to surface opportunities independently. Legacy businesses struggle to see opportunities to leverage data or AI.

How do we kick off the process and drive change?

For the business hesitant to adopt data or model-supported products, the best place to start is with pain points. Technical strategists can develop initiatives and recommend opportunities around what the business is currently complaining about.

In every business, one group or one set of customers always complains the loudest. These become some of our closest allies in the challenge of getting people to adopt.

In McDonald's, this is the chicken sandwich problem: 260 chicken sandwiches showcase a more extensive suite of issues beyond just delivering a single report. Again, it's time to dive into the workflow. What processes could potentially lead to 260 different chicken sandwiches being deployed across McDonald's locations globally?

My next step is to find groups disgruntled with this current process. While inept middle managers often love dysfunction, frontline workers hate it. Broken processes make their lives harder because frontline workers are the ones who end up supporting them. They have to cover up the shortcomings. Behind every broken process sits one or more teams who hate it.

People complaining about an existing solution are less resistant to new solutions. One of the biggest barriers to change is a currently working solution. When someone's complaining, they obviously don't have one of those.

The process is broken. The tool or the workflow is broken. The people engaged with it know that. These workflows are excellent targets for introducing data or model-supported products.

I can also rely on soul-sucking processes for low-resistance initiative ideas. What work do people hate doing? What do customers hate interfacing with when it comes to the business? In the McDonald's example, I discussed starting with the franchisee onboarding process. I could begin by talking with franchise owners and people who have gone through the process. I would ask a simple question, "What was the most challenging part?" Early initiatives are often that simple to discover.

Marketplace drivers can also force adoption and overcome resistance. A competitor threatening to pull ahead could move the ball forward. Right now, we're watching Google respond rapidly in a way that it hasn't for several years. Microsoft demonstrated the feasibility of introducing ChatGPT to search and caught Google flat-footed. However, their CEO immediately recognized the magnitude of the threat they were facing.

Bing's ChatGPT search could disrupt people and change customer workflows. All Microsoft must do to change search customers' behaviors is get a few weeks' worth of new usage and adoption. People use Google search because they've always used Google search.

TikTok has also shown Google's vulnerability to search disruption. Younger search users leverage TikTok more frequently than Google. They are looking for what they see as more honest, transparent results. In the arc of disruption, this fits the description of underserved customers with unmet needs. There's still time to get in and take market share.

Google had been extremely hesitant to touch the golden goose, its search business. This new threat has made it more than willing to implement changes. Fear is a powerful driver, so changes in customer demand and behaviors are powerful drivers for change too.

The same approach will work in more traditional industries. Pointing out a competitor who is pulling ahead can be a powerful motivator. I prefer to lead with hope, but fear can be useful every once in a while.

In the fear situation, involving other organizations in opportunity discovery is still a good idea. The competitive threat or changing customer behavior causes this new opportunity discovery session to be needed. It creates a strong connection back to the core strategy and starts building coalitions across the business.

It May Be Bottom-Up, But It Still Starts at the Top

Opportunity discovery should always connect back to the business. We meet the business where it is, and that also relates to its original goals. The first pass of opportunity discovery shouldn't be aimed at changing current goals. We must introduce ways technology can support the current business goals and objectives.

One of the mistakes strategists often make during opportunity discovery is trying to tell the business to do something because the technology makes it possible. We need to take the opposite approach. C-level leaders have given us their highest priorities, the business's strategic goals. We should work forward from the opportunities they see and define initiatives where data, analytics, and models can return value better than an alternative approach while supporting existing strategy.

Otherwise, we are taking autonomy away from C-level leaders, which is another driver for resistance to change. It cannot feel like technical strategists, product managers, or the data team is dictating strategy to C-level leaders. We cannot dictate solutions to frontline workers and teams. That process must be collaborative.

We must never forget that for the rest of the business, technology isn't their area of expertise. The less these frameworks touch on the technology, the more effective they will be.

Meeting the business where it is and where transformation is today helps with adoption. Most digital transformation initiatives have some process mapping or process discovery. It's an attempt to understand the business better that connects to transparency and opacity. These initiatives are an excellent way to integrate data and AI initiatives into the digital transformation process.

That brings up an even more significant challenge when answering the question, "Where do we start?" Mapping processes and workflows reveal the hidden giant. With all the potential opportunities and initiatives the business could be doing, what should it be doing?

I returned to what data does better than alternative technologies. What parts of the business are complex or time-consuming to interact with and people frequently must interact with to create customer value? The same question applies to customers in their workflows.

Applying for a mortgage can be painful. Ask a customer what the worst part of the workflow is, and it's typically all the information that's necessary. It's a pain to find all the documents, upload them, and then enter all the information required to get approved.

Is it possible to streamline this process? Probably. It doesn't take too much effort to scan documents and detect the types of information that the application requires. Amazon offers a web service that handles this type of document parsing.

Is it monetizable? In the current economic climate, most banks are reducing staff at their mortgage divisions. Application rates are falling, so they don't need as many people to service customers. While this feature could be monetized in different conditions, it's a bad idea right now. Banks are dealing with less demand than they have staff to support. That's the opposite of a high-value initiative.

Sometimes the value of opportunity discovery is in the opportunities you decide not to pursue. Establishing the data team as a strategic partner means saying no to low-value initiatives. The data team's resources are finite and should focus only on the most lucrative opportunities.

What's Next?

Large, foundational models create an entirely different class of opportunities. Multimodal functionality opens potential applications that cross industries and support use cases that technology could never serve before. New frameworks are necessary to support opportunity discovery.

These models also enable businesses to leapfrog the maturity models. Products can be built on top of these large, foundational models without ramping up a high-end applied machine learning research team. Businesses that understand the paradigm will seize immediate and long-term opportunities.

There's significant disruption coming. I'll introduce frameworks and describe the new product paradigms in the following chapters.

14

Large Model Monetization Strategies—Quick Wins

Entirely new business models will be built around generative AI and the wave of new companies like OpenAI, Anthropic, and HuggingFace. New partnerships are emerging every day. Amazon has partnered with HuggingFace, Microsoft with Open AI, and Google with Anthropic. Google also has its own version of these generative models called Bard, and generative models actually originated there before other businesses took them forward.

Is everyone going to need a partnership? No, but every business will need to understand the new paradigm, not just for generative models but for all of the other large-scale platform models that will come after this round.

Less technically mature businesses are leapfrogging larger competitors. A new paradigm of models enables products that used to be the domain of the largest tech-first companies. Now that's changed, and we need to think differently about the concept of an AI platform.

How will these changes impact businesses and the AI competitive landscape? What's being accelerated, and by how much? More important, how will businesses use these new AI model platforms to generate revenue and run more efficiently?

In this chapter, I'll answer those questions and more. I provide frameworks for monetizing large models like GPT and all the ones that will follow. Multimodal language models are just the beginning.

Large robotics platforms and supporting models will be delivered soon. Level 3 autonomous vehicles are available to the public, and fully autonomous vehicles are in service in large cities like San Francisco. The time to create a monetization strategy is now, and these frameworks will help you do it.

AI Operating System Models

A digital metaphor is extremely effective in driving this new paradigm home. It helps to have connections with more familiar concepts. Think of these large models as your baseline and a new type of operating system. Products will be built on these AI platform models like software, and applications are built on Windows, Linux, Android, and iOS. Few businesses will develop their own operating systems.

Software and applications are built on operating systems to get them into the hands of people. As these operating system AI models get smaller and more efficient, we will see them move from the cloud to running on PCs and, eventually, mobile devices.

Every major cloud platform will have AI operating systems. That's why Google, Microsoft, and Amazon were the first to undertake these partnerships. It is a critical piece of their cloud growth strategies.

In the 1990s, a company couldn't ship a PC without an operating system. How would people have used it? What would they have used it for? It would have had so much functionality missing. It's the same for cloud platforms. Those must have an AI operating system for customers to build on, or they'll leave for a cloud that does.

The conversational interface is our new keyboard and mouse and serves the same functional need. We need some way of interacting with the model, just like we need some way of interacting with our computers.

We can use natural language to interact with any application built on an AI operating system. Generative search is one example of a product built on AI operating system models. The earliest implementations were Bard for Google and GPT for Microsoft's Bing.

We don't have to create search strings with our new keyboards and mice. I can simply ask a question in a natural language, and the conversational interface makes it simpler to interact with the model. Follow-up questions are answered with the context of earlier questions.

Will we replace keyboards and mice completely? Not immediately. The metaphor is a framework to think about the equivalence between the PC revolution, which you may be familiar with, and the AI operating system models. That context will help you to see opportunities better.

What do generative models give us access to? A knowledge graph. That's what sits behind the first wave of AI operating system models. Internally, that's not actually how they work, but that's the functionality these models provide. Separating the technical details from the functional for opportunity discovery is critical.

Multimodal models support translating between formats. The model can extract and translate information from an image into text or turn a text prompt into an image. These tasks are more complex types of language translation. Instead of French to German, the multimodal model can translate from a video to a text summary of the video.

AI App Store

Let's get to the second metaphor. The AI platforms are becoming the new App Store. OpenAI recently released, and Anthropic and HuggingFace are building toward that. Third parties can give users of ChatGPT access to their applications.

A user can request recipe suggestions from one application and use another to order the ingredients for delivery. I can search for vacation destinations with Bing and use a travel app to compare prices for each one.

The big three cloud providers are creating a new type of operating system based on AI. That's where many enterprise applications will be built. Some companies will release them as part of their own application or platform ecosystem.

Even those companies will likely develop some applications to integrate with these new AI App Stores. By making it easy for ChatGPT and Claude users to access their applications, companies get access to a larger customer base. OpenAI is developing this AI App Store, and others will likely follow.

When Apple introduced the iPhone and then the iPad, there was an App Store built into it that allowed any company to submit an app to the App Store. Once approved, the app will be available on the device, and I can access it. No matter what it is.

Large AI operating system platforms are trying to replicate the business model. Developers will use the tools ecosystem developed by HuggingFace, Anthropic, or OpenAI, but also Amazon, Microsoft, and Google, their respective partners. Developers can use the tools ecosystem to create best-in-class and sometimes highly questionable applications.

Each will have an App Store where businesses on the Amazon or OpenAI platforms can sell all their products to anyone on that platform. Developers will work on one side with the tools ecosystem. On the other side, businesses will get access to an entire customer and user ecosystem.

There is also an emerging partnership ecosystem. Bain and OpenAI recently announced a partnership agreement that adds Bain's professional services wing to the platform. Bain supports building, developing, and deploying apps built on GPT, so lower technical maturity customers don't have to. That's a powerful combination.

Customers get the GPT series of models, the platform, and the App Store. They also get access to a services provider who can take a business from 0 to 100. Bain brings the ability to help partners integrate GPT into their businesses and products. It's a fast track to getting up and running in these new AI operating system and App Store paradigms.

All the pieces are starting to come together into what will eventually be a super platform. Users won't need to go anywhere else. OpenAI will give users access to apps and functionality to support nearly all their workflows. Each AI operating system and App Store will compete against the other, just like the mobile platforms did. The same dynamics that governed iOS, Windows, and Android will repeat themselves.

None of the major players is going away, but the landscape will change. There will be clear winners and losers. AI platforms that provide the greatest functionality and the best tools ecosystem, customer and partner ecosystems, service providers, etc., will win. All of these dimensions are being built on AI operating system models and their platforms.

It's an entirely different thought process. Apps are no longer built-in isolation just to run on something like an iPhone. Businesses are building their apps on AI operating system models to run at scale on emerging super platforms.

Businesses aren't just integrating models into their applications. They are building apps that integrate with AI operating system models. New models will also be developed on each AI operating system model.

The App Store is a good metaphor, but it extends only so far. There will be a significant difference between the applications built for the original App Store (digital applications) and the digital and AI applications built on top of these AI operating system platforms.

A massive range of solutions can be built by retraining these models. Businesses across industries will deploy retrained models to support functionality that the original large models weren't meant to or don't handle reliably enough. I'll explain those in the next chapter, but first, I must reveal the short-term opportunities available right now.

Quick-Win Opportunities

Evaluating early potential applications based on use cases is essential so initiatives don't result in vaporware. Workflows are tangible artifacts we can integrate solutions and technology into. Even advanced models allow us to evaluate value creation for internal users and customers.

This pulls from the arc of disruption framework. A solution could currently serve customers, but the question is, are they underserved? TikTok exposed a weakness in Google search functionality.

When TikTok introduced search, people 20 and younger began to turn away from Google. They used TikTok to find tutorials, informational videos, and product reviews. Customer behavior pointed out underserved use cases for this specific segment.

They had lost trust in Google's search results. They turned away from YouTube to find higher-quality tutorials and informational videos. Everything from DIY to technical walk-throughs was now the domain of TikTok search. Google lost credibility and utility because there were simply too many ads being displayed. Some search results were obviously promotional, filled with affiliate marketing links.

Underserved markets are the biggest opportunities for disruption. Bing exposed a different way that search customers are underserved. Complex search needs haven't been fully met either. It's exceptionally cumbersome to do a detailed search for something very specific. Natural language avoids us having to develop some convoluted search strings.

We don't realize we're underserved because we've had the same solution for so long. We're almost blinded to some of the opportunities due to habits. It's another reason why use cases and workflows are critical for opportunity discovery here. They help us evaluate enterprise and customer use cases pragmatically. The focus is on monetization strategy versus chasing hype.

A three-point assessment framework can help with opportunity discovery. The first point assesses whether there's actual value potential or if the use case is just smoke. Evaluating use cases with a workflow-centric view allows us to understand whether there are missing pieces.

This is a different type of gap analysis. The search is for places where users abandon their workflow. This can involve users going from a digital solution to something manual. Users may need to copy and paste information back and forth between multiple applications. Some workflows require multiple applications to complete, and users are constantly bouncing back and forth between them.

Each one of these areas of friction indicates an underserved need. When users depart from the standard workflow, we're seeing one of these underserved needs. The next step is to understand the value of improving this workflow. This assessment can be as simple as evaluating the workaround's cost. Assessing how well the business can monetize that workflow is equally critical. If the opportunity doesn't fit the existing business model, it's probably a bad fit.

It's also critical to evaluate implementation and support costs. Many of these solutions will be easily built, but integration and support will be where the real expenses appear. The more volatile or frequently changed the workflow, the higher the support costs will be.

As with any other model solution, reliability requirements must be assessed. The risk with large models is hallucination. Even though the models are broadly functional, they're not reliable enough to support every use case. It's safe to assume that without significant retraining, human-machine teaming is the limit of their reliability.

Competitive advantages and threats must also be assessed. Your competition is working on these as we speak. It's important to keep tabs on your competitors and what they're working on for these large language models. Sometimes significant value can be gained by developing features that deliver the business a competitive advantage or maintain its competitive standing. Operational efficiencies could result in competitors being able to put pressure on pricing. It's important to evaluate both sides.

Some implementations will have marketing and branding benefits. For these initiatives, the value proposition is similar to an advertisement. The novelty value might be high enough to perform better than some online ads do. As the cost of these models comes down, this is an interesting application to consider.

The Digital Monetization Paradigm

Most quick-win opportunities will fall under the digital paradigm. Opportunities here follow the paradigm of integrating these AI operating system models into existing applications. While not every product will fit this well, you'll find significant opportunities by thinking in this direction.

That's both good and bad. With all this potential, you're probably getting an inbox full of potential opportunities from across the business. How do you whittle all that down and deliver actionable advice?

The best approach is to explain what the models can do by providing examples. A little bit of education can go a long way in funneling ideas toward high value. It could be worth publishing the list of scenarios and existing implementations that could be feasible for the business from an integration standpoint.

Customer support has significant opportunities for integration. Microsoft has already showcased a few proofs of concept with GPT 4. In one, it's able to summarize conversations after customer support calls. Customer service agents no longer have to do this step manually. The application summarizes the complete conversation, writes up action items, and can even escalate issues to the next level.

These and dozens of other customer support use cases will be managed by third-party vendor software. Companies like Microsoft and Salesforce are all already rolling out products to support customer service use cases. It's important to showcase that some opportunities could be serviced better by buying a solution instead of building it internally.

Customers have a range of product questions. They often want to make side-by-side comparisons. Current solutions handle many of these use cases clumsily. Intelligent agents can take natural language queries and deliver high-quality, complex results. This is a better use case for building an internal solution.

Automated marketing is another rich landscape for opportunities. Marketers can now create content faster. Salespeople can pull information from their CRM systems to automatically populate emails. Content and email customization will achieve new heights in the next 12 months.

Individual use cases can illustrate deeper themes of what these AI operating system models are capable of. It helps people focus on where thinking about quick win opportunity discovery should go. Still, it's important to encourage creativity and to extend the themes to discover new use cases.

Generating answers has some interesting potential applications. Large language models can also provide recommendations based on complex search strings. Those looking for a present can provide the chatbot with details about the person they're buying for. They could detail some of their hobbies, interests, and demographic information like age. The chatbot could return a recommendation or potential gifts to the customer.

There's potential for customers to get an entire blog post written about the product and how it meets their specific needs. Recommendations can be extended to the point where the chatbot becomes a minimally functional salesperson.

Generating content is simply a variation on generating answers. With multimodal models, that content could potentially come in the form of texts, images, or video. We're used to transcribing audio to text, but it can now be done in the other direction.

Content Summary has several interesting applications. Models can turn white papers or long videos into a series of articles and social media posts. Content can be created on demand from multiple different formats. It can be translated from one format to another. Responses can pull from more than just the customer's request. Responses can also include context from the business's CRM to provide more customized answers. Product recommendations can also be made more specific.

These are all excellent thought sparks. Anytime you hear about a new use case, abstract out its first principles. Think about how the problem being solved could apply to different categories of problems your business faces.

Understanding the Risks

As with everything else, there are always risks. Most aren't getting enough attention. During opportunity discovery, constantly think about potential downsides. It's critical to advertise as many risks as possible up front as part of developing monetization strategies.

The first risk theme is quality. These models are amazingly performant, but as we've seen, there are areas where they begin to break down. Every model has functional limits, no matter how impressive they are at general tasks.

One of the biggest challenges with generally performant models is testing all the potential functionality a customer could throw at it. There's an entire field called *chaos engineering* to handle testing complex systems like these AI operating system models. In that testing paradigm, businesses throw all the worst-case scenarios they can think of at the application. There are typically hundreds of them, so testing these models is more complex than companies are accustomed to.

Safety nets must also be put in place. Scenario planning is essential here too. Determine the unacceptable behaviors and put safety nets in place to prevent those scenarios from happening. If you don't feel like you can appropriately risk-proof the solution, don't deploy it to production. Someone will inevitably take advantage of it, exploit it, and put that exploit all over the Internet. Many companies will find themselves exposed because they didn't do the appropriate level of scenario planning.

Regulators have yet to fully weigh in on where these models fit in their regulatory structure. New frameworks can take significant time to be adopted and implemented. The business must consult experts before moving forward with a monetization strategy to ensure they are not operating in jurisdictions where the company could get into trouble. It's also important to monitor for changes in the regulatory environment that could impact existing solutions. Every business needs a governance framework for AI operating system models.

Integration, usability, and user experience will all be critical. For companies like Best Buy or Walmart, using these intelligent agents to provide customer service will be widely accepted. For prestige brands where world-class customer service is critical, customers may not be as accepting. On the other hand, some customer segments will demand access to intelligent agents as part of the e-commerce experience. There will still be areas where customers want people to remain their primary point of customer service contact.

Security and privacy also still matter. Significant unknowns exist about what gets done with the data sent to these models. There must be clarity in the terms and conditions. It's critical to evaluate each third-party AI operating system model that you work with to ensure your and your customers' data are protected.

The bottom line is that considering risks is still absolutely critical. Scenario planning and risk mitigation are essential parts of monetization strategy. Always be asking what if? Don't rush headfirst into a massive mistake, no matter how many other businesses in the industry are doing it.

It's equally important to find risk mitigation strategies rather than making risk avoidance the centerpiece of monetization strategy. Manageable risk shouldn't prevent the business from innovating. There's an element of risk to every product. The goal here is to avoid taking ridiculous risks because the business didn't evaluate solutions thoroughly.

What's Next?

There are more opportunities on the horizon for AI operating system models and AI app stores. In the next chapter, I will explain how businesses can leapfrog competitors and deliver high-end models without building the capabilities internally.

Data curation and workflow mapping are about to get a lot more valuable. They support opportunities to build best-in-class models. These models level the playing field between small and large businesses. What's an opportunity to some will be a massive threat to others.

15

Large Model Monetization Strategies—The Bigger Picture

Larger opportunities are on the horizon, and businesses should be getting ready to seize them. In this chapter, I'll explain a new opportunity to leapfrog competitors and how it impacts the maturity models. Curated data sets have more value locked in them now that AI operating system models are generally available.

The previous chapter explored the digital paradigm and integrating functionality into existing applications. In this chapter, I'll explain the AI product paradigm opportunities and provide frameworks to discover and seize them. The first question is, should every business invest in developing large generative AI models? Spoiler alert. The answer is no, and here's why.

What Are the Costs?

You're probably wondering, "How much does training one of these AI operating system models cost?" As it turns out, quite a bit. Will costs eventually come down? They already are. When Databrick open-sourced Dolly, its version of GPT, it showed that a smaller labeled data set could train a highly capable model. Training costs were orders of magnitude lower than GPT and Claude.

Optimization is well underway for AI operating system platforms. Google's 540 billion parameter PaLM cost around $27 million to train. Meta has a much smaller 65 billion parameter model (that sounds crazy to say, much smaller, but it actually is). Training costs about $4 million. Admittedly, this model isn't as capable as GPT-4 or PaLM.

However, as a baseline, it performs well. Retraining Meta's and Databrick's models will be more feasible and cost-effective. The efficiency wars will continue to improve tools and make the unit economics work for more use cases.

Model training isn't where the costs end. Experts with specialized knowledge are required. People who develop the infrastructure and architect the model to distribute efficiently into the cloud are required. For data scientists, architects, and high-end researchers, demand is rising. Talent is costly and hard to come by. Not every company has access to building a team capable of developing a large model. Even as training costs come down, the talent puzzle remains.

Businesses also need people curating these data sets. Those costs will not immediately come down either. In the long term, maybe in three or four years, we'll start to see reductions, but these will continue to be costly resources in the near term.

Labeling itself is an art form. Different labelers have different label quality scores. One can be 95 percent accurate, while another labeler could be 92 percent accurate. Their error classes could be the same or completely different. Solving the various problems with design, collection, and consistency require specialized capability sets in and of themselves. Businesses will need talent for that too.

It's not just the people who label the data. Businesses also need people who do all the logistics work behind the scenes to make those labels as useful as possible and solve some of the hairy problems behind labeled data. Some costs are unavoidable, even in partnership scenarios.

Finally, model maintenance or continuous retraining is an iterative cost. Even if training costs drop, maintaining or continuously improving the model remains a significant expense. Maintenance costs will come down. As large models become more efficient, retraining will get cheaper. The tools ecosystem will also help here.

Costs will come down, but in the near term, these large models will still be out of reach for most companies in the next two years. So, does that mean most companies will have large models in 2 or 3 years? No, in 2 years, these models will be even more complex. Complexity will scale to take advantage of improvements in technology and optimizations.

AI operating system models and AI App Store platforms are massive undertakings. Will some companies choose to do this? Yes, but very few cases will make sense. For most companies, it's too expensive and isn't worth it from an ROI standpoint. There's just no justification for building it for yourself versus partnering.

To see how retraining will add value, it's helpful to understand a little bit about how they are trained in the first place.

How the Models Work

Understanding how these models work is essential because some of their inner workings will help you understand monetization better. The amount of money that it costs to develop the data sets, do the training, retraining, serve inference, and maintain them puts creating these models out of reach for most businesses. It's a considerable investment.

Most businesses will partner or develop on one of the AI operating system platforms. Companies will build new models and products by retraining large models with more granular data to improve or extend their functionality. It's not just apps being built on top of large models but also models being built on them.

AI platforms will potentially lock the business into an ecosystem unless they develop applications for multiple platforms like businesses do for iOS and Android.

Each model will be built around data the business has access to. If higher-quality data isn't readily available, it makes more sense to use an out-of-the-box model. However, companies with the best-in-class, proprietary data can retrain the model for their products.

The opportunities come from building models on or retraining AI operating system models to create highly reliable functionality for niche workflows. Retraining generalizes the large model to a broader range of use cases that OpenAI, Anthropic, and HuggingFace never anticipated or lacked the data to support.

It's worth understanding some of what's going on under the hood of AI operating system models. Simply put, generative models generate something: text, audio, images, and video. Large models can create new instances of any of those if there's sufficient training data. When training data is insufficient, opportunities exist to build on and retrain AI operating system models.

AI operating system models are highly functional out of the box, but they also have significant limitations. As I'll discuss in the next section, limitations are opportunities. How are they trained?

The baseline GPT model is trained on a massive data set in step 1. Next, OpenAI curated and generated another high-quality data set to retrain and fine-tune the model. Developing this new data set involves giving examples of precisely what the model's output should look like. This is a higher quality, more targeted, and more granular training data set.

In the next step, they created a reward model. The process starts by taking several different outputs from the same model and having a person rank them by quality. Reviewers look at the model output or responses and label them from best to worst.

A final retraining step is completed next, resulting in the generally accurate model, but it's just a baseline to build on. It performs well over a broad number of cases, but for many questions, the model is entirely wrong.

Despite the accuracy problems, these models are highly functional out of the box. Understanding the feedback loops and retraining and how they lead to a better model reveals the opportunity to develop new AI products. Many companies will take advantage of retraining to build new models that are even more functional.

Flaws Are Opportunities

The flaws in these models are actually opportunities. No AI operating system mode will be ubiquitously reliable, and we're seeing that play out. Google's Bard did horribly, even when answering some fairly basic questions. The same thing happened during Microsoft's ChatGPT integration into Bing. Tons of pieces are missing.

OpenAI undertook an interesting project in early 2023. It hired more than 1,000 software engineers to do the types of labeling and ranking that I talked about in the previous section. Each software engineer is given specific tasks with specific code to write.

They are creating a more complete labeled data set around software development and engineering. It will be used to retrain GPT to be better at developing code. This is one of Microsoft's big-push applications for OpenAI's GPT series of models. GitHub and VS Code have early versions built into Copilot.

Advanced debugging will be introduced to help developers find and prevent defects. This functionality will cover more than the simple ones that cause compiler errors or the semi-complex ones that cause runtime errors. A retrained model can help discover defects that could become issues at scale, potential security flaws, or optimizations that aren't obvious.

Microsoft is trying to handle more complex software development use cases and complex types of code. They are leveraging the same process of curating highly targeted labels for the data and then using it to build a more capable model.

They've recognized a gap in the model. There is not enough data on software engineering, which has led to inaccuracies. The large model doesn't handle all the questions and code generation tasks that customers need to make Copilot easier to monetize.

There could also be data quality problems in the original training data set. OpenAI and Microsoft trained GPT on GitHub's software library, especially open-source projects. Most open-source projects are very high quality, but some aren't. There's probably low-quality code lurking in their data sets, causing substandard answers and code to be generated.

Capturing the workflow itself and a bit of the detail about why this code is being written provides invaluable contextual information. That's why the coding tasks OpenAI hired software engineers to perform are so controlled. It's equally critical for labeling to be consistent and for labeler quality to be high.

Data is being developed to fill in gaps where the model didn't perform very well. The process creates metadata and context around workflows through the labelers. Having software engineers complete granular tasks creates high-quality data that will improve GPT through retraining. As a result, the out-of-the-box model will become broadly capable across a larger set of software engineering tasks, filling in coverage gaps in the workflows.

Flaws are opportunities to deliver new value by retraining AI operating system models. Curated data sets covering gaps in functionality will contribute to this new monetization paradigm. Curation requires access to the workflow, and that's what OpenAI is getting from the software engineering project.

The granularity of tasks and diversity of potential workflows are why 1,000 software engineers are needed to build the data set. Each task asks engineers to write a code block with particular functionality. OpenAI is essentially giving software developers the prompts and seeing what they produce.

Then another set of reviewers, code reviewers, you could call them, will evaluate the retrained model. They are given six or seven responses to a coding prompt to rank by quality. This data set trains the policy model. A policy model automates the reviewer's role making retraining possible at scale with less expert-labeled data.

To take advantage of these opportunities, businesses need access to workflows in controlled conditions and experts to do the labeling and reviews. With this retraining paradigm and high-quality, workflow-centric, labeled data, best-in-class models can be built for specific use cases and workflows.

The higher the workflow's value, the more valuable the retrained model will be. The better the business can curate data, the more it can reduce the costs, and the higher the margins will be.

You're probably starting to see the tip of the opportunity iceberg. If the flaws are the opportunities, anytime you discover a flaw, it's time to think about monetization potential.

Disrupting College

Large models will cause disruption, and how that plays out is not always obvious. We need another framework to deal with this challenge. Disruptions are known for the threats and opportunities they create. As dangerous as they are to existing products and business models, disruptions create opportunities for new products and business models.

I use a three-layered framework: disruption, implications, and adaptation. When new technologies like AI operating system models come to the market, disruption will follow, bringing immediate and long-term implications.

Once the implications become apparent, businesses, customers, and the marketplace adapt. The goal of evaluating disruption as part of the strategy planning process is to be more forward-looking. The company must see threats and opportunities coming instead of reacting after it's too late.

The first disruption example is happening in traditional college education. Educational institutions across the globe are grappling with the implications of widely available GPT-style models. What does a college do now that everyone has Anthropic, OpenAI, or Hugging Face models in their pocket? The challenge for education is directed at the nature of the curriculum.

Step 1 in the framework is assessing the disruption. That can begin by considering how customers, employees, and competitors will use the products built on AI operating system models. Students, teachers, researchers, and administrators have already started to use them.

Assessing the disruption moves to those groups' potential use cases. Homework is one specific use case, but students can use ChatGPT for any use case that fits into the memorization or summarization of facts categories. If students have one of these intelligent agents, the number of facts they must memorize drops significantly.

I realized this a few years ago, inspiring me to develop a different type of course design. It's the rationale behind systems, frameworks, and models. The memorization of facts is increasingly marginalized. We don't need to remember dates and times. We must understand how systems work and develop internal models or heuristics to manage them.

Frameworks serve that need best. That's why I teach them instead of forcing students to memorize facts. My teaching style is an adaptation to the changes I knew were coming to the educational world.

The adaptation is the final piece. In my case, the new course design concepts were my adaptation. A traditional college education will be challenged to adapt in the same way that many other course creators and I have. The essential parts of what we know are more complex than a set of facts to memorize. That means teaching in the large language model era must shift focus.

What should colleges do now that students have these models in their pockets? The flaws are the opportunity. These models are not accurate in every case; that's especially dangerous for students. Students don't know when the model is right or wrong. What opportunities does that create?

A textbook company could retrain its own version of Chat-GPT or Claude. The goal would be to develop a reliable model capable of answering questions about different college topics. The value added by retraining is to deliver a higher degree of certainty. The corpus or textbooks is the data set in this case.

Textbook companies could monetize that quite nicely. Instead of having online and digital textbooks, those companies can use them to retrain an intelligent agent. They could charge for access to the retrained model per semester, year, or college.

Students' workflows improve because they don't have to search for answers in their textbooks. They can ask the intelligent agent for answers. Bing and Google can be unreliable agents, so the value proposition is providing students with a product that will deliver a high-quality answer.

Generative AI could put textbook companies out of business unless they get ahead of the trend and adapt early. The unreliable nature of generative AI creates a new product opportunity that sidesteps their textbook-supported business models from being disrupted. Adapting their products makes them more valuable than ever.

The digital textbook transforms into something completely different. Textbook companies can offer not just a single textbook but an entire library of questions and answers. There are tons of other monetization strategies for this business model. They can sell access by college, student, semester, course, or series of textbooks. The product could be priced in any number of different ways.

Using this framework as part of the strategy planning process is critical.

- What's the disruption?
- What are the implications of that disruption?
- What are the adaptations that will happen as a result?

With that information, businesses can decide on the best way to position their product so they're no longer obsolete.

Advanced Content Curation

I believe advanced content creation is a generative AI use case that's flying under the radar. We're thinking about how large models can create content very simply. We should be paying more attention to how large models will disrupt streaming entertainment.

Let's go through the three steps: disruption, implications, and adaptation. A company like Disney or Netflix could use large models to create new shows; large multimodal models can handle text, audio, images, and video-generating tasks. One prompt can lead to multiple media types being returned.

Generating characters and having them read lines and interact with each other is quickly becoming possible. How much content creation will it take over? That's uncertain. There are several use cases, but we don't know for sure what's going to happen. Large multimodal models make it possible, and someone will figure out how to capitalize on that opportunity.

Developing the retraining data set will involve a large content provider. It might require actors and actresses to read and act out very specific scenes. Labels could focus on emotional content types and context around the scene. There'll be several labeling challenges to overcome, but the training data set will be developed. As a result, these models will become much more capable of producing longer-form entertainment content.

What are the implications? There are some obvious ones. It'll lower the cost of creating and refreshing an entertainment content catalog with new shows and movies. Content will be developed faster, so new series and films will release sooner.

There's also an interesting implication that content could be personalized. That won't be to an individual level; that would be too expensive. Creating three to five versions of every movie is more feasible.

Each version could cater to different viewer preferences and areas of interest. Some people enjoy character development. Others enjoy more action. One version could be a deep dive into the characters. The next may highlight and accentuate the action scenes. Finally, a third could be developed for younger viewers.

We may soon see new levels of personalization, so different audience segments, which usually wouldn't enjoy the same thing, can watch the same movie or TV show. The thin layer of personalization is possible because large models automating parts of content creation will bring costs down enough to make that use case feasible.

What are the adaptations, and what might happen because of this disruption? Novel concepts and stories become the focus of people's workflows. The ability to develop new stories and ideas for stories will be the new human-dominated creative capability with the highest demand.

It won't be as essential to do the script's granular pieces, but capturing those storylines and bringing them to life will be crucial. People will need to take the model-generated pieces and improve them. People will still be necessary to turn AI-generated content into high-quality movies or TV series.

Workflows will shift significantly to flow, character, and action development. Expert creatives understand what people want, and their content makes a genuine connection. AI-generated content is still coming to terms with workflows like those.

When costs come down, studios can take more significant risks on different types of content. The cheaper it is to produce a riskier series or movie, the more likely it is that studios will take that risk. The ROI will be there because the content costs aren't as high. Not everything needs to be a blockbuster to succeed if high-quality content can be produced at lower costs.

What are the opportunities? Obviously, curating those training data sets is a huge opportunity. Companies with access to an existing content library or an easy way to develop those training data sets have a gold mine on their hands. Content companies will pay a lot to reduce their costs. For some streaming services, lowering content costs is their only path to profitability and survival.

Companies spend billions on content development. When you identify an opportunity like this one, there are two sides to evaluate. The business could be a consumer and leverage the model to produce content in a new way. The company could also be a data set curator.

There are risks to consider. The business may be disrupted. This is a scary concept for many studios, actors, and actresses. How do you position yourself to survive this coming disruption?

Content creators will be competing against AI. We need options to turn the tide so that we don't compete against large models but collaborate with them. The business and operating models must adapt to leverage content creation engines and models to build better content.

This framework is designed to kick off these thought exercises and help businesses understand the pragmatic implications. The process should reveal opportunities for partnerships and threats. The goal is to develop ideas about adapting so the business model isn't wiped out. The business model may need to be redesigned around data set curation.

Don't be limited in your thinking. Use this disruption, implications, and adaptations framework to kick off this innovative process and find some practical, tangible, actionable ideas.

How Microsoft Successfully Monetized Their $10 Billion Investment

Monetization follows a different paradigm. The business typically monetizes a digital product in one or two ways. Data and AI products fit a different monetization process. The same model can be monetized multiple times.

Microsoft's partnership with OpenAI is an excellent example of the AI operating system monetization paradigm. Microsoft has been investing in OpenAI and GPT since 2019. Late last year, it added another $10 billion. How can Microsoft get a return on that investment?

It released ChatGPT with Bing in a way that got people's attention. Their shareholders rewarded them almost immediately. We will see this pattern repeated. The company will announce a partnership and a series of products.

One or more will be immediately available for the public to use. The release showcases the product and proves it isn't vaporware or hype. The business has an actual product that supports multiple customer use cases. The adoption cycle will be critical, but for now, I'm focusing on the monetization component.

Microsoft's partnership was immediately worth far more than $10 billion. Their market cap went up almost $100 billion over three months, from announcing the collaboration to the initial Bing demo. There were significant rewards for investors who held Microsoft through 2022's downturns.

How is Microsoft monetizing GPT to earn that higher valuation? The first project was GPT integrating into GitHub's Copilot and Power BI. Next, it integrated ChatGPT 3.5 into Bing. With GPT-4, Copilot became the face of generative AI functionality across its product ecosystem.

Looking further down the road, there are even more opportunities. ChatGPT 4 is already good at generating content. Integrating Copilot into Word and other Office 365 apps will make people more capable and efficient. We'll be able to build emails and respond to questions faster.

GPT 4 is a big step forward in accuracy, so it generalizes to new use cases, such as building out the basic framework for a PowerPoint presentation. It helps with blog posts, press releases, and event-based news articles. Microsoft has integrated Copilot into Office 365, creating opportunities to monetize at scale. If Microsoft can charge an extra dollar a month, it represents $4 to $5 billion in annual recurring revenue.

That's why platforms are so powerful. They open multiple ways to monetize these best-in-class models, and that's what Microsoft is demonstrating to us. Review Microsoft's platforms, and you'll find opportunity after opportunity.

Businesses should constantly look for new use cases and workflows when monetizing AI products. One product or idea for a business model isn't the end. Retraining the model or partnerships that businesses forge opens an opportunity landscape.

AI products and models don't just do one thing anymore. Models can adapt to multiple use cases and workflows to serve numerous needs. The more functional the retraining makes the model, the more monetization opportunities open.

Large Models Enabling Leapfrogging

Why are the AI operating systems and app stores such game changers? Companies don't need to build complex models internally. Partnering and building on AI operating system models lower the barriers to developing products with advanced capabilities. This allows companies to skip steps on the maturity model.

Levels 2, 3, and 4 are no longer necessary for some use cases. The business needs high-quality, curated, and labeled data sets. Businesses can leverage their data to retrain the models and go from level 1 to level 4 overnight.

Companies are using a combination of augmented reality and 5G technologies, as well as some reasonably simplistic models, to deliver functionality in a new way to repair technicians. These technicians are involved in automotive and aircraft repairs and maintenance. These businesses are giving technicians goggles. Basically, they look like safety glasses, but each lens is a video screen. They show the technician a heads-up display that overlays video on the real world.

The heads-up display shows instructions on performing a repair or maintenance task. The technician opens the hood, and the heads-up display identifies the parts and pieces the technician will work on to complete the task. The goggles overlay detailed instructions like precisely which bolts to twist off, what parts to remove, and what part is being replaced.

This is a significant improvement to repair and maintenance workflows. It can augment repair technicians with the instructions necessary to perform repairs, from simplistic to very complex, properly even the first time they complete one. The goggles walk an experienced technician through the process, so it's not a significant challenge if something changes about the parts or layout. The technician can put the goggles on, and the heads-up display will walk them through the new process.

It dramatically reduces the time it takes to train technicians and the time it takes to perform repairs. But what does that have to do with data? None of that's really a data use case. Basic computer vision is used to recognize what's in front of the technician and overlay the images.

What if the business wanted to add functionality so the technician could ask questions as they complete the repair? The step-by-step instructions might not have all the information the technician needs. It would be convenient to ask some basic or even advanced questions about "what if" scenarios.

What happens if something goes wrong? What if I break one of the bolts? Is there a recommended procedure for getting a stripped bolt out? What if I find additional cracks in one part?

A company that isn't at level 4 yet couldn't deploy an advanced chatbot to handle those use cases. They couldn't meet their technicians' needs for additional questions, so there would be parts of the workflow that they could not service. The business's low maturity level would limit the ROI of this amazing device.

With generative AI models, all the business needs is data. Do they have data that could answer these questions? The business can retrain Claude or ChatGPT with a data set built from its resources, manuals, instructions, videos, and specifications.

The more information available, the harder it is to sift through all of it to find exactly what the technician needs. Claud or ChatGPT can manage that data set without a problem. Once they're retrained, the resulting model can answer all the questions a technician has about any repair.

Partnerships change the maturity model, and companies can leapfrog levels. If they have the data to support the functionality, they can retrain the model and provide functionality that otherwise would be out of their reach.

Workflow Mapping Becomes Even More Critical

Workflows can be broken down into decision chains and task geometry. Decision chains are people's connected series of decisions when completing a workflow. If a recruiter reads and rejects a résumé, there are two parts to the workflow.

The tasks are reading and clicking the reject button. The decisions are more complex and opaque if all the application logs are the button press. Something about that résumé informed a decision to reject it. I want to build functionality into the application to capture that data.

We could put a series of checkboxes into the application. After the recruiter rejects the résumé, they can check the box that best explains why.

- *Checkbox 1*: Missing capabilities
- *Checkbox 2*: Missing education
- *Checkbox 3*: Underqualified from an experience standpoint
- *Checkbox 4*: Overqualified from an experience standpoint

This is a low level of effort on the recruiters' parts, and I at least understand what category to classify the rejection under. The more granularly I track the decision chain, the more it costs and the higher the labeled data set's quality. The additional time necessary for the recruiter to fill in that data isn't free. I may negate any benefits from automating the workflow in the first place.

Natural language processing and data curation are complex and require weeks of data science team time. The feedback needs a scheme and, eventually, a structured assessment rubric. This is simple in the early phases of maturity but very complex as the system moves from gathering structured categories to an open field of text attributes.

I would need a very high-end application to support tracking the workflow at this level.

Task geometry is the actual work being performed. In my retail customer greeting example, the sales associate does initial and follow-up greetings. At early maturity phases, we can leverage computer vision and store camera video feeds to put timestamps on the greeting and follow-up. This data isn't very valuable because I am missing most of the business context.

In the next maturity phase, I want to gather the greeting text and any activities performed supporting the greeting. That's beyond the current scope of data gathering. It's possible but infeasible from cost and logistics standpoints. Those parts of the task geometry remain opaque until my data-gathering methods improve.

I use the term *geometry* because some tasks overlap across roles. Greeting a customer in a shoe section or suit department has significant overlaps. Higher-level task categories help to increase the data set size. Data can be gathered across multiple roles while preserving the business context and any subtle differences between greetings.

In both examples, data gathering happens while salespeople and recruiters do their jobs. This is a decisive advantage most businesses don't realize they possess. A retail store controls the data-generating process for every workflow its people complete. They have the greatest (and lowest cost) access to those workflows. The same is true for a recruiting agency.

OpenAI has hired software engineers to generate data through controlled workflows. Software development companies have access to those workflows as they are completed internally on a daily basis. Adding functionality to gather workflow data intentionally leads to curated data sets, but there's always the overhead consideration. Labeling can be done in line with the workflow; some can even be automated.

Workflow mapping creates a catalog of data-generating processes that the business can access easily. This is a critical step in the opportunity discovery process for these longer-term opportunities. Workflows reveal the lowest-cost data sets the company can develop to retrain AI operating system models.

The other side is assessing AI operating system models' current capabilities. How well do they manage that workflow today? The workflows where large model flaws and business access overlap represent the opportunities.

Costs come into play at this point in the evaluation. In the retail greeting example, a high-quality labeled data set is infeasibly expensive to generate, so the business can scratch that off the opportunity list. It could be worth revisiting if the data team finds a low-cost way to get more data about the greeting task geometry.

In the recruiter example, there's also significant overhead in the natural language feedback option. The check-box option is feasible, but will the labeling be comprehensive enough to generate a high-quality data set? Costs will often force difficult compromises.

Customers and employees will be early adopters of the retrained model, which generates even more feedback. In the recruiter example, the model is retrained to manage selection and rejection based on résumés. Recruiters will evaluate the model's choices and provide feedback on accuracy.

This follows the ranking paradigm that OpenAI used to develop its policy models. The recruiter goes from performing the workflow to evaluating how well the retrained model performs the workflow. After enough feedback is captured, the model can go through its second retraining phase. Again, this process is part of the recruiting agency's everyday operations.

Businesses have an advantage over AI operating system models and app store platforms. Those companies must pay more to curate these data sets. They must hire people and develop domain knowledge without the same level of access.

As the model improves, the business becomes more efficient. Recruiters spend less time screening résumés and are more productive. The company is reducing costs and preserving margins to achieve short-term gains. At the same time, they are setting up to release the retrained model on the AI operating system platform's app store. Combining short- and long-term returns is critical to making these initiatives sustainable.

The shift to focus on workflows and intentional data generation are powerful constructs. These frameworks enable the business to capitalize on opportunities to partner with AI and take advantage of large models. The potential is enormous, and as enterprises realize how it's done, there will be a flood of new entrants. The differences between the winners and losers are the frameworks they use to go from potential to execution.

What's Next?

All the pieces are in place to begin building the data and AI strategy. In the next chapter, I explain how to gather all the background information necessary to meet the business where it is. As part of the business assessment framework, we begin implementing frameworks.

We're shifting from theory and planning to implementation and execution. In the following chapters, I'll explain how to put everything you've learned up to this point into practice.

16

Assessing the Business's AI Maturity

The assessment framework creates a baseline snapshot of the business's AI maturity to build from. The process avoids a significant misstep I see frequently made early in transformation initiatives when businesses just start implementing and changing things.

Diving straight into a playbook without understanding where the business is and what's been tried before rarely ends well. The initial assessment framework delivers much needed context about why the company is the way it is today. There's always a backstory that informs how we should move forward to get better results.

The frameworks are adaptable, and what I learn from the initial assessment tells me precisely what they must be adapted to. It's easy to develop unrealistic expectations and build an even more unrealistic strategy without it.

Most businesses have one or more silos. The assessment starts the process of building coalitions to help break silos down. The simple act of talking to people outside of the data team or strategy organization can be a huge step toward building relationships. People buy in when they are involved from the start and not treated as afterthoughts.

Assessing the business moves from implementation to execution. For the first time in the book, we're producing tangible artifacts and deploying the frameworks.

Starting the Assessment

The initial assessment gives the business enough information for data and AI strategy planning. It's the starting point for continuous transformation, the technology model, the talent strategy, and opportunity discovery. The goal is to identify where the company is on each capability maturity model.

I assess businesses on seven points based on the Harvard Business Review Framework. I like its labels and the thinking behind them, but my definitions and process are altogether different.

I will explain each point with questions that will help you start constructive conversations. The questions can also refine your thought process to develop your assessment rubric. Customization has been required at every company I've worked with. You're in the best position to create the rubric, and the framework is your guide to do it.

You could create surveys for each of the seven points, but I prefer to spend time working with each organization. Conversations start relationship building and deliver a more accurate assessment. In surveys, people are tempted to give overly optimistic answers. I trust one-on-one and group interactions more.

Assessments give you the opportunity to talk to people at all levels of the organization and every part of the business. Beginning the process by asking questions versus telling people what comes next shows an interest in what other teams think. This comes back to preserving autonomy, meeting the business where it is, and starting with experts.

Culture

As we've already discussed, culture is critical. If the business doesn't have the right culture, no one adopts any of this. Getting people to act on data can be a massive undertaking. I won't get too much further into culture because I've already spent so much time on it. It is worth explaining a few examples of incentivization structures that can help accelerate cultural maturity.

No one will adopt anything until we have evaluation and incentivization structures in place that measure organizations based on their ability to transform and improve. I've had success with bug bounty programs. In this case, the bug isn't a problem with the software or technology. It could be a problem anywhere in the business.

Bug bounties reward people based on problems that they find and the severity of the problem. If someone finds an issue that saves the company $250,000 a year, giving that person a $2,500 bonus makes good business sense.

There must be some tangible connection to significant business value or outcomes. When that connection doesn't get made, chaos ensues. People look for minor, nitpicky problems. The business doesn't need 1,000 people finding $200 problems. These bug bounty programs reverse the perception that people are punished for finding problems when solutions deliver significant ROI.

Another crucial step is to stop punishing people for listening to data. If a team makes a decision based on data and it ends up being wrong, they shouldn't be penalized. The team practiced the behavior that a data-driven culture enforces. The incentivization structure needs to align with behaviors and allow for imperfect outcomes.

Businesses shouldn't punish a roomful of experts for overriding the data. An individual ignoring data is usually a terrible sign. A group of experts who looks at data and says, "This doesn't make any sense," should be listened to. Trusting the business's experts is part of giving autonomy back to people.

Why does culture matter?

- *Alignment:* Everyone across the enterprise must be moving in the same direction. Culture is a significant part of that.

- *Adoption:* The value of an unused solution is always zero. Culture supports the adoption and transformations necessary for data and AI products to succeed.

- *Momentum:* Transformation is a continuous process. It requires commitment, or people will simply abandon it when things get hard.

Here are some focusing questions:

- Can business units articulate their value proposition for data, analytics, and AI?

- Have business units been trained to leverage data and AI?

- Do business units trust data and AI products enough to adopt them?

- How do incentives align with data-driven behaviors and best practices?

- Do systems and technology preserve autonomy?

Leadership Commitment

There are two sides to any business that's aligned and moving in the right direction. The first is culture, and equally critical is leadership. Committed leaders will champion initiatives and show the rest of the business they care about and are invested in the data team's success.

Most C-level leaders say they're committed, but often that extends only to allocating funds to the data team and infrastructure. Commitment is different and requires an expectation of returns, or it's unsupportable.

Why does it matter?

- *Buy-in*: Transformation is painful. There will be resistance and people who stubbornly refuse to adapt. Leaders must champion transformation and data initiatives, or holdouts will take it as a sign that the business isn't 100 percent bought in.

- *Support and sponsorship*: Transformation can take hold if it's sustained by leaders at every level. The C-level can get you a long way, but the middle layers matter too. Frontline leaders and managers are critical as well.

- *Incentivization*: Goals and KPIs are the best way to keep leaders focused on transformation. If leadership doesn't have a goal, they will eventually abandon transformation for something they have a KPI for and are measured on.

In many organizations, you start with leaders having no goals attached to transformation or data and AI maturity. Prioritization suffers greatly. When a leader must make a trade-off decision, anything that lacks a goal eventually falls down the prioritization ladder.

Data science initiatives stall because diverting resources from them has the fewest consequences. The data organization can be large and capable, but if data and AI aren't priorities at the leadership level, it doesn't matter. The company must transform in lockstep to prepare for these initiatives and products. That cannot happen with only bottom-up support.

Here are some focusing questions:

- Do C-level leaders have goals aligned with data and AI maturity?
- Do organizational leaders have goals aligned with adopting data and AI, literacy training, and initiative creation?
- What revenue and cost savings expectations do C-level leaders have for the data team?
- What percentage of the C-suite are data and model literate?
- Does leadership use data to improve decision quality and strategy planning?

The last question is an accurate gauge of commitment. Leadership must point to times when they have used data to change their minds. There must be multiple instances where leadership went into a planning meeting with one frame of mind and left after seeing the data with a completely different one.

Operations and Structure

The disconnect between transformation strategy and execution is a common cause of data and AI strategy failure. To set up for execution, operational and structural support for data, analytics, and AI are critical. No matter what we build in the data organization, it must integrate with what's in place across the rest of the firm.

Frontline organizations define the initiatives the business will pursue through bottom-up opportunity discovery. Before running the first rounds of opportunity discovery, I must evaluate the current operations and structure to find where we can integrate data and AI products into existing workflows and products. If I start the process in organizations where integration will become a bottleneck, I'm setting up initiatives to fail.

Bottom-up opportunity discovery generates a pipeline of ideas and returns ownership to frontline workers. I must evaluate the in-place innovation processes that support surfacing opportunities and getting them to the data organization. In most cases, there's nothing in place, but it's crucial to check first to avoid duplicating existing processes.

Frontline workers understand that they will have to do things to adopt and get the benefits from data and AI. They don't know what the benefits are and are probably more worried than optimistic. Starting the transformation process with opportunity discovery helps change the focus to benefits over fear.

Why does it matter?

- *Integration*: Data and models must integrate into workflows and existing products.
- *Opportunity discovery*: People at the frontline are the best equipped to discover and document opportunities to generate value and improve productivity with data and models.

Here are some focusing questions:

- Do people at the frontline of each organization have access to data, analytics, or models that support their workflows?
- What self-service data tools are in place, and what percentage of teams use them?

- What self-service solution with validation and oversight functions exists?

- Are frontline organizations provided with a learning path for data and model literacy?

- Is there a process for frontline workers to define opportunities and bring them to leadership?

- Are workflows designed to integrate data, analytics, and models for increased productivity or cost reductions?

The first question begins the conversation nicely because I get a yes or no answer. That leads to follow-ups. "Well, why not? What is it that's keeping you from it?" They might not have access because the infrastructure isn't in place, or they didn't get the budget for the tools they needed to access it.

There are often silos in the way. Frontline workers don't have access to data because no one talks to them, and they don't have a point of contact in the data team. Broken processes and communication bottlenecks are common problems that prevent access. Leadership will often have better access to data than frontline workers, so it's essential to ask the questions at multiple levels.

When I start talking to frontline employees about innovation and opportunity discovery, some are excited. Proposing a process to escalate their ideas usually gets a positive reaction. Every once in a while, I encounter a team whose mentality is, "Oh, so you're trying to give me more work and get free ideas out of me." I am careful of that because some organizations have more close-minded attitudes toward innovation than others. That's another setup to fail.

Part of this assessment evaluates workflows to find easy ways to introduce analytics or models and produce quick wins. I evaluate well-understood or documented workflows, estimate value, and assess feasibility.

Workflows and in-place technology must create enough quality data to develop reliable solutions. More times than not, the data doesn't meet the bar to move forward with an initiative. If that's the case, I need to assess what must be implemented before this team's first initiative can succeed.

Skills and Competencies

Skills, talent, and access to talent are the biggest barriers to data and AI execution, according to most C-level surveys. While the shortages and gaps have eased some, the costs of talent and acquisition have not. Skills and competencies are still a massive problem for businesses.

Why does it matter?

- *Access to talent*: The number-one bottleneck for transformation is hiring so the business cannot be reliant on external talent.

- *Continuous workforce development*: Transformation is continuous, and so is upskilling. There must be structure in place to achieve talent objectives.

This assessment is like inventorying skills, competencies, and capabilities. Few realize how many people are reskilling across the business. They're trying to future-proof their careers by transitioning into a technology-focused role. People are developing their data, analytics, and even data science abilities.

During the assessment, I find many employees at a midpoint of training into high-value roles. In most large retail companies, you can go onto the sales floor and find 5 to 6 people out of 50 working that day who are training for a technical role. Talent is everywhere, but most businesses let people slip through their hands.

The state of the business's talent will surprise you and make your job easier. There are already people with data and model literacy. Some employees can quickly upskill into hard-to-fill roles within the data organization. That's critical because reliance on external talent is unsustainable. Businesses cannot hire their way out of the current talent gaps and shortages.

Companies must implement a continuous workforce development program. Training, mentoring, and upskilling are transformation necessities. The business must meet some of its talent needs with an internal pipeline.

I sometimes get the old, tired pushback: "Well, what if we train them and they go work for somebody else?" That will happen, and there will still be attrition. Put KPIs around internal training and upskilling. The business will quickly realize if it provides employees with structured career paths, progression, and learning resources, they will stay.

Program participation upskills people from across the business into roles in the data team. They bring existing domain knowledge and relationships with them. Both are invaluable to long-term success. Give everyone who wants a chance to become a data professional access to career development resources.

Starting where the business is could include reevaluating the current hiring plan and internal training programs. Most companies have already undertaken a hiring audit as part of their cost savings initiatives. It's critical to validate the current plan, but starting with that baseline is always easier than revamping it all together.

Finally, employees won't trust the advancement process or put in the effort without structured documented career paths. Intermediate step roles often must be defined to manage transitional stages. If someone from marketing finishes the program, they should transition into an apprentice-type marketing analytics role. That's where they get experience building data products for the marketing team under a senior marketing analyst or data scientist.

I help HR create a library of career paths. Frontline employees have more trust and certainty in a documented versus ad hoc process. Employees who feel they don't have to go elsewhere to advance stay. That's critical because, again, it's unsustainable to hire externally.

Here are some focusing questions:

- Is there a data organizational build-out plan and supporting hiring plan?
- Is there an internal training, upskilling, and mentorship program?
- Have career paths been documented and advertised to all organizations?
- What continuous learning resources and support are available for the data team?
- Do external teams have the budget for training and upskilling?

Analytics-Strategy Alignment

This assessment point sets the stage for developing the technology model and high-level technical strategy. As I introduce the technology model, I must design it to consider what's already been implemented. I must integrate existing processes for initiative selection and prioritization.

It's also essential for me to gauge expectations. I need to understand the perception of data and AI's potential across the business. My goal is to understand the current sentiment around value creation and delivery.

Why does it matter?

- *The technology model*: This assessment creates a starting point to implement the technology model.
- *Alignment*: Strategy must drive technology, not the other way around.
- *Connection to value*: The connection brings the user and customer needs into the development process.

Here are some focusing questions:

- How are data and AI initiatives chosen and prioritized?
- How does the business currently use data and AI to create and deliver value to customers?
- What percentage of revenue growth is the data and analytics organization expected to drive?
- Do initiatives produce their expected value, and do the business and customers adopt them?

These are essential questions to ask anyone involved in the strategy planning or initiative prioritization processes. If either process exists, I can track back to strategy, some sort of plan, or even a vague construct that resulted in prioritization decisions. Anything that's been implemented in the past should be the jumping-off point for improvement. Ignoring even messy processes creates confusion and duplication.

These questions also help me get a snapshot of expectations for how much value data and AI can produce. I gain insights into what the data team has already delivered. Ideally, there is a track record of success and early partnerships to build on.

A self-assessment of the data organization is part of this process too. Alignment runs in both directions. The team will have to look inward and assess its own maturity.

Here are some focusing questions:

- What has the team delivered in the past, and what's the track record like?
- Are data and AI products working as promised?
- Were they adopted, and did they achieve their goals?
- Does the data team own all the data, talent, and resources necessary for the data science life cycle?

Assessing the data team's connection to business value will raise some hard questions that must be asked. Answers must be blunt, transparent, and unflinching. Honest introspection is difficult, but there's no path forward until everyone's cards are on the table.

It's far better to admit what's wrong at the beginning than to cover it up until you get to the point where you can't anymore. When that happens, data teams lose credibility.

Once this piece is documented, it becomes the starting point for developing the technology model and technical strategy. There will be technical, strategic, and cultural debt that we are stuck with. Start where the business is, no matter how brutal the reality is. Strategy must acknowledge reality so the technology model can be built on a solid footing.

This is also where C-level leaders determine how far the business will go on the maturity model. Opportunities dictate maturity to keep transformation connected with business value. The foundation for the transformation strategy gets built during this stage.

Proactive Market Orientation

Proactive market orientation is a framework for aligning products, initiatives, innovation, and customer or internal needs.

This point evaluates the current innovation processes, opportunity discovery, go-to market, and paths to production. I seek people and processes supporting monetizing, productizing, and commercializing the technology.

Data and AI are the most expensive technologies the business develops and uses. Products cost the most to deliver into customers' and internal users' hands. There must be a significant and obvious value and revenue generation to support all this expensive technology.

Once the results start rolling in, people transition from supporters to believers. When things get hard, costs rise, and setbacks occur, they're more likely to stay on board. When people have a concrete concept of what innovation and these technologies will do for the business, they buy in.

Why does it matter?

- *Cost justification*: Transformation is expensive and must have significant, obvious value.

- *Product and infrastructure road maps*: C-level leaders need visibility into the products that are possible only with data and AI.

- *Innovation*: Implementing processes to discover, build, and deliver innovative products to market is critical.

Here are some focusing questions:

- Who has the authority to say "yes" to innovation initiatives?
- Does the culture support the potential for failure and have processes to mitigate risks?
- Does the business have processes to align innovation with business value?

Once this assessment is complete, it's time to start top-down opportunity discovery sessions with C-level leaders. The technology model is further developed as part of the process.

The outcomes of bottom-up opportunity discovery should be shared with C-level leaders, too, so they can be added to the technology model.

Opportunity discovery leads to parts of the business and operating models being transferred into the technology model. That's the source of new initiatives and products. Once the first round of top-down and bottom-up opportunity discovery has been completed, the infrastructure and product road maps can be built. It's critical for infrastructure to be connected with the products and initiatives it will support. It's the only way to calculate ROI for things like data engineering and self-service tool purchases.

Maturity models help data and AI product managers break large initiatives into smaller pieces for incremental delivery. Some parts will fit on a road map with structured delivery schedules. Others must be managed by the research life cycle and put into the innovation pipeline framework. C-level leaders need visibility into returns, which comes through opportunity and cost estimations.

The road maps and innovation pipeline dictate the hiring and training plan. New hires and upskilling are likely needed before some initiatives can start. The data organizational buildout must be developed to support the transformation, product, and infrastructure road maps.

Employee Empowerment

Why does it matter?

- *Autonomy*: People need control and ownership over solutions.
- *Adoption*: People use what they trust, and users must feel like their feedback is part of the improvement process.

- *Coalition building*: The data team needs promoters and supporters who evangelize the benefits they have seen from early initiatives.

If everyone's transforming, that means everyone is part of the development process. Employee empowerment extends the concept of autonomy by giving people control of the solution. There must be integration points for people in the design, deployment, and continuous improvement phases. We must not only gather feedback but also trust it enough to act on it.

If users or customers say the product doesn't work how they need it to, we must take that seriously. Too often, usability and design complaints are treated like resistance to change. Sometimes that's the case, but more often, it's genuine feedback. A relationship and trust must empower employees to bring their concerns forward.

Users and customers tell us the truth about data and AI products only when they have autonomy and ownership over that solution. Relationships must be built, so they trust that the data team will act upon their feedback. If they don't have that trust, customers and users will just stop using the product.

They abandon data and AI products in silence and don't tell anyone they failed. Six months or a year later, when someone finally does follow up with them, we find out the hard way what went wrong. The frontline team often says, "Oh, yeah, it's still great." Application usage statistics show that no one has done anything with the product for months.

Those are the types of things that derail the return on investment for even the most brilliant ideas. Ground-floor execution requires the business to give employees at the frontline the trust, access, and processes to succeed.

I must figure out how much of this is in place. Typically, none of it is. Many frontline organizations have zero control, say, or autonomy. Solutions are dictated to them, and they just have to deal with it.

Hospitals are notorious for doing this to their nurses and staff. They just drop software on them. Administrators say, "Look, the hospital bought it, so you're using it." Whether it works for everyone's workflow or not, they are stuck with the technology.

Each department in a hospital has different areas of focus, workflows, and needs. A system that supports 80 percent of the hospital still misses many internal workflows. Poorly designed solutions can increase costs and contradict the goals that staff are measured on.

However, frontline hospital staff members don't have a process for escalating challenges. Other teams see what's happening and think, "I know what that means. If something's broken, I won't get any support either. If it doesn't work for me, I'll be in the same boat as they are."

Frontline workers won't trust technology without autonomy, control, and ownership over the solution. They are not receptive to change, let alone continuous transformation. The solutions that we deliver are continuously changing, improving, and evolving. They look at an update like, "Great, what will they break this time?"

That relationship must be fixed, and that's what I'm assessing. Do the people at the frontlines have enough of what they need from a process, support, and relationship-building perspective to make innovative products successful? There will be an uneven rollout if some business units do but others don't. Some parts of the business will love data; others will not.

Those that love data will continue training, upskilling, and adopting. Those who hate it won't do any of that. The coalition that gets built will be lopsided. Some vehemently opposed to transformation will have evidence to support their case for the business stopping to reevaluate. The data team delivered a solution that didn't work and never returned to improve it.

That's not the perception that the data organization wants. Building a coalition and getting the broad support necessary to move the technology forward is harder. A partial coalition won't get the budget or buy-in.

Employees need to be empowered to surface places where their workflows don't support implementing the solution. Their leadership team must be willing and incentivized to make necessary process changes so products can succeed.

In some cases, goals and incentivization structures must be updated. If a data or AI product handles part of a workflow that's part of a frontline employee's performance review, a critical part of their job is out of their control. That can be dangerous if the solution affects that performance negatively.

I have seen instances where a data or AI product slows one part of a workflow to optimize other pieces. That causes friction when goals aren't aligned with the product's impacts.

This assessment also helps me to see where cultural debt has been accumulating. Solving these issues in advance saves a significant amount of money and pain in the long run.

Here are the focusing questions:

- How are users integrated into the design, validation, and continuous improvement process?

- How are customer or user adoption and satisfaction tracked?

- Are the data team's leaders accountable for user and customer satisfaction goals and KPIs?

- Is there a process to prepare users and customers for products that leverage new technologies?

- Are automated feedback mechanisms built into data and AI products?

- Is there an escalation process to respond quickly to failures and defects?

I must put tracking mechanisms in place. Some are manual feedback channels like the ones I have discussed, but it's equally critical to implement automated feedback mechanisms. Platforms are potent constructs because they generate data every time someone uses them. Automated feedback channels are data-gathering components that exploit platforms' unique data generation opportunities.

I need automated feedback to handle scale. As more users and customers interact with the product, it gets too expensive to collect feedback manually. With customer-facing products, manually gathering high-quality feedback is often impossible. Customers don't call; they just stop using products.

The Data Monetization Catalog

Data is a novel asset class, but businesses don't view it that way. The data monetization catalog is an artifact of the initial assessment. The purpose is to change the perception of data from an intangible to a monetizable asset. Data needs a dollar value associated with it, or the value will continue to be murky.

The data monetization catalog itself is a simple construct. Data sets are documented in a traditional data catalog framework. Each data set gets an additional list field that contains all the use cases it currently supports. The connection to use cases is critical because it directly ties to monetization.

Use cases allow data sets to be linked to workflows. The monetization can be measured using a with and without method.

What was the workflow before introducing the data, analytics, or model? How did the product improve the workflow? What is the change in value between the original and new workflow? The data monetization catalog creates the map from the data set to use case, workflow, and value.

It's rare for an early-maturity business to have all the information necessary to build that mapping. Use cases can be disconnected from workflows, or there may not be enough insight into the pre-product workflow to quantify the improvement. Creating the initial mapping is still critical because it documents a baseline for future initiatives to build on.

In some businesses, there's no data catalog to build on. I must work with IT to track down all the data sources they support. There can be a massive shadow data library living across the business. Some data lives in spreadsheets on share drives or even individual's laptops. The data monetization catalog might kick off data governance and security initiatives at early-maturity businesses. Be aware of that going in and involve other teams as needed.

I typically find that most data sets aren't used to support any workflows. Only a tiny percentage of the business's total data is being monetized and delivering returns. There's a significant opportunity for cost savings in that realization. IT and the data team spend significant resources supporting low to no value data sets.

The data monetization catalog also sets a precedent. New data should be gathered only to support a use case and workflow. The days of collecting data because it might be useful someday are over. That's how data lakes turn into swamps and dumpsters.

The data monetization catalog also begs the question, what are the highest value data sets the business has access to? There's a prioritization framework in the making. Given all the data the company has access to, the highest value data gathering initiatives should move to the front of the line.

Data is a novel asset class because it can be monetized repeatedly by supporting multiple use cases. Data gathering initiatives should be evaluated on the primary use case, but the opportunity estimation must also consider secondary use cases that increase the initiative's ROI. The data monetization catalog reinforces this mindset and changes perceptions.

The connection to workflows enables the maturity models to be applied to data gathering and curation. Reliability requirements of current and planned initiatives guide decisions about the initial implementation, so it doesn't need to be rebuilt with each phase. The concepts of continuous transformation reach down to execution.

What's Next?

Assessments typically take 8 to 20 weeks, depending upon the business size. Putting time and effort into the assessment process helps us estimate the transformation rate. How fast can the business transform? Calling out the barriers, roadblocks, and impediments to transformation speeds up the process. We can prepare for only what we know about.

It's tempting to pretend that everything will go smoothly and every organization will transform at the same rate organically. They're all going to love data because it's awesome, right? That's not realistic. The assessment reveals the reality on the ground. It defines the current state of the business.

This reveals the hard work; we can't fear the truth. If we do, we cover things up. We can't just cover it up until it gets to the point where we can't cover it up anymore. The assessment is painful, but the process is necessary to gather all the information required to develop the data and AI strategy.

In the next chapter, I'll explain how to build the data and AI strategy document and deliver the next artifact.

17

Building the Data and AI Strategy

Building a data and AI strategy happens in stages. The process leverages the frameworks and information gathered during the assessment to deliver a plan. It's critical to document and share the data and AI strategy document with the rest of the business.

The value diminishes greatly if it stays buried in the data team or isn't shared beyond the C-suite. The data team's work will impact every part of the business, so the enterprise needs access to this document. This step is critical to starting from the same page and using the same playbook to move forward.

Defining the Data and AI Strategy

The data and AI strategy represents a guiding principle and needs a mission statement. Any initiative under consideration must be evaluated against this principle. Will it actually result in or contribute meaningfully to the business's core strategy and goals? Could the business achieve the same results more efficiently or effectively using another technology?

I was contacted by a late-stage startup looking at data products to grow revenue. The purpose was to accelerate its path to profitability. That became the mission statement and kicked off the data and AI strategy document. The business will leverage data products to accelerate its path to profitability.

As you can see, the first part of a data and AI strategy is simplistic. The purpose is to inform decision-making throughout the enterprise about why the business uses data and AI to create and deliver value to customers. The late-stage startup was able to evaluate any proposed initiative based on the mission statement. Is this a data product? The business was too early in its maturity journey to deploy AI products, so data and analytics were the limit.

Will this accelerate the path to profitability? The old timeline was 24 months, so any initiative had to generate positive returns in 6 to 12 months. It was an easy assessment point that prevented the data team from taking on work that wouldn't move the needle soon enough.

Creating the mission statement and top-level data and AI strategy begins by echoing one to three key points from the business's strategy. These explain why data and AI will support top-level strategic goals. The rest of the data and AI strategy document is designed to elaborate on and support them.

The purpose of including key points from the business strategy is to make the connection clear. The business does this for a purpose that isn't contrived or invented. Data and AI align closely with where the company is going, but the relationship must be defined. It's the first and last line for decision-making to help anyone across the business understand why it's using data and AI.

The strategy must address questions people have and are often too afraid to ask. Again, the purpose of strategy is to inform decision-making, so this section anticipates questions and attempts to provide some answers. Why is the business using data to support these goals instead of just continuing to leverage digital technologies? What is the value at a company versus technology level?

After the very simplistic strategy statements, the data and AI strategy document must explain and support those answers. The rest of the document explains why and how. Implementation is the how, and strategy is the why.

The Executive Summary

What comes next is an explanation of the vision and scope. The first section puts forward the connection to the business's core strategy. This section explains the extent of what the data organization plans to do and how far the company will mature to achieve its strategic objectives. The current state of the business is the first component, and it comes from the AI maturity assessment.

Presenting the maturity assessment findings gets everyone on the same page. In many companies I have worked with, C-level leaders believe the business is extremely mature, data-driven, and everyone has access to the data they need.

I speak to people on the frontline who say the exact opposite. They don't feel very data-driven. Frontline workers and teams can't get access to the data they need to do their jobs effectively. They encounter significant barriers and sometimes dead ends when they try to gain access.

People at the top tell one story, but the truth comes out when I build the data monetization catalog. The business believes it is supporting a range of use cases. In reality, use cases are not well supported by existing products. The value that C-level leaders thought data and AI were delivering hasn't materialized. This section can be a reality check, but that's essential to moving forward with a single vision.

Where is the business on the maturity model? Where are the gaps? Gaps can come from talent, transformation, strategy, prioritization, opportunity discovery, initiative planning, and a range of processes to support moving forward. Gaps can be found in product and organizational maturity.

A business with high-maturity technical capabilities can have a low strategy or product maturity. It sounds counterintuitive, but those can coexist in the same business. Companies can also have a knowledge divide, with some business units at a high data and model literacy level and others at level 0. Products can be uneven. Sometimes the assessment is a tale of two or three businesses, each at a different stage of transformation and maturity.

It's critical to talk to all parts of the business during the initial assessment and share the findings as part of the data and AI strategy document. I find these maturity gaps and divides in every business, even large tech and Fortune 500s.

The next part explains the transition. The current state is a tough reality, but the business has opportunities. First, we must lay out what's being done and the strategic goals for where the company goes with data and AI.

A large retailer was looking for ways to increase margins. The top-down opportunity discovery process led to the creation of a pricing model initiative. Data from across the business was necessary to deliver a model that led to significant increases in margins. Capabilities had to be developed to support level 3 maturity products.

A basic, low-maturity model would be incapable of achieving the strategic objective. Costs and returns were considered as part of strategy planning. C-level leaders decided to move forward with capabilities development and had the estimated returns to justify it. Expectations for revenue were set, and C-level leaders were invested in the data team's success.

This section explains which opportunities justify the business becoming innovators or leveraging the technology for competitive advantages. Sometimes, data and AI only align with the company enough to pursue competitive maintenance initiatives. The goal may be to keep up with the rest of the marketplace and new entrants. Some legacy businesses or those in uncompetitive spaces will take this road.

We must be ready for that answer too. As much as we want to be innovators, I have seen cases where there's no way to justify anything more than maintenance. Opportunities aren't aligned with the business in a way that allows it to leverage data and AI for competitive advantage, let alone move toward innovator status.

That's a possibility, but it still requires a strategy. In those cases, the data and AI strategy justifies not advancing to higher maturity levels. Businesses avoid the costly mistake of just building advanced data capabilities because everyone else is. Almost all companies will pursue a competitive advantage, but when it doesn't make sense, the right call is to wait for the next wave, which might align better.

Finally, a little bit of theatrics and marketing. The third part of this section defines what the business will look like in 1 year and 3 years. This is a very high-level technology model and opportunity discovery presentation. I explain what workflows C-level leadership decided to move from the business and operating models into the technology model.

I use those decisions to extrapolate what the business will look like when it's improving, delivering products, and the frameworks are in place. I emphasize the big bets that came from top-down opportunity discovery. I move on to the innovation strategy that these data and AI initiatives support.

This part should include an explanation and justification for the innovation mix. I may need to explain why margins are compressing or which competitors are entering the marketplace. Does the business see dwindling opportunities for growth from its existing product lines?

We find ourselves at a crossroads and must invest in innovation. The company will leverage data and AI for 30 percent or 60 percent of its growth. That technology will be the focus of advanced R&D to seize new opportunities.

It's worth covering one or two short-term steps on the road to those high-maturity initiatives. There must be some tangible work, and it's essential to keep innovation grounded in the reality of what's being done today. Innovative products and initiatives should have short-term monetization potential, even if we cannot articulate the exact timeline for the larger research initiative to complete.

Work is being done to make space in existing products and workflows for the innovations. These short-term deliverables are critical to keeping innovation from seeming too disconnected from core strategy. Otherwise, they are very likely to get deprioritized.

Finally, this part should also include the highest value bottom-up opportunities the data organization will deliver this year.

The Introduction

The introduction is meant for mid-level leadership but should be built to be actionable for a frontline worker. The last section explains why the business is moving forward with the technology, and the introduction takes that explanation down a level. This section speaks to people who will implement components of this strategy from the EVP to the director level.

All these leaders are thinking is, "What are you about to do to me, and what's in this for me?" The goal is to provide some level of certainty to people charged with implementation because that's the source of most pushback and resistance. Parts of the transformation strategy and road map are explained in this section.

This section contains specifics about who benefits from transformation and how. I assume I'm speaking to a more skeptical audience at this level. For them, the data and AI strategy sounds aspirational rather than practical. This section is built to address that perception and begin to change it.

Certainty about implications is critical. Data and AI products change how people across the enterprise operate. I anticipate questions.

- What parts of their workflow will transform to make space for this new technology?

- What aspects of their digital silo must be broken down, and who's running that process?

- What's the budget, and how much time do they need to handle that part of the process?

The introduction must address concerns about automation and job losses. It should explain how models will be designed to work with people and augment their capabilities. Without some explanation of the approach, people often assume the business is pursuing a strategy of replacement.

The best framing I have seen is "AI in the loop" and "augmenting, not replacing." The human-machine paradigm is built to make people more efficient and effective. AI will reduce operational complexity and allow the business to scale faster. The result will be a business that can seize opportunities instead of watching competitors take them away.

The data and AI strategy will impact their teams. They must have transformation goals and incentives. They need a budget and time set aside specifically for the support work they're being asked to perform. This section must acknowledge these needs and explain how they will be met.

Even while discussing the hard work ahead, I'm still creating certainty for those groups and avoiding speculation, which can lead to more pushback. Great people aren't afraid of hard work; it's uncertainty that they fear and resist most.

The introduction acknowledges that teams across the firm will need new capabilities. This gets into parts of the talent and staffing plan. The strategy for upskilling and development includes external organizations. It must come with budget and goals associated with transformation.

That must be part of the introduction. It tells external business units I'm on their side, and their leaders can expect me to go to bat for them. If they're asking for new resources or budget, I can use some of my cool AI glow to help them get what they need. A mistake I see most data and AI strategies make is to focus entirely on the data team.

The introduction must detail more than the cool technology, benefits, and innovation speak. It should also cover the work and support the data team will provide to the rest of the business. Coalitions are two-sided. The data team and this strategy must support the entire business. I make the partnership more concrete as a two-way relationship in these components of the introduction.

Strategy Implementation

Implementation begins with an explanation of what's already been done. People have been working in the business to deliver results with data and AI. It's worth calling that out for two reasons. We're giving credit where it's due and establishing a track record of success by explaining the results that have been delivered to date.

It's important to cover anything that's been worked on in the lead-up to delivering this strategy. We rarely inherit a clean slate. The initial assessment won't all be bad news, and it's essential to keep what's working. Implementation starts by calling out the components that will remain because they're successful. This phase is focused on improving. It acknowledges where the business is today, so why not start with what's working?

This section should detail the high-profile use cases that connect the data and AI strategy to strategic business goals. I include more detail about the highest profile use cases from the top-down and bottom-up opportunity discovery. I typically focus on the initiatives C-level leaders feel are most important to begin supporting the new prioritization framework.

I am anticipating the chaos to come. Change doesn't happen overnight, and rigorous prioritization frameworks don't take hold that quickly, either. Someone will test prioritization and the data organization's discipline early on. I'm giving the data organization's leader something to point out. They can push back by showing how their current work contributes directly to a very high-profile initiative.

With the large retailer, I was setting up for the battles to break down each data fiefdom. C-level leaders had expectations of revenue, and there would be consequences if those weren't met. Refusing to give the data team access to siloed data had implied consequences.

Derailing the data team with an ad hoc request threatens to push the pricing model initiative back. With visibility at the C-level, external teams don't want to be the cause of setbacks. I'm building the foundation for the defense of prioritization by including the highest-profile use cases built through opportunity discovery.

I must highlight near-term gains and returns the data team will deliver in the early product or capability maturity phases. Many of those high-profile use cases are long-term, but explaining what value is being delivered this year is essential. This section is much more granular than the executive summary.

The pricing model was delivered in stages. Each delivery added another data set, and retraining improved the model's performance. The bottleneck was access to quality data. Instead of trying to get all the data engineering done first and then delivering all at once, we broke the initiative down.

Again, I'm laying the foundation to justify pushback when another team attempts to derail the prioritization framework. Emphasizing incremental delivery and value creation are keys. I explain how the initiatives are broken up by maturity phase and what value will be delivered by each phase. This moves the data and AI strategy even further away from aspirational.

Explaining what's already been accomplished includes calling out the early partnerships and coalitions. These are the groups involved with early projects that progressed beyond the pilot stage and made it into production. The teams that are critical components of those successes or were pivotal in getting buy-in should be called out so they get some credit.

Sharing the spotlight is critical. These strategy documents get a lot of attention, so being included is a big deal for early supporters and adopters. They get a little bit of fame. Another piece of coalition building is supporting the data team's promotors and letting some C-level attention flow their way too. There's plenty to go around.

Introducing the Data Organization

Introduce the rest of the business to the data organization, no matter how small it is. Most of the company doesn't know who any of you are. It can feel like everyone knows the data team, but even in small to midsize businesses, most people don't.

It's essential for the company to get to know the people and what they do. Remember, this strategy document informs decision-making across the business. Part of decision-making is knowing who to go to.

Introducing the data organization explains things like the following:

- Who are these people, and what do they do?
- What is the difference between a data engineer and a data scientist?
- What's the organization's role in creating and delivering value?
- What revenue and business growth are the data team accountable for?

Introducing the team includes a charter and mission statement. These are aspirational, but they connect to core business strategy, some initiatives, and the teams the data organization supports. That is the beginning of creating context and the data team's place in the business.

- Where does this unit fit?
- Who supports the data organization, and who do they support?

- What parts of the workflow, infrastructure, products, processes, value creation, cost savings, productivity improvements, etc., does the data organization own?

Write this section so a frontline worker can read it and know where they would go with questions. The data team should have a central point of contact and escalation chains for different needs.

If someone is considering joining the data team, after reading this section, they should leave thinking, "This is a team I want to be a part of because it is working on some interesting things. Their role is well-defined by capable leadership. They deliver value and have built a place for themselves in the business."

That's the whole purpose of the data and AI strategy. Senior leaders should see the data team as capable of owning its value creation and strategic direction. That's a big step out of the cost center category. The data team goes from a cost center to a value creator by defining its place in the business and delivering what it promises.

Next Steps

This section should get into granular next steps. This can be a very lengthy segment in the strategy document. The next steps cover parts of the following:

- Data and AI product road maps
- Data and analytics organizational development plan
- Transformation road map
- Infrastructure road map
- Hiring and training road map

This section must provide someone charged with implementing or executing with enough information to know where to begin or go next.

I must set clear expectations for what the data team will do. As soon as the document is signed off, what work begins?

In the next steps section, I explain that implementation and execution are a data organization first initiative. The rest of the business has parts to play, and I must also define what they will do next. This section should include points of contact and responsible parties in each organization.

Points of contact handle data access, opportunity escalation, issue escalation, governance, security, and compliance concerns. Without those contacts, people on the frontline can easily become disenfranchised. Plan for the most common scenarios that could arise and ensure there is a point of contact to address it.

Needs, Budget, and Risks

Finally, highlight the needs and budget, obviously, but also risks. It's crucial to detail what could threaten this strategy. Risks include simple pushback and failure to adhere to prioritization frameworks. In low-maturity businesses, these are worth calling out.

Risks connect to top-level strategy by saying, "If one of these risks materializes, the business won't make its numbers. We've promised this to investors by putting margin preservation and revenue growth on the data organization's shoulders. We must stick to this strategy if we want to live up to those promises."

Risks set up for some of the inevitable battles ahead. Connecting data and AI strategy to the business's core strategic goals makes winning those battles easier.

Needs and budget are fairly straightforward planning items, so I won't dive into them too deeply. Most companies already have templates and frameworks for both. It's a best practice to leverage what's in place.

What's Next?

I touched on the data organization in this chapter, and in the next, I'll explain how to build it. Too many data organizations are developed by fear of missing out (FOMO). Data professionals are brought in before there's enough infrastructure and support to deliver products.

I introduce a framework to keep the data organization's growth aligned with the business's needs. I describe a three-phase framework to rapidly improve the data organization's functional and project delivery maturity. By the end of the next chapter, you'll be ready to create the data organizational built-out plan.

18

Building the Center
of Excellence

There is likely some data organization in place today. During the initial assessment, we discover how well it meets the business's current needs. That's a strong dose of introspection, but just like building out the data and AI strategy, nothing can move forward without knowing the current state.

This process can be difficult because resources are scattered across the business. They will likely need to be centralized to succeed. The data team may poach resources from other groups and organizations. They will need ownership over infrastructure and their budget, which other leaders could own.

Building the organization won't and shouldn't happen overnight. The pace of change must match the business's timelines. In most cases, more has already been built than the company can currently leverage. Data scientists were hired before the data and infrastructure were in place for them to do their work.

These early phases involve not only growing pains but also transformation challenges. In this chapter, I explain how a data and AI Center of Excellence (CoE) is built to minimize costs while moving maturity forward.

The Need for an Executive or C-level Data Leader

A C-level data leader should be brought in to help build the data and analytics organization. That's rarely done, so what we inherit has been built in several competing directions. The data team is often distributed across multiple organizations at early maturity businesses. Each team has developed independently. This is also common when the data team reports to the CIO or CTO, who builds to support the paradigm they're most familiar with.

Multiple, sometimes conflicting, views of what the organization should look like lead to a chaotic, unplanned build-out. When teams are scattered across the business, it's easy to develop different technology and tool stacks. Aside from the cost of maintaining duplicate stacks, integration across teams is more expensive. Resources from one data team can't be brought in to support other teams' projects.

When the business brings in a C-level data organizational leader, it is one of the most significant indicators of future success. C-level representation is essential, but it's also a sign of commitment. The CEO signals, "I'm invested in the data organization's success and the broader success of data and AI initiatives." It also creates a single vision for the organization's development and strategy implementation.

In some organizations, the technical strategist and C-level leader are the same person. I think that's too much for a single role, but at small or early maturity companies, that's the reality. That structure is feasible, but not for very long.

Navigating Early Maturity Phases

Data and AI products must integrate into something. Often in a business, especially at lower maturity levels, the software engineering organization is wholly separated from the data team. That makes it difficult to get resources back and forth from one side to the other.

The software engineering team has existing product lines and automation that they support. Digital transformation initiatives are often owned by their teams too. They typically own most of the data-gathering process and some data infrastructure.

The data team introduces features to existing products and develops new product lines. They also aggregate the data that's currently in digital silos. There's a significant overlap in the earliest maturity phases. If done well, the handoffs and integrations are a collaborative effort. When there's no plan in place, handoffs and integrations turn into nightmares that derail initiatives.

Talent and infrastructure will go through some level of transformation to reconcile the two worlds. Building the data organization has broader impacts across the technology organization. If frontline business units own data resources, the process involves them too. External teams will need new resources to complete the integration work.

Early-maturity businesses have underutilized data scientists doing reporting work and basic descriptive modeling. Many have been pressed into service doing data engineering and cleaning. People are hired into roles before their capabilities are necessary. There's burnout and dissatisfaction to address. Some skills may have degraded over time and need to be updated.

Technical strategists and data product managers should be part of the early team. Businesses typically don't think about them until later maturity stages. Keeping the team's work connected to value depends on those roles. Again, data scientists have been pressed into service and take on roles they haven't been trained to do. That's one of my main motivations for writing this book. I've been in your shoes.

There's a lot of early work necessary to fix what wasn't built properly in the first place. The goal is to develop a centralized data team that controls all the resources required to deliver products. It could be a long road to get there, but nothing else matures until the data team does.

The Data Organizational Arc

Scattered in-place talent and resources must be reorganized. When businesses start with data, talent is spread throughout the company. Analysts and even data scientists are in different business units. Data and machine learning engineers could be in IT or part of software engineering organizations. It's chaos.

For maturity to move forward, people must be centralized into a single data organization. It is sometimes called a Center of Excellence model. With resources in one place, the team can be built with a single vision and direction.

Infrastructure is centralized and unified under a single architectural design. Tools and workflows are standardized. Data is centralized and managed under a single set of best practices. Standardization and continuous improvement bring order to chaos and optimize the data organization's ability to deliver products.

Eventually, the organization builds products it thinks the business needs instead of what it actually needs. The data organization calls it *innovation*, but the rest of the company does not benefit much from initiatives.

New leadership gets brought in. The first round of leaders includes mainly technical leaders. The second round consists of business and strategic leaders. If the old and new teams of leaders find ways to collaborate, the partnership brings the data organization back into the business. They start working with the company on innovative and more mundane but equally high-value projects.

This all works until we reach the point where Meta was at the end of 2021. The centralized organization had its own leadership and had strong ideas about which initiatives people's time should be allocated to. It usually leans toward forward-looking innovation over immediate business needs. The innovation mix skews too far from exploiting existing opportunities. Obviously, that causes some friction across the business.

While innovation delivers high-value hits, the team will remain centralized and have a high degree of latitude over projects. When growth slows, like it is today at many companies, the mix of innovation versus immediate business needs comes under scrutiny. How committed is the C-suite to long-term investments?

At Meta, and many companies will follow their lead, immediate business needs win. Each business unit needs greater leadership control over data and analytics resources for its projects to succeed. The centralized leadership creates friction between business units and the team.

External organizations don't have control of all the resources they need to deliver their work. If the data organizational leaders have different priorities, more innovation typically, external teams can miss their delivery deadlines. The winner in these internal disagreements is always the group pulling in the most revenue. The more revenue the data organization can show, the more control it has over its work.

Some AI strategy KPIs are designed to show that data initiatives return more to the business than an alternative investment. This is another layer of defense for the data organization. The early attacks on the centralized organization's leaders come during the budget planning process. While leadership can defend its budget based on a higher return per dollar spent than the alternatives, the data organization retains its autonomy.

The goal is to hold the centralized structure together long enough to mature. Breaking the organization up too soon slows and eventually halts progress. Data science capabilities plateau and the decentralized organization matures in multiple directions based on each business unit's needs. Again, the result is chaos.

At Meta, it looks like its leadership accomplished the mission. Its outgoing leader built the transformation plan from centralized to decentralized data science capabilities. Meta's team was redistributed across product lines and embedded into those organizations.

Long-term, that is always the endgame. This structure puts domain experts and data experts as close as possible. The result is better products.

The next challenge is to maintain the innovation mix. Innovation initiatives can disappear overnight if a structure isn't established to preserve them. In Meta's case, each product organization must maintain innovation levels in line with the data and AI strategy. I assume the leadership of each organization has goals tied to those initiatives. That is a successful framework to keep innovation alive while refocusing on mainline products.

Benefits of the Center of Excellence Model

There is a strategic driver for the CoE model. For some, it's a knee-jerk response, but that's the wrong way to look at this. The CoE is a centralized business unit built around a specific technical capability. The justification for creating one should be that the business needs to ramp up and mature that technical capability rapidly.

In early-maturity businesses, resources are scattered, and there is a lot of duplication when it comes to infrastructure and tooling. Best practices are tough to implement. The time it takes to get buy-in from multiple business units becomes a significant time sink. Much-needed change comes too slowly.

That's the main challenge that a CoE resolves. A scattered approach to data science isn't optimal when it comes to improving the capabilities, implementing best practices, removing duplication, and ramping up.

It's also critical for the data organization to own its budget. That speeds up organizational development significantly. The value of a data CoE can be undermined if it lacks autonomy. Having another organization or leader control the budget removes the data organizational leader's autonomy.

The data organizational leader is also the best person to advocate for the team's budget when there's pushback. When another leader owns the budget, they don't have the same level of commitment to the team and making it successful because it's only one part of their scope of responsibilities. Especially if it's a CTO or CIO, the most important KPIs they're accountable for may not be connected with early maturity data initiatives or organizational development.

Budgetary control also makes managing the tools standardization and infrastructure ecosystem development easier. There are fewer risks of stalls and restarts due to budgetary shortfalls. The best people to own and specify the budget are the domain experts.

The CoE should be built around what needs the most improvement. If it's functional areas like data engineering, data science, machine learning engineering, and MLOps, teams should be built with those capability functions in mind. Teams are built around each functional area, and by putting all the resources into the same team, improvement cycles happen faster.

This works only when the data organization owns all the necessary resources to complete the data science life cycle. Until that happens, the team doesn't truly control its delivery timeline. I can't count the weeks I have wasted waiting for IT to allocate resources for model training or access to data. It's impossible to estimate when an initiative will be done if the data organization isn't sure how long to pad for disruptions like these.

Implementing consistent processes and best practices is far easier when everyone involved has the same reporting structure and final decision-makers. Everything they need to complete an end-to-end data science initiative is under that team's control. Improvement decisions don't require external input to be implemented. Infrastructure consolidation by committee is a painfully slow and inefficient process.

Once the functional areas are improved to the point where the capabilities are built out, the next step is reorganizing into project teams. Project velocity and initiative efficiency become the focus for the next series of improvement cycles. Project teams begin with a focus on product quality and reliability. Velocity and efficiency come next. Finally, initiative selection and value creation go through improvement cycles.

The move to improving value creation eventually leads to decentralization. The resources are distributed into the frontline business units and product teams they support. A type of cross-training happens once data organizations decentralize. Teams become specialized around the business unit or product. Domain knowledge and expertise seep into the data team when they live next to what they support.

The advanced research team remains in the CoE. Data scientists and applied researchers working on high-maturity initiatives must remain separate from frontline business units and product teams. This team is the seed that will grow into applied sciences. Every business will eventually make the same move that Mercedes' racing division has, but that's a long way off.

Connecting Hiring to the Infrastructure and Product Roadmaps

Knowing who to hire and when is the toughest job in building the data organization. There are two primary strategic considerations. How much does the business need to build, and how fast does it need to be built? There's an easy connection to opportunity discovery.

For each opportunity the business has chosen to go after, the final question in the arc of disruption dictates a timeline. Eventually, the opportunity will be gone because customers are fully served. Competitors entering the market or the need for new revenue can accelerate the timeline. That represents the ticking clock for the business to beat.

Evaluating the business's data and AI opportunity portfolio on this metric provides a basic velocity measurement to determine when products must be delivered. The slower capabilities development and staffing levels increase, the less of each opportunity will be left to take advantage of. In noncompetitive or slow-moving marketplaces, this is much less of a factor. Time and value must be considered together.

The product road map breaks out into individual initiatives. Each phase requires capabilities to execute. The infrastructure road map breaks down similarly, and each component requires capabilities to deploy and maintain. In a few cases, people will be necessary to develop infrastructure components.

Each initiative maps to the capabilities required to execute. As initiatives mature, so too must the data organization's capabilities. More experienced people will be necessary, some with niche capability sets. How does the business ramp up to meet an aggressive timeline?

For some businesses, relying on third-party vendors to support rapid capabilities build-outs will make sense. Partnering with vendors on infrastructure projects can accelerate their implementation. With product initiatives, the goal is different.

Third-party vendors have extensive experience building data and AI products. Partnerships can include knowledge exchanges and training. It's expensive, but not when compared to the cost of missteps and slow product development maturity.

Many companies attempt to overcome the experience problem by hiring high skill workers. I've seen this approach several times, and it costs more in the long run for a few reasons. Obviously, talent is very expensive and difficult to source. It can take 6 months or longer to fill senior++ data roles. A lot of early maturity work still must be done, and top talent rarely wants to be involved. That leads to high rates of attrition.

Mid-level talent is easier to source and retain. Partnering with a third-party vendor can serve to upskill internal talent to handle future projects. This approach has significant benefits if the business must build capabilities and bring products to market quickly. More forgiving timelines don't need these measures, but many companies face a time crunch.

Getting Access to Talent

I covered this at a surface level in an earlier chapter. Still, it's worth getting deeper into the need for an internal talent pipeline as part of the data organizational build-out plan.

Before hiring can begin, the data organization must create well-defined roles. This challenge doesn't get nearly enough attention, but poorly defined roles increase talent costs and time to hire. The unicorn data science roles are still typical and completely delusional.

Some hiring managers expect one person to be an entire department. It's become impossible to be a unicorn, given the field's growing tools and infrastructure landscape, as well as the advances in each domain. The data science life cycle is simply too broad and complex.

Roles must be divided into parts of the life cycle that a person can feasibly own. Talent is easier to source and less expensive when roles stop being defined aspirationally. Conventional wisdom got skewed by hype, and companies believed they would save money by hiring one person.

The team hires someone who's really good at a single part of the data science life cycle and mediocre at the rest of it. The products they deliver are equally lopsided from a quality standpoint. Someone else must be brought in to clean products up, or nothing succeeds in production.

Removing duplicate tools and infrastructure is equally critical to keep job requirements rational. Outside of the increased maintenance costs, hiring becomes a nightmare. Job descriptions must include multiple requirements for the same workflow, and finding people who can work with multiple stacks is difficult.

Those job descriptions send out an unintended signal. Senior++ data professionals read them and know what kind of dysfunction lurks under the covers. Most will actively avoid companies that have low-maturity job descriptions. Organizational maturity helps attract top talent; well-defined roles are a big part of that.

Once roles are defined, career paths can be developed too. Data organizations need individual contributor, strategy, and leadership tracks. It's essential to allow individual contributors to have leadership-level equivalents. Many very senior data professionals leave or are forced to take leadership roles to continue advancing because they top out in the individual contributor track.

Structured career paths are critical for retaining top talent and another sign of maturity that attracts them in the first place. However, they also enable internal training and upskilling programs. These are critical for building a farm club and an internal talent pipeline. The reality is that external talent sourcing is unsustainable during the data organizational build-out phases.

There's not enough talent in the marketplace to meet the current demand. Businesses must develop people internally and need programs in place to succeed.

Companies will be forced to train and upskill their way out of the talent shortage for the next 3 to 5 years. We don't have any other infrastructure to train as many people as we need except for internal training and upskilling programs. There's just no other feasible way.

College is too expensive and not accessible enough. Data boot camps have varying levels of quality, with most releasing graduates who are unprepared to handle professional roles. Graduates have limited capabilities. Most require significant retraining, so we might as well start doing that work inside of the business in the first place.

You'll also find a huge source of talent inside the business. I didn't realize this until I spent time with people in frontline organizations. When I talked to sales associates and warehouse workers, I was amazed by how many were already upskilling on their own. Businesses have access to a rich source of people already interested in software engineering and data roles.

They are taking online programs, and some are even going back to school for a degree. However, there's no structure.

Most don't have a learning path or road map for their target role. There is no assistance or guidance for them. On the other side of the equation sit dozens of open data and software roles. Each takes several months to fill and costs $25,000 or more to recruit candidates.

Most businesses have talent who are upskilling on their own. Internal training programs provide them with guidance, access to learning materials, and structured career paths. These programs don't cost more than external hiring processes, and the results are more sustainable. They can become significant sources of talent to help fill most companies' shortages.

The business gets literacy in two different directions. People from frontline teams have business and domain expertise. They understand the functional area or business unit. They spread their business acumen into the data team and bring their relationships.

In all honesty, most people who start an internal data program will never finish it. They hit the upper-level math or programming and say, "OK, this is not for me." The classes that they do complete teach them data and model literacy. Even if they don't decide to take on a new career path, essential training is still delivered, and the frontline team has a more capable employee.

There's no downside to these programs.

Common Roles for Each Maturity Phase

I'll wrap up with my timeline for bringing in each role. There's no cookie-cutter framework, but this talent timeline fits with the maturity model best. This describes the ideal order and what you would do if you were building the organization from the ground up.

- *Level 0*: Traditional software engineering roles and data analysts.
- *Level 1*: Data engineers, C-level data Leader, data and AI strategist, and data and AI product manager.
- *Level 2*: Data scientists, machine learning engineers, MLOps engineers, and additional data team leaders.
- *Level 3 to 4*: Machine Learning platform architects, automation engineers, applied researchers, model QA engineers, and information scientists.

Data governance and ethicists are also necessary, but they may not live within the data organization. They play an oversight role, so they may need a different leadership structure to avoid the fox guarding the henhouse.

What's Next?

We're nearing the end, but the last piece is one of the most important. In the next chapter, I'll explain data and AI product and monetization strategies. The book's titled *From Data to Profit*, and the final chapter focuses on realizing those profits. It's time to go to market and generate returns.

Data and AI Product Strategy

Product strategy is the connection between implementation and execution. Without this component, everything that comes before it doesn't result in anything except for a lot of paperwork. Taking a product-centric view is critical from the earliest phases.

The word *product* makes us think immediately about customers. The data organization can also treat internally facing products the same way. A product mentality means we're designing for the real world. The data and models won't just live on a laptop or some development environment. Treat each initiative like a product, and it has the best chance of becoming one.

Top-down and bottom-up opportunity discovery has been completed. The business needs a strategy and some frameworks to convert those opportunities into products that can be built and monetized. This is where a data product strategy takes over.

Products are pragmatic by nature, and that leads to some tactical questions. What is a data product? How do I define a data product? How do I put a price tag on this data product? How do we explain the side of data products people purchase, are willing to pay for, and the business will monetize? This chapter focuses on answering those questions and more.

The Need for a Single Vision

Products start as digital products and mature to include data, analytics, and more advanced models. They need a sense of continuity through their maturity journey. The challenge is similar to retailers' struggles in adopting e-commerce and integrating the new channel into their brick-and-mortar businesses.

The biggest challenge was creating a connection between the two and a consistent customer experience across them. Successful retailers brought the best parts of online into brick-and-mortar, and vice versa. They translated the elements that made the retailer great in the brick-and-mortar world into the e-commerce world.

As our products transform, we bring customers along for the journey. Without a single vision, the disconnected set of products can quickly lose people along the way. We're seeing that happen now with many Metaverse products. Meta is working to get people off their mobile phones and into a completely virtual world. There's no connection between products and platforms, so adoption has been extremely slow.

How does a user get from what they do on Facebook, WhatsApp, and Instagram to what they do in the Metaverse? There's a loose social connection with the ability to get into virtual rooms, but very little connects a user's mobile experience with those virtual worlds. There are games but no connection between playing on Facebook and in the Metaverse.

As a result, there's no easy path to convert users from Meta's social media platforms to its virtual reality Metaverse. Customers can't find a connected experience that unifies the technologies. Meta's headsets and Metaverse have left their users behind instead of taking them on the technology maturity journey. Businesses face the same danger moving through the data and AI product maturity journey and continuous transformation in general.

We must define a common thread and need another framework that unifies them all. That's the vision for data, analytics, and model-supported products. The vision provides that unifying factor, explains where products are going, and brings customers along for the maturity journey.

Each business unit has a different idea of how to monetize this new technology, and in many ways, that's a positive. That level of customization is where the business will eventually mature to achieve. Business units must have the ownership to take data and AI products in the direction that will be most lucrative for them.

The purpose of a vision is not to take control of what gets built. A vision for products explains the transformation journey. A single vision is critical; we need something we can build around. I'll begin with defining a data product and work backward to create a vision that unifies data and AI products.

Defining Data and AI Products

Is everything that uses data a data product? No. Consider the login screen that prompts us for our username and password. Data is used to keep track of our credentials, but the login is not a data product. The primary value-creation mechanism is digital. Data is a secondary player. When data is the primary value generator, a digital product becomes a data product.

Netflix recommends content to customers. What does a content recommender system do for its customers? It manages the complexity of browsing through Netflix's content catalog. It's more important than it appears from an outside perspective, and the customer workflow reveals the value proposition.

A subscriber opens the Netflix app and looks for something to watch. They are unable to find anything and leave dissatisfied. Their probability of canceling their subscription rises dramatically each time this happens.

To keep subscribers, Netflix must maintain the perception that "Netflix has a ton of content I enjoy watching." Anything that might change that perception to "I can't find anything that I enjoy watching on Netflix" poses a threat to revenue. That shift in perception is a major cause of churn across content providers.

There's a connection between the model-supported recommendations and a KPI (churn) that the business cares about. It's revealed by the workflow and potential customer outcomes. Netflix wants customers to leave satisfied and has data to define the workflows that cause the desired outcome.

There are two initial user states. First, the user knows exactly what they want to watch and just needs to find it. In that case, search functionality is important. Recommendations help customers avoid searching in the first place. Highly accurate recommendations lead to fewer steps between the customer and the content they want to watch.

Second, they don't know what they want to watch and are looking to find a new series or movie. Recommendations have a significantly higher value in this workflow. There's too much content on Netflix to browse through it all. The recommendation system reduces the complexity by shrinking the catalog to what the customer is most likely to enjoy.

Monetization is indirect because it prevents the loss of revenue instead of generating new revenue. If Netflix tried to charge customers $1.99 for recommendations, that probably wouldn't fly. The model makes money by preventing churn. Every time the recommendations succeed for customers who don't know what they want to watch, the model has reduced the likelihood of them unsubscribing.

This fits nicely into a problem statement for the data team. Say 80 percent (I'm making that number up for illustration) of customers leave the platform four times without finding something to watch, and they unsubscribe. The recommendation model must prevent enough people from reaching that fourth time to justify the initiative's expense. Any improvement to the model must pass this basic litmus test.

Estimating the opportunity size is simpler with a workflow-centric framework. The data team can bring forward an opportunity to reduce churn by 7 percent by increasing recommendation accuracy for an underperforming customer segment. Seven percent is the opportunity size, and the initiative definition allows for a cost estimate.

TikTok has a different type of content recommender system that curates users' content timelines with videos it believes they will like. It reduces the complexity of discovering new content because there's simply too much for users to scan through themselves. Customers don't pay for TikTok directly, so the monetization path goes through advertisers.

Accurate recommendations increase a user's time on the platform and the number of ads that can be served. The point is to reduce the complexity of discovering new content and optimize time on the platform. This feature tracks to a simple workflow.

The user scrolls through their feed. If they don't find something they engage with or enjoy, they leave the app, and TikTok loses the opportunity to serve ads. Eventually, the user will uninstall the app for good. The longer TikTok can keep users engaged, the more ads it can serve and the more revenue it makes.

The next product example comes from a recruiter's applicant tracking system. Recruiters need to find the most qualified candidates from hundreds of résumés. Reading through each résumé isn't feasible, so most recruiters skim them, and they often miss out on great candidates as a result. Recruiters need an application that reduces the complexity of reading hundreds of résumés per job.

This could be monetized internally and externally. A recruiting agency could deploy this as an internal-facing product. Recruiters who worked for the agency would be the users. Value creation would come from reducing the time it takes to screen résumés for each job opportunity.

It could also be made publicly available for external customers. Other recruiting agencies would buy the product to improve their productivity. Instead of being monetized once internally by the agency that developed it, this would allow the platform to be monetized multiple times.

Many platforms will begin their lives as internally-facing utilities. Once the business realizes the true scope of the opportunity, it will likely make the platform available publicly. It's similar to McDonald's transitioning to a franchise business model and Amazon moving forward with a cloud-focused business model. Businesses will realize they have something more valuable with greater monetization opportunities than the product they originally sold.

Amazon Prime's automated pricing system reduces the complexity of pricing millions of products on the platform. If pricing analysts or customers had to perform the work manually, not as many products would make it onto the platform. It's monetized internally by reducing the cost of pricing decisions, but there's more to it than just reducing Amazon Prime's reliance on labor.

Decisions can be made faster by automation than they could be by people. The number of pricing changes per day has an upper limit too. In some cases, making pricing changes in near real time may be advantageous based on demand or other factors. People don't scale to do that very well. They also can't process new information fast enough to make those decisions.

The number of times a person can revisit a decision based on new data has an upward bound. The number of times a model can revisit a decision with new data doesn't. The result for Amazon Prime is more revenue and sometimes higher margins too. The more accurately the model predicts a customer's price, the more sales are made.

There's a complex balancing act that makes the model's ROI challenging to calculate. Total sales must be balanced against margins for the pricing model to succeed. If a lower total number of units sold resulted in higher profits due to better margins, that would be a successful pricing strategy.

In an overstock situation, the business could be balancing profits against the cost (and opportunity cost) of the products taking up warehouse space. Indirect costs of the overstock could offset lower margins making a lower price desirable. For complex use cases like pricing models, mapping the problem space becomes critical to monetization.

Uber leverages a similar pricing model during surge times. It's gotten them into trouble a few times because models have issues dealing with the ethical side of surge pricing. If Uber increases pricing during a natural disaster or mass casualty event, we call that predatory pricing. That's a data point the model doesn't always have.

It's critical to assess reliability requirements for edge cases like Uber's and decide if this use case can be trusted to a model. Top-level frameworks like core-rim extend to products on the ground floor.

The Business's Four Main Platforms

Four platforms explain the approach to developing data and AI products around a unified vision. Businesses have four types of platforms.

- An operational platform that supports tasks people do as part of value-creating workflows

- A product platform that supports delivering value to customers

- A decision platform that supports decisions made as part of value-creating workflows

- A large model platform that integrates with or leverages one or more of the AI operating system platforms

Every product fits into one of these four platform categories. The product vision explains where each platform is today, the journey ahead, and where it will be in three to five years. The initial assessment defines the starting state for each platform. The product and infrastructure road maps define the journey and where the products will be in the near future.

Each platform follows a different monetization path. The operational platform is monetized through cost savings and improved productivity. The decision platform is monetized by the improvement to decision outcomes. This is measured directly with the KPIs the decision impacts. The product platform is monetized for new revenue leveraging the customer and partner ecosystem. The large model platform is a revenue-sharing model.

The vision explains why parts of the platform will follow the maturity model frameworks. It's more than a story about the journey itself. The vision describes how each new technology serves the workflows better than the last. It explains how the old experience transforms into the new one and how customers or internal users will migrate from the prior technology to the new one.

Diverse products will be built on each platform. The vision goes one layer deeper to make the connection between them.

Leveraging Data and AI Strategy Frameworks

Unifying diverse products that span multiple technologies seems complex on the surface. Some of the data and AI strategy frameworks can be extended to reduce complexity significantly. This begins with the business, operating, and technology models. Those have direct ties to product strategy and vision.

The way products evolve is dictated by that top-level framework. C-level leaders decide which parts of the business and operating models will be transferred into the technology model. The purpose of the product vision and strategy is to move those decisions forward.

The operating model connects to the value stream and internal workflows. That creates a straightforward mapping to products built to support workflows. Here's an example of how that process works.

During top-down opportunity discovery, the chief human resources officer (CHRO) brings forward the opportunity to move candidate discovery and initial screening from the recruiting workflow into the technology model. As hiring slows, the focus has shifted to sourcing hard-to-find talent. Layoffs have led to significant reductions in recruiting team sizes. HR has been challenged to increase service levels with fewer people. They've turned to the technology organization to meet that challenge.

Following the arc of disruption framework:

- There are multiple examples of working implementations for candidate discovery and screening models.

- Case studies detail the ROI companies have achieved with these systems.

- The business has the necessary capabilities. It has data and access to data-generating systems around those workflows. There is a clear monetization path. Internal users must be prepared for the transition from digital to data and model-supported products.

- The current solutions do not meet business and user needs. For the sake of this example, let's assume there's no solution from a third party that meets the business's needs, even though there likely is.

Candidate discovery and initial screening are well-defined recruiter workflows. Products must be built to automate those workflows and improve existing service levels. The core-rim model defines what the business trusts technology to manage and which parts of the workflow people must manage. The human-machine product framework explains the product maturity level.

The work and autonomy of discovering candidates can be handled by technology in a human-machine collaboration paradigm. Selecting and screening cannot be completely turned over to models. There are compliance and regulatory considerations. The reliability requirements for many decisions are too high, so these will be human-machine teaming and tooling use cases.

Technical strategies facilitate the decisions around product maturity and continuous transformation. It starts with a digital or application strategy.

- How much of each workflow can be serviced with the least expensive technology?
- Do these use cases have a scale that requires the cloud?
- Do these use cases have complexity or uncertainty that require data and analytics?
- Do these use cases have high-reliability requirements that can be supported only by more advanced models?

Each technology can be evaluated based on its unique value-creation properties and advantages. Those are defined by their individual technical strategy.

Initiatives must be designed to develop the product. They begin at the product maturity model's level 0 with an assessment of the technology that is currently serving the workflow and the currently available data.

- What opportunities are there to improve the digital product and service more of the workflow? What is the ROI? What new data-gathering opportunities do those initiatives create?
- What opportunities exist to leverage existing data sets and introduce data into the workflow? What is the ROI?
- What data-generating processes does the business have easy access to that can produce high-value data sets? What opportunities does that data gathering create?
- Are there opportunities to partner with an AI operating system model and leapfrog maturity levels based on the data the business has today or has easy access to curating?
- What experiments are possible based on the level of access the business has to this workflow? What opportunities offer returns that could scale faster than the cost of developing more advanced models?

The frameworks extend from top-level concepts to initiative planning and execution. These questions serve as the basis for quickly moving from opportunity discovery to the data and AI product road maps. The questions define how each product will likely progress on the maturity models. Designing initiatives this way from the earliest stages establishes the vision and strategy for each platform. Decisions are made with the current, next, and potential long-term transformations in mind.

Each product is built on one of the four main platforms. Its product maturity journey follows a cohesive arc. It's easy to call out the training and preparation necessary to support each transition. Users and customers have a clear story to follow.

Workflow Mapping and Tracking

Some of you may remember Clippy, which is the soon to be rebranded Copilot. It shipped with earlier versions of Microsoft's Office Suite. Clippy had some pretty significant problems, and most people who spent a few minutes using Clippy quickly understood what those problems were.

One, it was terrible at predicting when it was necessary. That was a sign that Microsoft didn't really understand its customers' workflows. Clippy would show up at all the wrong times, and when it did, Clippy made it harder, not easier, to do our jobs. The assistant became an impediment because it prevented us from focusing on the task at hand.

Instead of improving Clippy based on user feedback, Microsoft just kept doubling down on Clippy's functionality. The company had grown out of touch with its customers, so it couldn't see the best solution would have been to eliminate the feature altogether.

Microsoft failed to ask a critical question before implementing Clippy. What is broken about the current customer workflow that Clippy will fix? Anytime we introduce data, analytics, or models into a workflow, it should be with the purpose of making an improvement.

If the workflow isn't broken, it's unlikely that customers will change behaviors to adopt the new feature or product. If a customer's needs are fully served, what's the point of serving them in a different way? A costly mistake many companies have made is introducing AI because it's assumed to lead to superior solutions. That's simply not the case. For many customer workflows, digital functionality operates just fine.

Microsoft's demonstration of GPT integrated into the Office 365 suite shows a different approach. Users can still follow their existing workflow. Copilot is integrated and available if they want it. However, it is not thrown at them. What Microsoft has done with its demos is to show why people would want to adopt it. Each example demonstrates a solid value proposition for Copilot.

Microsoft has learned to wait until the customer sees a problem before introducing the potential solution. This is a unique property of large platforms. Anytime customers use the product built on that platform, they generate data. When businesses gather that data intentionally, they can understand when workflows are completed successfully and when they fail.

Broken workflows are opportunities to improve the product's service level. As I'm writing, I often have to leave Word to find some information from the Web. I don't always remember who initially introduced some of the concepts I discuss, and I should give them credit. This is an example of a broken workflow.

I'm forced to leave the application I'm writing the document in and start using a different one to conduct that search. I could be moving from Word to Bing or Google search in this workflow. Either way, the broken workflow opens an opportunity to improve the platform's functionality. Why not allow me to search directly from Word?

Allowing users to search directly from Word would enable me to continue my workflow without moving to another application. As users, we're so conditioned to bouncing back and forth between applications that we barely notice it anymore. However, it makes more sense to put the functionality in a place that's as close to the user's needs as possible.

In this workflow, information from Word could actually be useful for my search. Allowing me to highlight some text I had written and ask a question about it would be a significant time-saving improvement. ChatGPT enables that functionality. This is an opportunity to introduce models into my workflow and improve the value that Word delivers.

Platforms' power is also the ability to track the success or failure of features like these. If the application detects a broken workflow and recommends the search functionality, how often do users click it? The times when users decide to do the in-app search, how often do they incorporate part of the search results into their document? How often does their workflow remain broken and they use another application for search?

These types of usage metrics can tell the business whether we're on to something valuable. It allows for a closer relationship with the customer. Workflow analysis and tracking are powerful constructs that platforms enable.

Assessing Product and Initiative Feasibility

Should we dive in and take every opportunity that's presented? No, and I've developed a quick way to decide which ones we should pursue and which aren't worth the time. The first point to consider is always monetization.

If the business can't monetize the feature, we've reached a dead end. In the search example from Microsoft Word, how would Microsoft monetize that? One possibility is serving ads as part of the search results. Another is making the functionality a paid upgrade. Both options fit Microsoft's business model, so they are potential opportunities for new revenue.

My next consideration is, will the customer adopt it and actually pay for it? In theory, this is an interesting use case, but will it result in revenue? This often gets overlooked because the technology and its newness overwhelm common sense. Again, I'm going to return to the workflow for my answer.

Today, customers do not directly pay for search. As a result, I can immediately eliminate charging an additional fee for this functionality. If they're not paying for search today, this isn't the feature that gets customers to start.

Customers do tolerate minimal ads in their search results today. The ad-supported monetization channel has potential. This feature not only monetizes searches happening today but introduces a new opportunity to do searches. There's potential here for an entirely new class of search to emerge. That has a compelling value proposition. As a result, this passes my second feasibility test.

My last assessment point is whether the business can build this. Obviously, a company like Microsoft can. It's important to touch base with the data team at this phase. There's often a gap between a feature that is possible to build and a feature the business can build. Not every company is Microsoft.

However, with AI operating system platforms like GPT, this type of functionality becomes significantly easier to develop and deploy. Leveraging a partnership is the right way to go for most businesses.

Technical feasibility gets way too much attention. It's essential, but monetization should always come first. It's not worth talking to customers and seeing if they will adopt it. It's also not worth the effort to see if the data team can produce it. The mistake I often see companies make is they go to customers and the technical team first. The result is an avalanche of potential features.

I prefer to take the approach of bringing the best of the best forward. I can quickly evaluate monetization potential. From there, I rank opportunities by their returns. Only the highest-value opportunities should progress forward. Having 30 different opportunities doesn't mean I should be evaluating every single one of them.

All of this leads to the next most obvious question. How much can we charge?

Pricing Strategies for Data and AI Products

I'll cover three different types of pricing models, but that doesn't mean this is all there is. A new product paradigm opens the opportunity to define novel pricing paradigms too. Don't limit yourself to these three but use them as defaults.

The first is consumption-based pricing. This is what Amazon Web Services relies on for their pricing model. The more of one of their services you use, the more you pay. Many of their services are priced per hour. Others are priced by how much data you send. The common theme is the more you consume, the more you pay. This has several benefits.

OpenAI has introduced a tiered consumption model. Its 3.5 version of ChatGPT runs at a significantly lower cost than the newly released GPT-4. It reduced the cost of GPT-3.5 to drive adoption. It's inexpensive to try it and see what it can do. As a result, the unit economics work out for more use cases.

Sitting right next to 3.5 is the latest version. It's more accurate and capable of handling more use cases. OpenAI is training its customers to see higher value in a more reliable model. Pricing is also a powerful tool in setting customers' perceptions.

The danger of consumption-based pricing is commoditization. OpenAI is training its customers to differentiate based on model reliability. It's only a matter of time before a competitor releases a model that equals GPT-4's reliability. Once that happens, what will make a customer choose OpenAI instead of its competitors? Price.

Consumption-based pricing eventually leads to a race to the bottom. Models have so far been unable to establish a brand preference. OpenAI is definitely the cool kid on the block, but it is nowhere near Nike's or Apple's standing. Customers will choose the lower-priced option if everything else is equal.

With every pricing model, there are pros and cons. It's important to remember there is no right decision, and each pricing model requires an evaluation of trade-offs. That's why it's essential to consider multiple pricing models before landing on one. Pick the model that aligns best with the opportunity, customer workflows, and business model.

Subscription is the next pricing model. Quora released a mobile application called Poe with access to multiple large language models. Users pay a monthly fee rather than per transaction. This pricing model makes sense for Quora, which is partnering with each of these large model platforms.

Some users, especially businesses, prefer set, stable pricing. For Quora, the benefit is revenue stability as long as the company can keep the customer churn rate low. Customers also often forget to cancel their subscriptions and end up paying for an application for much longer than they actually use it.

The downside to subscription compared to consumption is churn. When a customer decides to unsubscribe, the relationship is typically terminated. Consumption-based pricing enables the opportunity to reduce the amount of usage. This keeps the relationship intact, even though revenue has decreased significantly.

With a subscription pricing model, once the user unsubscribes, that's the end of it. It is much harder to get them back on the platform as a subscriber again.

Partnerships and revenue sharing is the third pricing model. This is what OpenAI and Microsoft have. The advantage here is the ability to build on top of best-in-class functionality. OpenAI has a best-in-class large language model. Microsoft has best-in-class enterprise and productivity application suites. The partnership allows both to leverage the other's advantages for their own monetization.

Apple took this approach when it released the App Store. Apple had developed a strength in the mobile device realm. Apple was not a mobile game or productivity application powerhouse. The App Store allowed them to monetize partnerships with best-in-class application developers. Companies that create amazing mobile games use the App Store for access to distribution. Application developers got access to the ecosystem, and Apple got a cut of the revenue.

The danger of partnerships is that revenue success depends on the quality of partners you choose. Microsoft chose well with OpenAI. However, from the beginning, there was always a risk that OpenAI would not be able to deliver a best-in-class model. If their research into GPT had failed to thrive, the partnership would have also failed. All the money Microsoft put into the relationship would have been lost.

The opportunity has been discovered, validated, estimated, and priced. It's time to define the product at a high level so the data team can build it.

Problem, Data, and Solution Space Mapping

People on the project team need enough information to make good, value-focused decisions. Technical individual contributors make more business decisions than most people realize. They must have enough context around the business problem being solved to make those decisions well.

Defining the problem space can be as simple as defining the workflow and the problem with the workflow today. It can also be an explanation of the underserved customer need. This product will change the workflow, so the problem space definition explains why.

In the Netflix example, customers came onto the platform, searched for content, and left without finding something to watch. The change is targeted at the content search portion of the workflow to prevent the customer from leaving unsatisfied.

The next point of evaluation is the data space. The data team needs access to data generated by the workflow to deliver a solution. Does the business currently have that data, or does it have access to the workflow to gather it?

In the Netflix recommender system example, the platform gathers data about the content discovery workflow. Examples of successful and unsuccessful content discovery workflows can train a model to make content recommendations. Exploring the data space allows for an initial feasibility estimate and early product design.

Finally, the solution space describes the finished data, analytics, or model-supported product. The project team can define the technical solution but needs help connecting business or customer metrics. If the product is designed to reduce customer churn, the solutions space should include the metrics we expect the product to impact and the magnitude of those impacts.

In the Netflix recommender system example, it's necessary to explain the connection between the workflow and outcomes. If a subscriber leaves the application more than four times without finding something to watch, they churn at an 80 percent rate (again, these are made-up numbers for this example).

The recommender system introduces data into the subscriber's content discovery workflow to prevent them from leaving unsatisfied.

The project team uses the solution space definition to understand how their decisions and model performance deliver value to the business or customers. It helps keep the technical solution connected with the problem space.

Managing the Research Process

Innovative initiatives require a managed process to align the work with business value. A research life cycle is often without a definite end date for data and AI products. The artifact is also uncertain—some research results in nothing.

This makes it extremely difficult to apply existing frameworks. Managing the research life cycle requires a gated process. Each gate represents a review meeting. During that meeting, the data science team presents their findings and their next steps.

Results need to be reviewed and validated. This step involves determining whether the team has found anything significant.

If no artifacts have been developed, it's time to move on to the next step and evaluate what the team wants to do in the next cycle. This is where the value-centric decision is made. The team must explain why they're confident these next steps will result in further progress. That doesn't necessarily mean they'll produce an artifact. The goal is to make progress because explaining when they will be done may be impossible.

The review team needs to decide if it's worth continuing. The next steps must still be aligned with the original goals. The expected progress must be promising and represent a significant step forward. The review team's answering an important question. Is this the highest-value research project the team could focus on right now?

When initiatives depart from business needs or progress slows considerably, it's time to consider ending this initiative. The business isn't saying no to innovation altogether. The decision is made that there is a better research initiative to begin. Like everything else, this is an evaluation of trade-offs. The review team is determining the most promising use of this research team's time.

Shelving a research initiative today doesn't mean that's the end of it. In my experience, many shelved initiatives often get revisited. Often progress needs to be made on other fronts before the research can move forward and be successful. Even in those cases, the worst thing the research team could do is spin their wheels waiting for something to improve elsewhere. It's a better use of their time to move forward on more promising lines instead of churning on something that's reached a dead end.

Without a managed research process, most initiatives go off the rails or extend longer than they should. It's important to be reevaluating the innovation and research initiatives continuously. How often the review meetings happen depends on the business's risk tolerance. The more risk the business is willing to take on, the longer the gaps between review meetings can be. The gaps should be fairly small in businesses that are less comfortable with risk. It's often appropriate to be reviewing progress weekly.

The AI Evangelist: Community Building for Platform Success

Products and platforms need coalitions to support them. There must be more than just the data team saying, "Isn't this all amazing?" Data and AI strategists and product managers are often the first AI evangelists. The end of this journey requires us to hand off one last piece.

The more the company begins to rely on data products, the more evangelists will surface. Eventually, most businesses will have the full-time role of data and AI evangelist.

It's like a developer relations role, except it starts internally-facing and then turns outward toward customers. The goal is to get the business to adopt data, analytics, and model-supported products. There's an unspoken reality in any new technology paradigm. Customers don't show up ready.

Data and AI evangelists' top-level focus is building a community of potential users who could be interested in the products. We have data and AI evangelists because customers don't always get it. Forward-looking tools have a difficult time getting adopted on their own. Customers need to see the new paradigm in action to wrap their heads around what they might do with it.

So, this person builds a community around the tools and leverages those tools to solve the community's problems. The data and AI evangelist show the community what's possible. They are constantly doing demos and teaching people to use the available tools. The community grows around this passion for building and solving problems.

Data and AI evangelists are rare because few people are technical and know how to curate a community. The community becomes an ecosystem where some people are customers for the primary product line. Others are partners who will monetize in different ways.

Data and AI products live on platforms that enable ecosystems with partners and a different approach to competition. The data and AI evangelist looks at partners and says, "OK, normally, we would be competing for these customers, but how can we work together to serve both of our interests?"

Community building is where data and AI evangelists add the most value. The role focuses on teaching and building the ecosystem the company will monetize for the next 5 years. It's a techno-strategic role that understands a new construct of gaining followers and curating a community and ecosystem of people who will monetize on the platform in different ways.

All the frameworks and strategies keep going, but someone else takes the product forward to be used and improved by a growing ecosystem.

What's Next?

What comes next is the hardest part for me. I must let this book and the frameworks go. It's time to watch you take these ideas forward. You'll adapt the frameworks and build amazing data and AI products. These frameworks will be extended in the coming years to manage new technologies.

I'm handing the next chapters over to you. What comes next? You tell me, and I can't wait to hear about it.

Index